Theory and Practice

Papers and Session Materials Presented at the Twenty-Fifth
National LOEX Library Instruction Conference
held in Charleston, South Carolina
8 to 10 May 1997

edited by
Linda Shirato, Director
LOEX Clearinghouse
and
Elizabeth R. Bucciarelli
Reference and Instruction Librarian
University Library
Eastern Michigan University

Published for Learning Resources and Technologies
Eastern Michigan University
by
Pierian Press
Ann Arbor, Michigan
1998

ISBN 0-87650-354-7
Copyright © 1998, The Pierian Press
All Rights Reserved

The Pierian Press
Box 1808
Ann Arbor, Michigan 48106

LIBRARY ORIENTATION SERIES
(Emphasizing Information Literacy and Bibliographic Instruction)

ISBN*	Number	
354-7	29	*Theory and Practice*
348-2	28	*Programs That Work*
347-4	27	*New Ways of "Learning the Library"—and Beyond*
342-3	26	*Change in Reference and BI: How Much Help and How?*
338-5	25	*The Impact of Technology on Library Instruction*
328-8	24	*Bibliographic Instruction in Practice: A Tribute to the Legacy of Evan Ira Farber*
327-X	23	*What Is Good Instruction Now? Library Instruction for the 90s*
291-5	22	*Working with Faculty in the New Electronic Library*
294-X	21	*Judging the Validity of Information Sources: Teaching Critical Analysis in Bibliographic Instruction*
267-2	20	*Coping with Information Illiteracy: Bibliographic Instruction for the Information Age*
258-3	19	*Reaching and Teaching Diverse Library User Groups*
252-4	18	*Defining and Applying Effective Teaching Strategies for Library Instruction*
251-6	17	*Bibliographic Instruction and Computer Database Searching*
250-8	16	*Teaching the Online Catalog User*
201-X	15	*Marketing Instructional Services: Applying Private Sector Techniques to Plan and Promote Bibliographic Instruction*
182-X	14	*Bibliographic Instruction and the Learning Process: Theory, Style and Motivation*
145-5	13	*Teaching Library Use Competence: Bridging the Gap from High School to College*
131-5	12	*Directions for the Decade: Library Instruction in the 1980s*
124-2	10	*Reform and Renewal in Higher Education: Implications for Library Instruction*
109-9	9	*Improving Library Instruction: How to Teach and How to Evaluate*
092-0	8	*Putting Library Instruction in Its Place: In the Library and in the Library School*
078-5	7	*Library Instruction in the Seventies: State of the Art*
070-X	6	*Faculty Involvement in Library Instruction: Their Views on Participation in and Support of Academic Library Use Instruction*
063-7	5	*Academic Library Instruction: Objectives, Programs, and Faculty Involvement*
061-0	3	*Planning and Developing a Library Orientation Program*
039-4	2	*A Challenge for Academic Libraries: How to Motivate Students to Use the Library*

* Pierian Press's ISBN identifier is 0-87650. This identifier should precede the number given for a book (e.g., 0-87650-327-X).

Table of Contents

Table of Contents iii

Preface vii
        Linda Shirato

Articles

Why We Need a National Information Literacy Institute 1
        Cerise Oberman

Preconference Workshop

The Program Portfolio: Promoting Reflection and Dialogue; Preparing for Change 9
        Linnea Dudley, Diane Dustin, Catherine Neis, Paul Beavers,
        Mary Jo Blackport, and Michael Kruzich

Instructive Sessions

INSTRUCTIVE SESSION NO: 1
Implementing an Information Technology Training Program: Marketing, Managing,
    and Evaluating the Get Ready Pilot Project 15
        Jill Holman (University of Oregon)
        Table 1 17
        Table 2 18
        Table 3 19
        Appendix 22

INSTRUCTIVE SESSION NO: 2
Using Presentation Software in Instruction Sessions: Design Principles and Presentation Skills 25
        Julie Long (Saint Mary's College)

INSTRUCTIVE SESSION NO: 3
Designing and Implementing CLUE, an Interactive, Multimedia Instructional Program 29
        Abigail Loomis and Lee Konrad (University of Wisconsin-Madison)

INSTRUCTIVE SESSION NO: 4
Of Course the Library Is Important! Getting Library Instruction Included
    in a Freshman Experience Course 35
        Marsha A. Miller (Indiana State University)
        Table 1 39
        Table 2 42
        Appendix 1 45
        Appendix 2 47

INSTRUCTIVE SESSION NO: 5
Training Course Instructors to Teach Library Instruction 49
        Pixey Anne Mosley (Texas A&M University)
    Table 1 52
    Appendix 1 52

INSTRUCTIVE SESSION NO: 6
Reinventing Bibliographic Instruction: The BGSU Experience 55
        Julia K. Nims (Bowling Green State University)
    Appendix 1 64

INSTRUCTIVE SESSION NO: 7
Presentation Basics: Skills, Techniques, and Learning Styles 65
        Jan Orf and Marianne Hageman (University of St. Thomas)
    Appendix 1 71

INSTRUCTIVE SESSION NO: 8
Constructing Web Pages for Course-Related Library Instruction: A Business and
    Government Information Perspective 73
        Patrick Ragains (University of Nevada)
    Figure 1 74
    Figure 2 76
    Figure 3 79
    Figure 4 80

INSTRUCTIVE SESSION NO: 9
Teaching Library Users to Evalute WWW Resources 83
        Dena Siegel and Susan Levendosky (Ball State University)
    Figure 1 84
    Figure 2 85
    Figure 3 87
    Figure 4 88

INSTRUCTIVE SESSION NO: 10
Life on the Information Super-Treadmill: Management Issues in Creating a
    Departmental Web Page for Reference and Bibliographic Instruction 91
        Jeanie M. Welch (University of North Carolina at Charlotte)

INSTRUCTIVE SESSION NO: 11
Successful Marketing of Faculty Bibliographic Instruction: Faculty Bibliographic
    Instruction at Andrews University 95
        Wolfhard Touchard (Andrews University)
    Appendix 1 97
    Appendix 2 98
    Appendix 3 99
    Appendix 4 100
    Appendix 5 102
    Appendix 6 104
    Appendix 7 106

Discussion Groups

A Team Approach to BI: or, Growth Is Good for You (So Stop Complaining!) 109
        Deborah Davis (Valdosta State University), Carolyn McPherson (Valdosta State
        University), Beth Stevens (Armstrong Atlantic University), and Rosann Bustos
        (Augusta State University)
    Slides 110

Multiple Literacies and Competing Agendas: How Does Information Literacy Fit In? 121
        Tasha Cooper (Lycoming College) and Loanne Snavely (Pennsylvania State University)

Library Instruction Lessons Learned the First Year 123
        Laurel Carter (Hanover College)

Poster Sessions

POSTER SESSION NO: 1
"Mystery to Mastery"
        Sariya Talip Clay, Sallie Harlan, and Judy Swanson
        (California Polytechnic State University, San Luis Obispo)
Part 1 - Mystery to Mastery 125
Part 2 - California State University Information Competence Project 126
Part 3 - Unit Information Competence Course 127

POSTER SESSION NO: 2
"Classroom for the New Millennium"
        Donna Lehman and Charlene Loope (University of South Carolina, Columbia)
Part 1 - Classroom for the New Millennium 128
Part 2 - Technology Purchases 129
Part 3 - Classroom Design 130
Part 4 - Management of the Multimedia Classroom 131
Part 5 - Instruction in the Multimedia Classroom 132
Part 6 - Software Used in the Classroom 133
Part 7 - Tips for Teaching in the Electronic Classroom 134
Part 8 - Classroom for the New Millennium: Additional Resources 136

POSTER SESSION NO: 3
"The Carleton Library Experience"
        Terry Metz (Carleton College, Northfield, Minnesota)
Part 1 - Library Instruction Web Pages 139
Part 2 - Background 140
Part 3 - Advantages of Web-Based Library Instruction 141
Part 4 - Disadvantages of Web-Based Library Instruction 142
Part 5 - Tips for Instruction Page Development 143
Part 6 - Learn More about Web-Based Library Instruction 144

POSTER SESSION NO: 4
"The One Minute Paper"
        Sharon Lee Stewart (The University of Alabama)
Part 1 - The One Minute Paper 151
Part 2 - Introduction 152
Part 3 - Advantages of Classroom Assessment 153
Part 4 - Angelo's* Seven Axioms of Classroom Assessment 154
Part 5 - One Minute Paper 156
Part 6 - Appropriate Uses of the Minute Paper 157
Part 7 - Use in Library Instruction 158

Bibliography

Library Instruction and Information Literacy—1996 161
        Hannelore B. Rader

Roster of Participants   178

PREFACE

The 1997 LOEX conference held in Charleston, South Carolina, was one of the most popular and well-attended LOEX conferences in many years—undoubtedly owing, at least in part, to the wonderful location. As guests of the librarians at the College of Charleston, everyone enjoyed this charming city. Very special thanks are due to Phillip Powell of the College of Charleston Library for his hard work in making this conference possible.

The theme of the conference, "Theory and Practice," aimed to incorporate current theory about library instruction as well as to look at how that theory was translated into everyday practice. Thus, there was a wide array of presentations and discussion groups covering almost every aspect of present-day practice. Presentations ranged from teaching with the Web to discussions of workload and burnout. Two preconferences were also a part of this conference, one a repeat from previous years on metalearning (and thus not published again here), and one on using the program portfolio method to implement change in a library program.

Our keynote speaker, Cerise Oberman, surprised us with an overview of the past 20 years of theory and practice, and a new proposal for the future. Noting that a number of years of improving theory and practice in instruction had *not* resulted in a similar increase in training opportunities for instruction librarians at library schools, she suggested a radical step: the founding of a National Institute for Information Literacy. This institute would be a training place for intensive study for beginning librarians, and perhaps much more. Since that time, the National Institute for Information Literacy (NILI) has begun to take shape. Working with the Association of College and Research Libraries, planning has already begun to have some sort of institute in place by 1999. This institute undoubtedly will have an impact on the instructional practice in libraries of the future. LOEX is happy to have played a small role in the beginning of this new venture. It should influence "theory and practice" for many years to come.

Linda Shirato

ARTICLES

Why We Need a National Information Literacy Institute

Cerise Oberman

When Linda Shirato contacted me several months ago about speaking at this year's LOEX conference, I was excited because it was LOEX. And I was sentimental because it was LOEX in Charleston, South Carolina, and this is where I started my career—at the College of Charleston Library. In fact, just a little over 20 years ago I stood, in a then-slowly disintegrating Francis Marion Hotel presiding over the First Annual Southeastern Conference on Bibliographic Instruction. The fact that I had never even heard the term bibliographic instruction before I arrived at the College of Charleston in 1976 did not dampen my enthusiasm. It was here, in Charleston, where I also first became interested in active learning as a pedagogical tool for promoting critical thinking. And it was here that I had the marvelous opportunity to work with several other disciplinary faculty to begin the Freshman Abstract Reasoning Program. Although I am clearly a Yankee who has migrated back north, I have deep professional roots in Charleston. It is particularly wonderful to return to Charleston to be a guest speaker at LOEX, since LOEX played such an instrumental role in my own professional development as a new instruction librarian.

The topic of this year's conference, "Theory and Practice," was also exciting. I have spent most of my 20 years in this profession struggling to articulate theory for library instruction while all the time wrestling with its pedagogical implications. So LOEX's conference theme this year seemed tailormade for me. I felt certain I had something to share with practicing instruction librarians on this topic. Perhaps a historical overview of the struggle to bring a conceptual foundation to library instruction? Or a discussion of how library instruction improves critical thinking? Or an examination of successful programs that have achieved a seamless integration of theory and practice?

But, a funny thing happened on my way to Charleston…and it happened a few months ago when I was sitting in a hotel room in Washington DC, listening to a library director and a library school educator discuss the future of library instruction practitioners. I had made a particular point of attending this jointly sponsored midwinter ALISE (American Library School Educators)/ACRL Instruction Section discussion, entitled "Reinventing the Information Profession: Preparing Librarians for Their Teaching Role in the 21st Century." As a dean of a library, and, therefore, an employer, I am vitally concerned about what and how new librarians are learning about library instruction. And as an occasional adjunct library school faculty member, I have strong feelings about what new librarians should be learning.

I arrived a few minutes late and took a seat in the center of the room. I listened quietly as the prepared questions were asked of the library director and the library educator:

- How best to prepare library school graduates for teaching responsibilities?

- What are the specific skills necessary for well-prepared instruction librarians in the twenty-first century?

Oberman is dean of libraries and information services, Plattsburgh State University of New York.

- What emphasis should graduate education place on instruction?

The panelists' responses were thoughtful and measured, each of them citing the need for librarians to be knowledgeable about cognitive psychology, educational design, evaluation, and various aspects of computer science. These were appropriate answers, but not new ones. And the question-and-answer period that followed seemed like a rerun of an old familiar movie to me. Eager young librarians in the audience were asking the same questions I had asked 20 years ago when I was one of those eager young librarians. Whose responsibility is it to prepare librarians to teach if graduate schools don't? Given staff constraints how do we hope to educate a large number of students to the growing complexities of the information world? How can we hope to prepare librarians for teaching positions when many library schools continue to ignore or minimize its importance in the job market?

To tell you honestly, I left that discussion group woefully discouraged. While it is true that the library instruction movement has made significant strides over the past 20 years, particularly in developing a set of concepts that are widely embraced by most practitioners, it has not been successful in convincing our own profession that it is an integral part of librarianship. This is true on both sides of the educational infrastructure: graduate education still resists recognizing instruction as central to the preparation of librarians and the higher education institution in which the trained graduate works often does not fully embrace instruction as a core competency for librarians.

It was that realization that made me rethink what "theory and practice" I wanted to discuss here today. I decided I needed to talk about the "theory" of library instruction in the context of its growing recognition within higher education and the failing of our own profession to adequately embrace the theory and implement the "practice."

Some of you may be aware that Charleston used to use a catchy slogan to promote itself: "Charleston:—the South's best kept secret." I think a slight variation of that slogan epitomizes library instruction until recently: library instruction—higher education's best kept secret. While library instruction was flourishing in many academic libraries as a result of the renaissance of instruction in the seventies, it nevertheless remained peripheral to the core curriculum and was often marginalized in its significance to the educational enterprise. In 1989, the publication of the ALA Presidential Committee on Information Literacy Final Report[1] marked the beginning of a change. This report, and subsequent efforts on the part of many individuals, dragged bibliographic instruction out from the shadows and made a powerful case, aimed at educators, that information literacy was critical to the education of students.

I will confess, here and now, that I was not an early fan of this newfangled notion of information literacy. Information literacy was, in my opinion, little more than a masterful repackaging of the very ideas that bibliographic instruction had been extolling for years. In fact, I would have argued (and probably did), that the corpus of work completed by individual librarians, as well as the ACRL Bibliographic Instruction Section (BIS), had been little more than co-opted and renamed.

Clearly, my initial stubbornness blinded me from seeing the major benefits of this name. Freed from the jargon of librarians, the ideas extolled by bibliographic instruction, now information literacy, were easily and quickly embraced by an audience that was far more influential than the individual practitioner and far more widespread than ACRL BIS.

In fact, this new marketing of existing concepts provided for a radical turn of events: the growing recognition and acceptance of the importance of information literacy outside of librarianship. Fueled by the explosion of complexities introduced by educational technology, information literacy appears to have gained an important foothold in the current national conversation on the changing role of higher education. Let me share some examples.

Educom, a national consortium of colleges and universities and other organizations serving higher education, which is "dedicated to the transformation of higher education through the application of information technologies," recently published a "white paper" on *The Need for a National Learning Infrastructure*. This publication, which posits a radical agenda for higher education, notes that "increasingly, viewing a college education as mastery of a body of knowledge or a complete preparation for a lifetime career is becoming outmoded. Instead, we recognize that graduates need to have acquired skills, such as critical thinking, quantitative reasoning, and effective communication, along with such abilities as *finding needed information* and working well with others."[2] This explicit reference to "finding needed information" in a document that is calling for a major reshuffling of curriculum priorities is significant.

Another example of the emerging importance of information literacy to higher education is evidenced by a recent article in *Educom Review*, which caught the attention of many librarians. This article, notable in part because it was not written by librarians and was published in a non-library journal, embraces the notion of information literacy and calls for its marriage to technology to form a new concept of "technological literacy."³

Even more significant is the relatively recent incorporation of information literacy as an evaluation criterion by accrediting bodies. On this front, the Middle States Association has taken a leadership role. Their accreditation guidelines state that "Of paramount importance in assessing the effectiveness of library utilization is the ability in the self-study process to describe and document the strategies and activities used to provide an effective program of bibliographic instruction and information literacy."⁴

Howard Simmons, the former executive director of the Middle States Commission and a non-librarian, who was instrumental in incorporating information literacy into Middle States standards, explained the importance of information literacy from an accrediting perspective:

> ....information literacy must be seen as a concept inextricably connected to the improvement of the undergraduate curriculum—and not just a hobbyhorse of librarians and eccentric accrediting officials like me. In my judgment, information literacy—when it is narrowly conceived—will continue to be viewed by some as a peripheral activity unless it is an integral component of the teaching and learning process. Broadly construed, information literacy should be seen as a strategy for improving a student's ability to learn how to learn.⁵

Middle States is committed to not merely identifying information literacy as a part of evaluative criteria, but working toward creating institutional programs that are integrated as part of the institution's curriculum. As part of this effort Middle States has set a course to raise awareness and educate institutions about the important role of information literacy as a component of accreditation. Middle States recently conducted a program targeted at bringing together faculty, librarians, and administrators to discuss issues of information literacy, with particular attention on how to begin the process of inclusion. The most recent Middle States Annual Conference, held in October 1996, included a panel on "The Transformed Academy: Technology & Information Literacy," in which a librarian (me); a college president, Donald Farmer; and Steve Gilbert, from the American Association of Higher Education, presented three perspectives on this issue.

Other initiatives by accrediting bodies are not as advanced as Middle States. However, the environment is ripe for change. Esther Grassian recently reviewed this issue at the California Academic and Research Libraries Conference and encouraged the audience to make a concerted effort to push for incorporation of information competency into accreditation standards.⁶ Let me reiterate and reinforce Esther's call for action.

The American Association of Higher Education's (AAHE) Teaching, Learning and Technology Roundtable Project is also making note of librarians. The head of this national project, Steve Gilbert of AAHE, yet another non-librarian, told me recently he was eagerly looking for librarians who would be interested in AAHE's Teaching, Learning, and Technology Roundtable (TLTR) training sessions. These TLTR workshops focus on bringing different institutional voices together to discuss teaching and learning within the context of technology. Their purpose is to "encourage, guide and assist individual campuses in developing their own campuswide planning and support systems (roundtables)." Ideally, teaching, learning, and technology roundtables consist of teaching faculty, administrators, bookstore operators, computing staff, and librarians. This effort is key to assisting an institution in the difficult work of maximizing use of technology, coordinating efforts of different constituencies, and, most importantly, developing strategies for improving teaching and learning through technology. The roundtable concept also assists in turning rancor into harmony and multiple directions into unity. Librarians have a significant role to play in this institutional conversation. Sometimes it is to educate colleagues about information literacy, sometimes it is to explain the conversation on student learning.

There is little doubt in my mind that higher education has begun to understand the importance of information in our society and the integral need to prepare students to be information-literate. Twenty-five years after the renaissance of library instruction we have at least one regional accrediting body recognizing that information literacy is core to a college-educated person. We have colleagues outside of librarianship heralding the need to take a closer look at information literacy as a part of a larger issue of properly preparing students for future careers; we have the American Association of Higher Education courting librarians as critical players in designing student learning environments. So what can possibly be wrong with this picture?

When I was sitting in that hotel room in Washington, DC, listening to one of the few library educators who teaches library instruction and listening to a library director who is a supporter of library instruction, it became perfectly clear to me what was wrong. Our own profession has still not fully embraced or recognized the place of library instruction within our profession. Of course, this is the height of irony.

I am here today to argue that academic libraries must recognize information literacy as a foundation building block for student learning. If the library is to consider itself as an integral contributor to a student's education, then information literacy must be the central component of that contribution. This is an easy concept to embrace abstractly. However, it is the more difficult job of actualizing this concept that we must face. After all, it requires that we think of the library as, first and foremost, a teaching unit.

The notion of a teaching-library is not new. In fact, it has been around for at least 30 years. The rightful pioneer of this movement is Louis Shores. In the early 1960s he spearheaded the Library-College movement. This movement, fed by Shores' analysis that enrollment rates in college and universities would be rising steadily, was intended to offer an alternative to traditional lecture-based education. Shores explained that a "Library-College is a college in which the dominant learning mode is independent study by the student in the library, bibliographically guided, intellectually aroused and spiritually stirred by the faculty."[7] Shores was a proponent of the librarian as educator and advocated that librarians should shed their clerical and management roles for the more appropriate educational role.[8] While the Library-College movement never did catch on as a concept, it is an early example of an attempt to redefine the academic library as an educational center and the academic librarian as an educator.

A decade later, Alan Guskin, Carla Stoffle, and Joe Boisse published an article championing "The Academic Library as Teaching Library: A Role for the 1980s." Like Shores before them, their argument for a redefinition of the mission of the academic library was in response to the changing environment of higher education. This time, however, it was the reduction rather than the expansion of qualified high school applicants for college admission and the ensuing financial pressures that would bring to bear on all facets of the university. These changes were already being experienced by libraries: stagnant book budgets, personnel freezes, emerging technologies. In the face of these changes, the authors offered a new model for libraries: the teaching library. They maintained that "One major way in which the library can respond to the present challenges in higher education, maintain itself as a viable campus unit, and realize its potential as the symbolic heart of the campus is to become the "teaching library."[9] While many of the standard functions of the library would be maintained in this "teaching library," it is the emphasis of teaching from which all else flows. Guskin, Stoffle, and Boisse, unlike Shores, offered a step-by-step guide to transforming the present library into that of a teaching library. They were fully aware of the political and administrative land mines that must be crossed and provided a map of how to move from there to here. The teaching library, they argued, "may well become a model of institution (and constituent units') responsiveness to the educational changes of the next decade."[10]

But here we are, almost at the end of a second decade since that article was written and three decades since Louis Shores advocated for a Library-College and there are few signs that the academic library is transforming itself into a teaching institution. It is true that library instruction has been increasingly embraced and practiced in most academic libraries, in some form. But it has made few inroads into general education. It is true that today library instruction is often required as part of many library positions. But, it is far from being a requirement for all librarians. It is true that library instruction has gained recognition outside of the library world. But, inside academic libraries it is often a program that struggles for recognition in the academy and often, even among other librarians.

So today I propose, for the third time in four decades, that academic libraries embrace the notion of teaching as a core function of the library. This means serious and far-reaching change to the status quo. It means reordering priorities. It means moving resources. It means rethinking organizational structures. This is not a small task. Yet, the circumstances around us (perhaps for the first time in the relatively short history of library instruction) allow us the luxury of pursuing this objective with support from outside of librarianship.

We all know that the academic library is already being reshaped by powerful external forces: stagnant or reduced purchasing power for materials, increased outsourcing opportunities for technical operations, an explosion of electronic products, the networking of the campus, the networking of the world, the national trend toward merging libraries and computer operations, a need for staff to respond more swiftly to change. These forces are significant and will, if they already haven't in your library, reshape the identity of both libraries and librarians. However, I want to be clear that a move to an instructional model should not be a reactive position to legitimize the role of the library or the librarian. Rather, it must be a proactive position, which takes full advantage of the unique skills and education that librarians have to assist in preparing students and faculty for the millennium. It is an opportunity to recast our roles by embracing the educational mission of our profession.

Let me use my own institution as an example of the change that is allowing us to move toward a teaching library model. Plattsburgh State University of New York is a comprehensive public institution. Its student body is close to 6,000 students and it offers 50 undergraduate majors and a select number of masters' programs. There is a general education program, which includes a required one-credit course, "Introduction to Library and Information Research." There are 13 librarians.

In the last nine years, our library has changed more than I ever could have envisioned. Change has been prompted by both external and internal pressures. These pressures range from diminishing state budgets to the unrestrained growth of technology, from the introduction of a cooperative network instruction program with computing personnel to the organizational merging of the library and computer operations.

While each of these changes has been significant in its own right, the most profound change, from my vantage point, has been the organizational restructuring within the library. It is profound, because at its core this restructuring involved the redefinition of librarians' responsibilities. Up until this point, the responsibility for our instruction program, which includes a required one-credit course that is part of our general education program, course-related instruction, and network instruction, was squarely held by reference librarians. It was standard procedure that other librarians would teach the one-credit course, but they taught one rather than two sections, and rarely were involved in course-related instruction. Reference desk responsibilities were also partially shared among librarians, but non-reference librarians were, at best, involved only tangentially.

The restructuring of the library's organization began with the identification of a core set of responsibilities for all librarians. The four responsibilities are 1) serving as liaison to several academic departments (which was already a responsibility of all librarians); 2) serving equal shifts on the reference desk; 3) serving on two programmatic groups (the library restructured itself around six programmatic groups); and 4) teaching two sections of the required library instruction course. (Let me hasten to add here that the existence or absence of a required credit course in library instruction is not germane to my argument. Library instruction, regardless of the form it takes—course-related, integrated into an English 101 class, Web-based, or present in an information-literacy-intensive course, taught by a librarian or a teaching faculty member—all require an enormous investment of time on the part of the academic librarian.)

More to the point, the shift in responsibilities undertaken by the librarians at Plattsburgh State sends a strong message. The message is that the library and the librarians consider that the instruction program, which is part of the general education core, is one of the four library-wide factors which define the broad-based role of the library. In my estimation, this has moved our library a few steps closer to formulating our identity as a teaching library.

Moving toward a teaching model requires strong support and commitment from the institution's administration, the library's administration, and, most importantly, the library staff. It is, however, within our ability and control to move our institutions and affect this type of change, particularly given the recognition and support that information literacy is receiving in the larger sphere of higher education.

So let us fantasize for a moment: all academic library directors wake up tomorrow and dedicate themselves to transforming their libraries into teaching-libraries. Could our profession fill that need? After reviewing the evidence, I must sadly conclude "no." In 1980, 11 of the 67 accredited library schools offered separate courses in bibliographic instruction.[11] In 1993, ten library schools in the United States and Canada offered full courses in library instruction. This in spite of the fact that a 1987 survey of how instruction librarians acquired the proficiencies necessary for instruction clearly identified library school education as the critical place to receive their training.[12] A 1996 article, which asked the question "Do Instruction Skills Impress Employers?," answered it with a resounding "yes."[13] While this survey sampled a limited numbers of employers, the authors were impressed by a degree of interest that employers expressed in bibliographic instruction. Although these employers did not conclude that there is any "best way for librarians to learn instruction," the majority of them identified library school courses as one of the best mechanisms.

It certainly has become more common over the last ten years to see special graduate library instruction courses offered in the summer by practicing librarians. This is good and it's heartening, but it's not enough. It's not enough because these courses are hit and miss. Since they are often not part of planned curricula, it is difficult for graduate students to plan to incorporate them into their courses of study. Moreover, the number of opportunities that are available to take such courses are few in number.

ACRL, often in conjunction with ACRL BIS (now IS), has through the years played a vital role in providing continuing education opportunities for instruction librarians. Varied programs at ALA conferences, discussion groups at ALA midwinter conferences, and a host of preconferences focusing on instruction have educated and re-educated several generations of librarians. Add to this the annual LOEX conference, the newly established "LOEX" of the West conference, the Canadian Instruction in the Use of Libraries conference, and any number of regional and state associations that make instruction their focus in any given year and the ground looks well covered.

Well, it is in one sense and is not in another. As the dean of a library that has embraced the notion of becoming a teaching-library, I can say that all of our future hires will be evaluated, in part, indeed in large part, on their interest in and ability to teach. Of the four core competencies that our library has identified for librarians, I am relatively confident that a new librarian will arrive at our library doorstep with a reasonable grasp of collection-development principles. I also expect that a new graduate will arrive with a reasonable understanding of reference services and basic knowledge of the bibliographical apparatus that he or she must tap to provide this service. And, I am willing to accept the responsibility for inculcating a new librarian into the unique organizational structure in which our library operates. However, whose responsibility is it to train a new librarian in the 84 proficiencies identified by the ACRL BIS Education for Bibliographic Instruction Committee?[14]

After 20 years, I guess I'm just getting pretty cranky. I am tired of asking the question, "Whose responsibility is it to prepare librarians to teach?" I am tired of gathering data, talking with library schools, sitting in ACRL IS committees. It is time for more definitive action. If we are serious about moving academic libraries toward a teaching-library model, then we must have a dependable, ongoing commitment to educating those individuals who are interested in participating in such an enterprise.

It is time, I think, for something new! Therefore, today I am putting forth a proposal to establish a National Information Literacy Institute. This institute would focus on delivering a curriculum that would marry theory and practice together. It would offer an intensive training program targeted not only at continuing professional development, but also at equipping new librarians or librarians new to teaching with the proficiencies that are necessary to make the transition to a teaching-library. The institute's curriculum would be the product of collaboration among practicing instruction librarians, library school faculty, and appropriate faculty drawn from other disciplines like computer science, psychology, and education. The institute's curriculum would serve as the basic foundation for teaching librarians and might include in its curriculum

- A historical overview of bibliographic instruction/information literacy;

- An introduction to the basic concepts of information literacy;

- An examination of the role of information literacy in higher education;

- An introduction to different pedagogical techniques, including active learning, cooperative learning, lecturing, and technology-enhanced, and their appropriate use;

- A study of the role of evaluation and, more importantly these days, assessment;

- Practice in the development of an appropriate curriculum or presentation;

- A review of trends and projects in higher education that are supportive of and critical to information literacy; and

- Practice in teaching.

The institute would specialize in an immersion program specifically targeted at preparing the librarian with the foundational tools needed to begin the long road toward becoming an effective teacher. Prior assigned readings and assignments would ensure that participants arrived with common understanding and that learning was the main objective of the institute's program. Given practical concerns, I am envisioning that this institute might be offered no more than once or twice a year for a duration of seven to ten working days. There is no reason that the institute need reside in a single location. In fact, it may be desirable to move around the country.

An institute of this type would provide several direct benefits to the profession: 1) to employers like me, it would guarantee a basic and reliable learning opportunity for a new hire or a librarian who chooses to pursue teaching. I could, therefore, look more readily at graduate library school students, with little or no instructional experience but an identified interest in instruction, as hiring possibilities; 2) to library school students, it would provide an opportunity to be immersed in information literacy as part of their graduate education, if their home graduate library schools did not provide that opportunity; 3) to practicing librarians who have not taught before, but who find themselves interested in jobs that require teaching, this institute offers an opportunity to quickly become familiar with the basic history, activities, pedagogy, and proficiencies that will be needed; 4) to library schools and practicing instruction librarians, this offers a synergistic opportunity, which will naturally result in a much needed exchange of ideas and the building of an important coalition between theory and practice. This cooperative venture would provide a way to systematically and continuously tailor the institute's program to the changing needs of the academic library and academic librarians.

Over time, the institute might want to develop specific targeted immersion programs on targeted issues such as development of asynchronous learning models or developing and implementing assessment instruments. It might even provide seminars for library administrators who are interested in moving their institutions toward a teaching-library model. However, its first and most critical mission would be to prepare instruction librarians.

This is the first time I have broadly shared the idea of establishing a National Information Literacy Institute. For all I know, it may not be a new idea. But I do know that this profession needs to take more direct responsibility for the preparation of its practitioners. While this institute would neither be a substitute for those library school students who have the good fortune of taking full-blown instruction courses nor a substitute for on-the-job training, it would ensure that the profession has a mechanism for training and preparing the next generation of academic librarians.

We are at an important crossroads—higher education recognizes the value of information literacy and wants librarians to be partners in the educational process. The way we respond to that invitation will inevitably shape our future role. Let our response be strong and positive. Let us begin by ensuring that academic librarians have the benefit of common experience and education. Let us begin by taking the initiative and building a National Information Literacy Institute.

NOTES

1. American Library Association, *American Library Association Presidential Committee on Information Literacy: Final Report* (Chicago: American Library Association, 1989).

2. Carol A. Twigg, *The Need for a National Learning Infrastructure* (Washington, DC: Educom, 1995).

3. Jeremy J. Shapiro and Shelly K. Hughes, "Information Technology as a Liberal Art: Enlightenment Proposals for a New Curriculum," *Educom Review* 31:2 (1996): 31-35.

4. Middle States Association of Colleges and Schools, *Characteristics of Excellence in Higher Education: Standards for Accreditation* (Philadelphia: Middle States Association of Colleges and Schools, 1994.

5. Howard L. Simmons, "The Concern for Information Literacy: A Major Challenge for Accreditation," in *The Challenge and Practice of Academic Accreditation: A Sourcebook for Library Administrators*, ed. by E.D. Garten (Westport, CT: Greenwood Press, 1994).

6. Esther Grassian, "Doing the I.C. Limbo (and Trying Not to Slip!)," paper read at California Academic and Research Libraries Conference, San Diego, California, 1996.

7. Richard Hume Werking, *The Library and the College: Some Programs of Library Instruction*, 1976. ERIC Document ED 127 917.

8. See Werking also for a more indepth discussion of Louis Shores.

9. Alan E. Guskin, Carla J. Stoffle, and Joseph A. Boisse, "The Academic Library as a Teaching Library: A Role for the 1980s," *Library Trends* 28 (1979): 281-296.

10. Guskin.

11. Maurene Pastine and Karen Seibert, "Update of the Status of Bibliographic Instruction in Library School Programs," *Journal of Education for Librarianship* 21 (Fall 1980): 169-171.

12. Diana Shonrock and Craig Mulder, "Instruction Librarians: Acquiring the Proficiencies Critical to their Work," *College & Research Libraries* 54:2 (1993): 137-149.

13. Christine Avery and Kevin Ketchner, "Do Instruction Skills Impress Employers?," *College & Research Libraries* 57 (May 1996): 249-253+.

14. Shonrock and Mulder.

PRECONFERENCE WORKSHOP

The Program Portfolio: Promoting Reflection and Dialogue; Preparing for Change

Linnea Dudley, Diane Dustin, Catherine Neis, Paul Beavers, Mary Jo Blackport, and Michael Kruzich

Introduction

The program portfolio is a self-study methodology developed by the Michigan Library Association's PREMIER project. PREMIER (Promoting Research Education: In-service Educational Resources) is a community-based professional development program through which experienced academic librarians volunteer their services as consultants, and as presenters, in in-service workshops designed for specific institutions. (For more information on PREMIER see the 1996 LOEX Conference proceedings.)

As a study, the program portfolio provides PREMIER with information about the current state of a library instruction program. This type of portfolio, which is derived equally from portfolio assessment and the personal teaching portfolio, brings together pre-existing documents within a synthesizing structure. Its ten basic categories were developed in a series of open meetings of MLA's Information Literacy Roundtable, which were attended by librarians from colleges and universities throughout Michigan. The PREMIER port-

Dudley is the coordinator of reference services at Marygrove College, Detroit; *Dustin* is public services/reference librarian at Monroe County Community College, Monroe; *Neis* is head of reference and serials at Aquinas College, Grand Rapids; *Beavers* is assistant director of Wayne State University Purdy/Kresge Library, Detroit; *Blackport* is assistant director of Olivet College Library, Olivet; and *Kruzich* is coordinator of Research Education at the University of Michigan-Dearborn, Dearborn, Michigan.

folio is intended to be a living, multipurpose document, the potential uses of which include orienting new faculty, librarians, or other staff to an institution's information instruction practices; serving as information or evidence for accrediting bodies; or as a checklist for administering a library instruction program. The program portfolio's greatest value, however, lies in the experience of putting it together. The process of creating the portfolio is actually a consciousness-raising experience, with numerous opportunities for both reflection and communication. The portfolio process helps instruction librarians and others first to examine past practices and present or anticipated needs, and then to determine priorities for the future. Experience with diverse institutions over several years has shown the program portfolio to be an effective self-study instrument in terms of time and money, helping to facilitate needed change and strengthen academic communities.

Workshop Goals and Objectives

The first goal of the workshop was to present the program portfolio as a self-study methodology: the participants would understand the concept and applications; identify document types and specific documents from their own institutions appropriate to the basic categories; consider activities to supplement pre-existing documents; and practice interpreting sample portfolio materials from other institutions.

A secondary goal was to present a model of community-based professional development, which includes consulting and educational services—in other words, to give participants a mini-experience or "taste" of PREMIER by simulating a collaborative consultation and planning an in-service workshop.

First Activity: Basic Portfolio Categories

The workshop's first working session was a full group discussion, which identified the portfolio's basic categories and generated numerous examples of useful documents and library or institutional sources for documents. It should be noted that different institutions may place the same type of document in different categories, or in more than one category. The category definitions are taken from PREMIER's instructions for developing a program portfolio; the documents themselves are listed in no particular order.

- **Institutional information—Provide a description of your college or university: academic programs, student population and library holdings and facilities**—Published information sources include directories of higher education, for example, the *College Blue Book*, and the *American Library Directory*. Typical in-house documents include the institution's catalog or bulletin; institutional and library mission statements; Web pages; other self-studies; strategic plans; and institutional or departmental annual reports. Additional suggestions unique to the Charleston workshop were copies of student satisfaction surveys and reciprocal borrowing agreements (to identify other constituencies).

- **Library instruction policy—May be a formal document, a draft, or any existing equivalent which identifies philosophy, goals, strategies and procedures**—Documents or sources: ideally, a formal library instruction policy that is regularly updated; alternatively, departmental mission statements; library or departmental manuals; faculty handbooks that mention library instruction services; guidelines for adjuncts; request or in-take forms; memos; job descriptions; information literacy competencies; task force or committee reports; library's response to LOEX or other surveys.

- **Instruction librarians—Narrative statements which reflect on teaching experience are encouraged**—Job descriptions; resumes or vitae; biographies from Web pages or other professional biographies; statements of teaching philosophy. Workshop participants also indicated that the percentage of time devoted to instruction and status, faculty or not, of librarians would be relevant and important information to include.

- **Overview of present policy—Annual reports or statistics; try to include a range of years to show changes or trends; include budget information here. A narrative introduction or summary statement can be very helpful as well**—Other possibilities: general education or catalog course descriptions that mention library instruction; an inventory of the library's instructional technology resources; collected summaries of instructional sessions to coordinate reference and instruction services.

- **Specific examples—Can include orientation materials as well as credit courses, course-integrated and course-associated instruction**—Syllabi; assignments; scripts; outlines; summaries; notes; excerpts from librarians' teaching journals; handouts.

- **Collaboration—Highlight instances of team teaching between librarians and classroom faculty but include any other collaborative activities**—Syllabi; lesson plans; research assignments developed with librarian in-put; shared assessments of learning outcomes.

- **Assessment–All current learning outcomes assessments, cognitive, behavioral or affective; include how the assessment information is used**—Tests; student papers or bibliographies; student research portfolios; printouts; research appointment forms; observation of student research behavior; online catalog statistics and reports; assignments; in-class student writing; other classroom assessments.

- **Performance evaluation—Procedures and criteria**—Peer (or other) observation; excerpts from performance agreements; self-assessment statements; statistics; student evaluations of library instruction; faculty evaluations; thank-you letters from students or faculty; video tapes.

- **Professional development–Internal or external, local or national, individual or institutional**—Memberships, including library membership in LOEX; conferences; programs; workshops; mentoring.

- **Public relations/communications–Both formal and informal**—Letters or memos to faculty or other staff; fliers or brochures; library newsletters; articles in other campus publications; articles in off-campus publications; Web pages; posters.

It should also be noted that while no institution would have all of the above documents, these lists still are not definitive or exhaustive, and, in fact, institutions are encouraged to create additional categories as needed.

Second Activity: Enhancing the Documents

The second workshop activity was also a full group discussion, this time exploring alternative documents or activities to supplement existing materials. Participants were encouraged to look beyond the walls of the library and to "make the intangible tangible." The activity focused on four critical categories:

- **Library instruction policy: in the absence of written policy statements**—Suggested activities: convene a focus group (librarians, instructors, others?) to help identify perceptions and assumptions, correct or otherwise; take an oral history approach to try to understand the origins of de facto policies and procedures.

- **Specific examples: in addition to printed documents**—Suggestions: overheads; CAI programs; presentation software; videos or other audiovisual materials; flip charts; "show and tell" materials such as sample printouts.

- **Collaboration: examples of communication and community building**—Suggested alternative documents: telephone log; meeting notes; e-mail messages. Suggested activities: liaison work; librarian service on faculty or institutional committees; outreach, including library interventions in problem assignments; research assistance to faculty members; collaboration in grant applications; Internet training for faculty; librarians' academic advising; librarians teaching outside of their discipline; social opportunities. Comment: "Collaboration begins in many ways!"

- **Public relations: whatever makes you visible**—Suggestions: hold events in the library; work with alumni or friends groups; use any additional opportunities to at least informally discuss or suggest instruction; calendars may actually become portfolio documents.

Case Study Sessions: Analysis, Consultation, and In-Service Planning

The case study groups worked with a university, a college, or a community college. Example: the portfolio materials were donated by three of the PREMIER site libraries.

Analysis/Interpretation

After previewing the discussion questions, the participants began skimming the portfolio excerpts (approximately 30 pages from various portfolio categories). Although this kind of brief overview is clearly not sufficient for a real understanding of a library's instructional practices, the intention was to give participants a sense of how the assembled documents become a mosaic of information, which can be viewed either in parts or as a whole. Although conclusions differed from one group to another, the first hour's discussions covered these topics:

- How do the stated goals and objectives of library instruction relate to the institutional mission?

- How do they relate to the overview of the program?

- How is the program supported in terms of facilities, personnel, and other resources?

- Is there evidence for active learning in the librarians' instructional strategies and methods?

- Are critical thinking issues being addressed?

- What degree of collaboration exists between course instructors and librarians?

- How are outcomes measured, and how is that information used for ongoing improvement?

Consultation

In the next, brief, discussion section, the participants were asked

- What are the strengths of this instruction program?

- Are there changes that would strengthen the existing program?

- How might those changes be prioritized?

- Which changes are short term and which would be considered long-term projects?

Planning an In-Service Event

The remainder of the time (actually interrupted by a fire alarm) was spent designing a professional development or continuing education activity to encourage or support one of the recommended changes. Among other things, participants were asked to consider

- Who should be in the audience: librarians, classroom faculty, administrators, all of these, others?

- Where should the in-service take place? In the library? In "neutral" territory? What are the pros and cons of each?

- What are the advantages and disadvantages of in-house and guest presenters or trainers?

Finally the participants were asked to write one learning objective, to design one corresponding learning activity, and, if time permitted, to plan or select a short- and a long-term evaluation method.

Discussion Results

Community college case—The greatest strength of the program was seen to be the proactive librarians themselves, who also were perceived to be flexible in meeting the needs of course instructors. The recommendations were for a better in-take form (short term), still greater collaboration with faculty (short and long term), more professional and support staff and an electronic classroom (long term). The goal of the in-service was to encourage collaboration; the audience was therefore to include both librarians and some faculty members who were currently less participative in information instruction. The planned learning activity was to jointly critique and revise sample library assignments.

College case—Program strengths were recognized as the clear statement of information literacy goals and objectives, and the successful integration of information literacy into more than one required course, including a first-year integrated skills course. Recommendations were for more administrative support, closer collaboration with the campus computing department, and continued development of information literacy goals and objectives for second-, third-, and fourth-year core courses. The planned event, that grew out of the last recommendation, was a workshop that would bring faculty and students together in a learning situation involving information technology.

University case—There were three groups working on the university portfolio, and each identified a different set of strengths. For one group it was the strong relationship among the missions of the campus, the library, and the library instruction program, all of which emphasized a commitment to teaching and learning. That group also praised the three-session library component that is part of some of the composition courses, and the practice of scheduling student appointments for in-depth research consultations. Another group singled out the emphasis on critical thinking, and the knowledge and use of the Kuhlthau information search process. The third group highlighted the program's well-articulated policies and the positive relationships between faculty and librarians.

Recommendations included finalizing an outcomes assessment plan; publishing a definition of collaboration co-written by classroom faculty and librarians; doing a needs assessment to better focus library instruction; experimenting with alternative teaching strategies to better manage the instruction workload (short-term goals); developing an advanced or senior information literacy component; hiring more professional and support staff; and improving access to instructional technology, including an electronic classroom (all long-term goals).

One in-service plan that focused on the need for assessment would involve library and classroom faculty working together to design practical and meaningful information literacy assessments. Another suggested that librarians and faculty brainstorm together to develop multiple teaching strategies, including point-of-use tutorials, to maximize student learning without increasing the library instruction workload. The learning activity would be "thinking out of the box" to generate alternative approaches.

Conclusion

At the close of the workshop, one participant wrote, "Really helped me focus on what's got to be done." The portfolio process encourages librarians and others to look at library instruction resources and practices through multiple lenses, identifying strengths and accomplishments as well as opportunities for change. Peer consultants, working in collaboration, enhance and extend the visioning experience. The Charleston workshop brought together experienced librarians with an exceptionally high degree of commitment to information instruction, but the resulting range of observations, recommendations, and suggested educational activities is typical of PREMIER's multiple viewpoints—multiple voices approach to professional development.

Inevitably, the large- and small-group discussions of the workshop involved the libraries and programs of the participants as much as the sample portfolio documents and the institutions which they represented. As participants compared notes on similar needs and problems they were helping each other as well as the case study library; this is what makes the collaborative consulting experience so interesting and rewarding. PREMIER volunteers, addressing instructional and administrative issues, often say that there is no "right" way, no one answer, but rather a multitude of models that can be borrowed, blended, adapted, revised, and shared again. This is equally true of the PREMIER portfolio concept, as another participant wrote: "I think I can utilize parts of it and then create our own spin on it." Experience has shown the program portfolio to be an extremely flexible tool, which can be restructured or reinvented by different institutions, to reflect different circumstances and to serve different purposes, including that of catalyst for change.

INSTRUCTIVE SESSIONS

Implementing an Information Technology Training Program: Marketing, Managing, and Evaluating the Get Ready Pilot Project

Jill Holman

GET READY is a new instructional program to teach the basics of information technology to incoming students. We designed this pilot project to learn about the most effective method to reach our new students. In implementing a new instructional program, we found that three skill areas are critical for success: marketing, managing, and evaluating. Learning some theoretical material in these three areas will help you improve skills, which in turn increase the success of your program. The Four Ps of Marketing, (product, price, place, promotion) offer an excellent framework for developing comprehensive outreach to the students. Coordinating diverse people, resources, and activities can be done better with knowledge from the project management literature. Evaluating using sound research methods is important to justify expenses, plan improvements, and document successes. This paper is not a formal report of our pilot study. Rather it aims to discuss what is of practical use (with a bit of theory for background) to other librarians in implementing information technology training programs. Before examining the areas of marketing, managing, and evaluating, an overview of the GET READY pilot project is in order.

Background and Overview

Students are not all computer whizzes! GET READY, partially funded by a grant from the Oregon State System of Higher Education (OSSHE), is the University of Oregon's pilot project to determine the best way to teach 3,000 incoming students basic information technology using the most effective means of presentation and distribution. In Fall 1996, GET READY taught 275 students the basics of using computers for e-mail, the World Wide Web (WWW), and the library system. This pilot project compared three instructional methods: lecture with a self-paced, Web-based assignment; video with a self-paced, Web-based assignment; and hands-on sessions led by peer instructors.

GET READY was proposed in response to faculty and student needs. Faculty did not want to spend class time teaching information-technology skills. Students were having a hard time picking up the skills and wanted to focus on their subjects. While the University of Oregon Library's extensive Internet curriculum had been very successful, it was still not reaching a segment of our population and, because Internet workshops extend through the term, faculty sometimes wanted to incorporate technology before students had the opportunity to take a workshop. GET READY was devised to create a technological common ground among new students, so faculty could assume students had certain information-technology skills and so students could participate fully in their classes.

Upon receipt of the OSSHE grant to fund the pilot project of GET READY, the project team (assistant university librarian for public services and collections, assistant university librarian for administrative and instructional media services, head of reference, academic education coordinator, and curator of special collec-

---

Holman is Get Ready Pilot Project coordinator and science reference librarian, University of Oregon, Eugene. <http://libweb.uoregon.edu/getready>.

tions) hired a librarian to coordinate the project. The coordinator was to be .25 FTE February-June 1996 and 1 FTE July-September 1996.

First, we determined desired educational outcomes for the four topic areas: computer basics, e-mail, the World Wide Web, and the library system. The coordinator and project team brainstormed, held faculty focus groups, and solicited faculty input via e-mail. Desired outcomes included students' being able to perform certain tasks such as "read and send e-mail" and being exposed to terms and concepts such as "URL" and "netiquette."

GET READY had two main peaks of activity. The University of Oregon has a series of orientation sessions during July called IntroDUCKtion. About 80 percent of students attend to take placement tests, register for classes, and learn about resources available on campus. During IntroDUCKtion, the first peak of GET READY activity, we registered students for the program and conducted a preparedness survey. The survey was designed to help us better understand students' comfort levels, experience, and knowledge relating to information technology, specifically basic computer skills, e-mail, the World Wide Web, and library systems. We found that we were on track with our goals for GET READY because students still were not arriving at the University of Oregon ready to use information technology. Although 97 percent of the students in our preparedness survey had used computers, use focused on word processing and game playing. Only 47 percent had experience with the WWW and only 37 percent had used e-mail.

The students who registered for GET READY do not really represent our study body. Whether it is due to differences in actual skill, confidence levels, or willingness to participate in this kind of training, we had a high 72 percent of female students register for the program; approximately 53 percent of our incoming students are female. Similarly, 17 percent of minority students registered, whereas only about ten percent of our incoming students are minorities. We had a high 89 percent of registered students report they had home computers. Our findings compared to the national average of 30 to 35 percent[1] are an unexpected disparity. The percentage of students from places other than Oregon did not vary much between GET READY and the incoming students (43 percent and 39 percent). Age was not too surprising—the majority were 17- and 18-year-olds. We had about ten percent of our registrants over 21-years old; we had a small number of returning graduate students in GET READY. Although the pilot project was geared towards the incoming freshmen, incoming graduate students also have a need for this type of information-technology training.

Meanwhile, we developed the instructional modules over the summer. We determined that each of the three groups (lecture with a self-paced, Web-based assignment; video with a self-paced, Web-based assignment; and hands-on sessions led by peer instructors) would have about 3.5 hours of training. First, a team of librarians developed the outline for the hour-long lecture and video. Our approach with the video was an upbeat exposure to the basics of e-mail, the World Wide Web, and our library's online system. We knew they would not remember most details, so we aimed at alleviating fear and simply introducing them to the electronic tools, their appearances, and their functions. We also emphasized all the various places where students could ask for help. Two librarians were chosen as stars of the video. Our television producer/director from the library's Instructional Media Center directed the video. The coordinator acted as producer of the video, arranged props and locations, coached on content, and helped to edit the video. Our video stars were also our lecturers.

A team of two technology-oriented librarians, one education librarian, and our Web guru created the self-paced, Web-based assignment. The team included units on using Netscape, searching the Web, exploring online help systems, searching the library system, using e-mail, and mailing lists. They discussed general concepts and gave specific examples and lots of sources for further information. Interactive exercises throughout asked the students to try tasks and they received immediate, automatic feedback. The Web tutorial can be viewed from the GET READY Web site at <http://libweb.uoregon.edu/getready>.

Preparation for the hands-on sessions included advertising for and hiring ten peer instructors to teach the classes. Most were upper-level undergraduates and a few were graduate students. All were experienced with information technology and most had some experience teaching. The librarian in charge of the hands-on sessions developed a two-day training for the instructors, which focused on the purpose of GET READY, the material that was to be covered, and some techniques for teaching well. During the GET READY training, two sessions met at the same time, one in our Mac classroom and one in our PC classroom. The class was 3.5 hours with a snack intermission. After the break, the groups switched rooms in order to utilize the other platform. The project team also gathered relevant handouts and created a GET READY packet for each student.

The second peak of activity was in September during Orientation Week, the week before classes began. This is when the actual training was held. We held a main and a make-up lecture, a main and a make-up screening of the video, and 14 hands-on sessions.

GET READY Participation	
470	Registrants
411	Preparedness Survey Respondents
275	Training Participants
147	Comment Form Respondents
60	Evaluative Survey Respondents
6	Focus Group Participants

Table 1: Summary of Participation in the Pilot Project

People also viewed the video at their convenience in our instructional media center. About half (56 percent) of the registrants attended, plus some walk-ins. Very few students utilized the Web tutorial. We had a comment form at the time of training, an evaluative survey eight weeks later, and focus groups at the end of the term. See table 1 for a summary of participation in the pilot project.

Now that we have an overview of the project, let's delve more deeply into why we chose to compare three instructional methods. Fill in the blanks according to the situation at your institution (numbers in square brackets are estimates at the University of Oregon):

A) Number of Incoming Students = [3,000] _____

B) Number of Hours of Instruction Desired = [4] _____

C) Number of Electronic Classrooms Available = [3] _____

D) Number of Instructors Available = [10] _____

Let's assume you have **3,000** incoming students and you can fit **25** in an electronic classroom; then you need to have **120** classes. Let's assume you want **4** hours of instruction to cover computer basics, e-mail, the WWW, and your library system; then you need **480** hours of classroom and instructor access. Your goal is to have them ready for the start of their classes, so you hold the training the week before classes begin. You will schedule tightly by offering the training **8** hours a day for **6** days, or during **48** hours in the week; you will then need **10** electronic classrooms. Let's assume that an instructor can teach for **3** days, for **4** hours a day (a fairly heavy teaching load), and that you want **2** instructors for each class of **25**. From table 2, see that scheduling **1** classroom requires **8** instructors and thus you need **80** instructors total.

You would need ten classrooms and 80 instructors to provide four hours of training to 3,000 students in a week! Very few institutions have these resources. Let us see how we might reduce the necessary resources.

A) Number of Incoming Students—What percentage of new students really need information-technology instruction?

Certainly not all of the new students require instruction. However, the notion that all students are computer whizzes is not yet true. In our GET READY preparedness survey, 97 percent of the students had used computers, but the kind of use focused on word processing and game playing. Only 47 percent had experience with the World Wide Web and only 37 percent had used e-mail. Remember, these students were not necessarily skilled; they simply had been exposed to the WWW and e-mail. Thus at least 63 percent (1,890 in our example of 3,000) of new students needed some information-technology training to be successful on campus.

B) Number of Hours of Instruction Desired—How brief can the instruction be and still be useful?

In GET READY, we knew we could not teach students everything they needed to know, so we aimed at getting them over their initial anxiety, getting them started with the basics, and being sure they knew of the many opportunities they had for help when they later needed it. The lecture lasted an hour and the video lasted 45 minutes; students in these groups were satisfied with the program and found it effective.

C) Number of Electronic Classrooms Available—Can video or lecture be used in conjunction with a self-paced, Web tutorial for experiential learning, instead of hands-on sessions?

Students who used the Web tutorial liked it, but participation was low. Apparently, students need a great deal of motivation to learn on their own.

D) Number of Instructors Available—Can peer instructors be used instead of faculty?

Students in GET READY did not respond to peer instructors as well as we thought they would. Even though the peer instructors were experienced with information technology and trained in teaching, the students found them impatient and unprofessional. Students responded better to the lec-

	Day 1	Day 2	Day 3	Day 4	Day 5	Day 6
1st 4 hrs	AB	AB	AB	CD	CD	CD
2nd 4 hrs	EF	EF	EF	GH	GH	GH

Table 2: Sample Schedule for a Classroom. Each letter represents an instructor

ture/demo format and their experienced, personable librarian facilitators.

We have learned that students are not arriving on campus with the skills they need; at least 63 percent of them do need some information-technology training. It is not feasible to hold librarian-led, hands-on sessions for all students who need information-technology training and peer instructors were not a viable alternative in our case. Luckily, students were satisfied with as little as an hour of training in the lecture/demo or video format when we aimed to introduce them to electronic services and additional resources available. For basic information-technology training, we need not be overly concerned with instructional method.

> The moral of this story is
> DO SOMETHING!
> Even if the training you can offer is less than what you would like, students still need it and will appreciate it.

Marketing

After completion of the pilot project, we have realized our training was quite good and that now our main goal is to increase participation. The Four Ps of Marketing (product, price, place, and promotion) offer an excellent framework to develop comprehensive outreach to students and increase their participation. In addition, there are subdivisions to the Four Ps: there is the tangible product and also an augmented product; there are additional costs beyond any monetary price; components of place include location, timing, and atmosphere; and types of promotion include personal promotion, incentives, free publicity, and paid advertising. Let us examine our outreach activity in July, a main peak of activity for GET READY, in light of the Four Ps (see table 3).

The University of Oregon has a series of orientation sessions during July called IntroDUCKtion. About 80 percent of new students attend to take placement tests, register for classes, and learn about resources available on campus. At IntroDUCKtion, we registered students and distributed our preparedness survey. Our tangible product was Internet training and our augmented product was student success. There was no monetary price and other costs were kept to the ten minutes it took students to complete the preparedness survey. The location was a low-stress information fair held during an outdoor lunch. The sun shone and a band played upbeat music. Timing was convenient for students since they could walk through when they chose and the atmosphere was casual and fun. We had personal promotion as library staff asked the students if they had heard about the library's new Internet training program. We relied on the Internet itself as incentive for participation. Related departments such as the computing center and academic learning services offered free publicity by talking about GET READY in their informational sessions. We also placed advertisements in students' packets; additionally, we sent out some mailings.

Our outreach in July was nearly ideal from a marketing perspective! We had a variety of promotional techniques, costs were low, and the setting ("place") was fun and convenient. Our registration was successful. We had 320 students sign up at IntroDUCKtion during the 14 hours of information fairs. Additional personal contacts brought more participants. All 29 freshman electronic interest group students registered because their instructor required it. All 50 allotted slots for international students were taken when a librarian introduced the program to them. Advertising through the mail brought us more participants, but at a lower rate than personal contacts. Only 100 students registered through the mail, mostly from IntroDUCKtion. Only 14 registered from a 350-person mailing of at-risk students. Only ten registered from a 31-person mailing of School of Education (Early Intervention Program) graduate students.

After this delightful success in July, we made a mistake. We thought we were done. Students saw the value of our program and had registered. They would be motivated to take the training when they arrived in September. We were wrong!

We failed to view our contact in September from a fresh marketing perspective. Let us examine our outreach in September, when we held the GET READY training, in light of the Four Ps (see table 3). Again, our tangible product was Internet training and our augmented product was student success. There still was no monetary price, but other costs increased. The

	Definition	GET READY in July	GET READY in September
Product	*tangible* *augmented*	Internet training student success	IT instruction, IT skills success in courses
Price	*monetary* *other*	no fee 10 minutes to complete survey	no fee time, convenience, image
Place	*location* *timing* *atmosphere*	low-stress info fair convenient casual, fun	hard-to-find locations restrictive, assigned time confusing self-authorization, barrier to self-paced learning
Promotion	*personal* *incentives* *free publicity* *paid advertising*	library staff at info fair Internet as incentive publicized by related departments ads in student materials, mailings	impersonal and confusing mailing Internet as incentive not publicized by related depts reminder in program

Table 3: The Four Ps and Get Ready

training lasted 45 minutes (video), one hour (lecture), or 3.5 hours (hands-on sessions). Lack of time is a considerable factor for students during Orientation Week because they are new to campus and need to buy books, open bank accounts, make friends, and generally orient themselves to campus life. The image of the training is another potential cost. We know that many library patrons are reluctant to ask questions at the reference desk because it means they do not know something; this same danger exists for information-technology training. We did not want GET READY to seem like remedial training; we want GET READY to seem like "the happening thing" to do. Concerning "Place," some of our locations were hard to find, especially to students new to campus. The timing was not always convenient because students were assigned time slots. The atmosphere was lacking in that students had to initiate their computer accounts before their sessions and this was immensely confusing to them. We still relied on the Internet as an incentive and we had advertising in their New Student Orientation program. Instead of personal promotion, students received an impersonal and complex mailing and students did not receive publicity about GET READY from other departments.

Our outreach in September was much less than ideal from a marketing perspective. Our product was the same, yet we had increased non-monetary costs and negatives associated with "Place," especially timing. We neglected to continue that personalized promotion that worked so well in July. Our attendance was a limited success: Only about 50 percent of registered students attended. There is a strong message here: Unless participation is required, it is critical to the success of an information technology training program to use marketing principles to increase participation. For each contact with students, have a comprehensive outreach plan. See the appendix for additional marketing suggestions, some of which were brainstormed during the LOEX conference instructive session.

> Use the Four Ps of Marketing to create a comprehensive outreach plan *each* time you contact students.

Managing

Ponder this scenario: Library administration conceives a new instructional program for teaching basic information technology to incoming students. They receive a grant for a pilot study. They choose a librarian interested in both instruction and technology to coordinate the project. The coordinator, without having any real authority, must collaborate with a variety of people doing very different activities.

What are potential problems with this scenario?

The group at the LOEX conference instructive session brainstormed the following problem areas and questions:

- Staff are too busy to contribute.
- How do you get staff to buy into the project?
- The coordinator lacks authority.
- The project needs a better definition of priorities.
- Staff will need to use new skills.
- How do institutional politics affect the project?

- The library/institution will need an infrastructure of equipment and resources.

- When staff work on the project, who will replace them and do their work?

- Support staff are needed for a project like this.

Being new to this type of situation, the coordinator turned to the management literature and found that her situation was not unique at all. Let us look at some of the main ideas from the project management literature.[2] First of all, the goal of project management is to *Get Done*! with the following three caveats: finish on time, within budget, and according to specifications.

To complete the project, the project manager has two main objectives. The first is to avoid pitfalls. It is not possible to strive for a perfect project. Problems occur and the manager's job is to minimize their negative effects so that there are only acceptable losses. There are three main areas that can cause pitfalls. The first is organizational characteristics. This includes institutional politics and "the divorce of responsibility and authority" that most project coordinators must navigate. The second is poorly identified customer needs, which is also important from a marketing perspective. The third area that can cause pitfalls is poor planning and control.

After pitfalls, the second objective of the project manager is to "make things happen." This may sound simplistic, but it is no easy task and requires the coordinator to take on many roles. The leader of the project coordinates, influences, motivates, networks, negotiates, supports, whatever is needed. Second, to make things happen, the leader must remember WIIFM, which stands for "What's in it for me?" This means that the coordinator must think about those she approaches and how contributing to the project might be beneficial for them. How will this project help their students? How will this make them look more successful in their jobs?

Reading the management literature is useful to gaining an understanding of project management. Knowing that the situation is not unique can help the project manager feel more comfortable with having responsibility without having authority. The experienced manager learns to expect mishaps, delegate as much as possible, and MBWA, "Manage by Walking Around." The literature gives many practical tips to help the coordinator avoid pitfall areas and successfully complete the project.

> Use the management literature to understand the context and improve the coordination of your project.

Evaluating

The last area of critical importance in successfully implementing an information-technology instructional program is evaluation. Evaluation is important when you are substantiating user needs and when you are justifying the success of your program. Let's review the basic steps in the evaluation process. As always, know your goal/purpose. Know how you will use the information and explain this to the participant. Keep it simple and short. Be sure to pretest your methods and revise. Increase participation with reminders and the Four Ps of Marketing. Enter, analyze, and interpret your data. Use graphics for better communication of your results.

In considering research methods, more research methods are better. You want different types of information and you want to gather them at different times. How you ask questions matters, to both the content and the layout. In formal research, it is a good idea to have a control group. For example, in drug studies, two groups will be treated exactly the same way, except one group will receive the drug and one will receive a placebo. If the group receiving the drug does markedly better than the other group, it is assumed that the improvement is because of the drug. An example of using a control in instructional research would be to have two sections of the same course, give one group instruction, and see if the students receiving instruction perform better. Another wise technique is conducting a pretest/post-test comparison. In this way you can show that students know more after your instruction than they did before. Be sure to obtain both qualitative and quantitative information; both lend credibility to your findings. Strive to make your findings both valid and reliable. Your results are reliable if you were to conduct the study again and get the same results. Your results are valid if they answer your research questions. For example, asking students to rate their skills with information technology is a fairly valid way to measure their comfort levels, but a more valid way to measure their actual skill would be to test them or give them some tasks to perform.

GET READY was a strong pilot project because we incorporated a variety of evaluative techniques. In GET READY, we conducted a preparedness survey to check on student needs and our objectives and found that we were on target in focusing the training on e-mail and the WWW, as discussed earlier in the section, "The Problem with Librarian-Led Hands-On Sessions." We had a pretest/post-test comparison of their information-technology knowledge, use, and comfort. We did have a control in that we included students who did not take the training. We found that students' knowledge during the pretest was at the D level on our eight-question quiz. (There were two questions each to spot-test knowledge of computer basics, e-mail, the WWW, and the library.) Non-attendees remained at the D level, whereas GET READY attendees achieved a B average on the quiz. Generally, use of and comfort with information technology increased for both attendees and non-attendees, only slightly more for attendees. It is interesting to note that library use and comfort of attendees increased from the pretest, but non-attendees' library use and comfort actually decreased from the pretest.

We held a quick survey at the time of the training where we found that students were very satisfied with the training, no matter which instructional method they had. (Hands-on sessions got the only negative rating and that was only two percent of the hands-on respondents. Lecture got the most "well-done" ratings with 78 percent of lecture respondents choosing "well-done.") We had an evaluative survey eight weeks later where we asked about effectiveness. We found that students rated the training as effective, no matter which instructional method they had. (Video sessions got the most negative ratings with 28 percent of the video respondents responding negatively. Hands-on got the most positive ratings with 93 percent of hands-on respondents responding positively.) The evaluative survey also gave us ideas for improvement such as timing and content preferences that we have used in planning for next year. We held focus groups at the end of the term to solicit additional input. We gained more ideas to use next year and garnered the following types of comments:

"It makes me more confident about starting school."

"I helped everybody in the dorm set [their e-mail account] up because it was clear to me."

"If I didn't know how to search [on the WWW], my computer would almost be useless because I have to do that for a lot of my classes. I had to find my Congressman's address and [because of GET READY] I knew how to do it."

"Very informative and helpful."

"Teachers were upbeat and knowledgeable."

"Now I'm not completely lost."

Evaluation is critical in implementing an information-technology instructional program successfully. A variety of techniques makes your research stronger and gives you the evidence to substantiate user needs and justify expenses. The evidence also can be used to document the success of your program and plan improvements for next year. The last section of this paper explains the plan for GET READY 1997.

> Use as many evaluative techniques as possible—they give the evidence you need to justify expenses, plan improvements, and document successes.

Plans for GET READY 1997

A major and fortunate change for 1997 is that students will receive their computing accounts during IntroDUCKtion in July. We will hold GET READY sessions at IntroDUCKtion in order to reach them when they are interested, rather than months later. (Here we improve on last year's program as discussed in the Marketing section.) A librarian and member of the computing center staff will facilitate the sessions using new, updated video modules. The video segments will cover the bulk of the information, including more specific applications of e-mail and the WWW, and then the facilitators will answer questions and demonstrate additional capabilities and skills. Open houses in the computing labs will follow these sessions so that students can access their accounts, change their passwords, visit the GET READY Web site, and ask staff questions. The Web tutorial will include more interactive components and a formal quiz. We will encourage students to visit the Web site and complete the tutorial over the summer.

In addition, we will hold several open enrollment lectures during Orientation Week and the first two weeks of classes for the students who do not attend IntroDUCKtion. We have added e-mail classes to the Internet curriculum, which is offered throughout the term, for additional hands-on learning opportunities. Web and library system classes are also available in this curriculum. We will promote GET READY as a "happening thing" students won't want to miss and incorporate additional marketing suggestions from the appendix. Evaluation will continue. Hopefully, we can test/survey students at IntroDUCKtion before they attend GET READY sessions. We will have a brief evaluation at the sessions. We will get some information from the quiz on the Web tutorial. We will administer a follow-up survey in the fall term and hold focus groups.

Our plans for GET READY 1997 will incorporate many improvements as a result of what we have learned in the pilot project, especially in the critical areas of marketing, managing, and evaluating. Remember, marketing offers an excellent framework for developing comprehensive outreach to the students and it is important to use the Four Ps each time you contact students. Coordinating diverse people, resources, and activities can be done better with theoretical knowledge about managing projects. The management literature offers important context and helpful tips to the coordinator of an instructional program. Using solid research techniques to evaluate your program is important to justify expenses, plan improvements, and document successes. Use the theoretical material discussed in this paper to improve your skills in marketing, managing, and evaluating and ensure the success of your instructional program. Do not be overly concerned with instructional method or length of the training. The students need help getting ready to use information technology on campuses. You cannot teach them everything they need to know, but you can help them become more comfortable and more knowledgeable. You can help them to understand the basic patterns, to ask better questions, and to know where to go for help later when they need it. Good luck in developing your own information technology instructional programs!

NOTES

1. Neil Weinberg, "Getting Granny to Surf the Net," *Forbes* (6 May 1996): 119-122 and Stephen H. Wildstrom, "Wanted: A PC for the Masses," *Business Week* (15 January 1996): 18.

2. Most of this information is from J. Davidson Frame, *Managing Projects in Organizations: How to Make the Best Use of Time, Techniques, and People*, rev. ed. (San Francisco: Jossey-Bass Publishers, 1995).

APPENDIX: MARKETING SUGGESTIONS

Product *(tangible and augmented)*

Think of product as IT instruction, IT skills, success in courses, success in the future, entertainment.

Price *(monetary and other)*

Assuming there is no monetary cost to the student, reduce additional costs involving wasted time, inconvenience, frustration, image/stigma.

Place *(location, atmosphere, timing)*

Schedule in conveniently located, wired, newly refurbished rooms. Extend training to one and a half hours.[1] Hold sessions during Orientation Week, IntroDUCKtion, and the second week of classes.[2] Hold half the sessions in the afternoon, one-quarter in the morning, and one-quarter in the evening.[3] Improve signage leading attendees to the sessions.

Promotion *(personal, incentives, free publicity, paid advertising)*

Increase quantity and variety of promotion. For example:

- staff library tables during IntroDUCKtion and Orientation Week;

- be sure all public services people are knowledgeable and can recommend GET READY;

- work with academic advisors and faculty to require students to participate (professors could give extra credit to students who participate);

- get an article in the *Emerald* student newspaper;

- get related departments such as the computing center and academic learning services to give GET READY publicity;

- target to groups such as athletes, Honors College, residence hall clubs;

- charge $5 fee, refundable upon completion of the program;

- have prize give-aways for students who complete the program;

- take out an ad in the *Emerald* and in the New Student Orientation program;

- hang signs in the library and the student union;

- use personal testimony from last year's GET READY students;

- increase Web tutorial promotion; and

- debunk myths such as:
    - "All information is on the Internet, free and easy to use."
    - "My professors will teach me if I need to know."
    - "This would be easy if I were meant to do it."

SELECTED RESOURCES

Marketing

Kirkendall, Carolyn A. ed. *Marketing Instructional Services: Applying Private Sector Techniques to Plan and Promote Bibliographic Instruction.* Proceedings of the 13th LOEX conference. Ann Arbor, MI: Pierian Press, 1986.

Weingand, Darlene E., ed. "Marketing of Library and Information Services." (Special Issue) *Library Trends* 43:3 (1995): 289-509.

Managing

Forsberg, Kevin, Hal Mooz, and Howard Cotterman. *Visualizing Project Management.* New York: Wiley, 1996.

Frame, J. Davidson. *Managing Projects in Organizations: How to Make the Best Use of Time, Techniques, and People.* Rev. ed. San Francisco: Jossey-Bass Publishers, 1995.

Pinto, Jeffrey K., and O.P. Kharbanda. *Successful Project Managers: Leading Your Team to Success.* New York: Van Nostrand Reinhold, 1995.

Evaluating

Babbie, Earl. *The Practice of Social Research.* 6th ed. Belmont, CA: Wadsworth, 1992.

Evaluating Bibliographic Instruction: A Handbook. Chicago: Bibliographic Instruction Section, Association of College and Research Libraries, American Library Association, 1983.

Kiess, Harold O. *Statistical Concepts for the Behavioral Sciences.* Boston: Allyn & Bacon, 1989.

Shonrock, Diana D., ed. *Evaluating Library Instruction: Sample Questions, Forms, and Strategies for Practical Use*. Chicago: Library Instruction Round Table, American Library Association, 1996.

Producing a Video

Bergman, Robert E. *Managing Interactive Video/Multimedia Projects*. Englewood Cliffs, NJ: Educational Technology Publications, 1990.

DeLuca, Stuart M. *Instructional Video*. Boston: Focal Press, 1991.

Elliott, Geoff. *Video Production in Education and Training*. Dover, NH: Croom Helm, 1984.

Hausman, Carl. *Institutional Video: Planning, Budgeting, Production, and Evaluation*. Belmont, CA: Wadsworth Pub. Co., 1991.

NOTES

1. When asked about the amount of instructor contact, 93 percent said they wanted more or a lot more. (Even the hands-on students wanted more instructor contact.)

2. When asked about the timing of the training, 74 percent of students wanted training during Orientation Week.

3. When asked about time of day of training, 46 percent of respondents wanted afternoon, 29 percent wanted morning, and 25 percent wanted nighttime training.

Using Presentation Software in Instruction Sessions: Design Principles and Presentation Skills

Julie Long

Introduction

When I began my career as a children's librarian almost 30 years ago, the presentations I gave were storyhours to preschoolers, booktalks to elementary school children, and talks to parent groups about the value of reading to their children. My audio and visual aids were the books themselves, flannel boards, puppets, records, and the oral tradition of storytelling. The change to academic librarianship 15 years ago introduced me to a different audience, different visuals, and a different content to present. However, whether it is a storyhour for preschoolers or a marketing class for sophomores, certain factors remain the same: the need to know the audience, deciding what content to present, and determining how best to convey and deliver the content.

As my library and Saint Mary's students became more "wired"—OPAC, CD-ROM indexes, e-mail accounts, Web access—I felt like the element of "how best to convey content" was lagging behind the times. In 1995, I received an institutional research grant to look at software to enhance the library's instruction program and my teaching techniques. I purchased two presentation packages, Microsoft's PowerPoint and Adobe's Persuasion, and one authoring package, Authorware by Macromedia. After looking at such things as features, ease of use, and institutional support of a particular package, I decided to use PowerPoint in my instruction sessions. The guidelines and principles that follow, however, are generic and are applicable regardless of the presentation software chosen.

Why Use Presentation Software?

Why should we consider incorporating or using presentation software in instruction? The pat answer, of course, is this is the electronic age; today's students have grown up with MTV and computer games, and are attracted to the visual media. But the fact of the matter is, there are concrete benefits to seeing as well as hearing a presentation. From an instructional point of view, using presentation software can

- help clarify the spoken word,
- help students visualize information,
- provide a framework for notetaking, and
- hold students' attention.

Memory retention studies indicate that a person retains 20 percent of what she sees, 40 percent of what she sees and hears, and 75 percent of what she sees, hears, and does. Hopefully, the more senses we can engage, the more learning will take place. Taking a lesson from the business world, four reasons to justify adopting a new way are that it is faster, cheaper, easier, or better. I think using presentation software meets all four reasons. Once the software has been mastered, preparation time decreases; making changes or integrat-

---

Long is a reference and instruction librarian at the Cushwa-Leighton Library at Saint Mary's College, Notre Dame, Indiana.

ing slides from different presentations takes very little time. If presentations are run directly from the computer, the cost of making transparencies can decrease and delivery of the presentation becomes easier. Lastly, I think it can make us better at what we do by helping us think more creatively about the content and the way we convey it.

Incorporating Presentation Software

How, then, do we incorporate this software into our instruction sessions? The guidelines we have used in the past for preparing instruction sessions and accompanying visuals are valid for preparing technology-enhanced lectures.

- Be organized and prepared.

- Clearly define the topics or points you expect to cover in the session.

- Repeat the message using the technique of "tell them what you're going to tell them; tell them; tell them what you told them."

- Avoid information overload.

Five Areas of Design

With an understanding of some basic design principles, we can use presentation software to create more attractive visuals that result in more stimulating instruction sessions. As we build up a collection of presentations, we can mix and match slides from previous presentations to create new ones. What we need to keep in mind is that the purpose of the visual medium is to enhance the content we are teaching. It is important to draft frames that "read right" so that good information is not buried or lost in the design. We want our students to both consciously and subconsciously see what is important. Avoid the "too" concept. The use of too many bulleted points, too many graphics, or too many colors will result in clutter and confusion and obscure the points we are trying to make. The five areas of design we need to be aware of are overall layout, fonts, color, graphics, and builds and transitions.

Overall Layout

Two key principles to bear in mind in the overall layout are simplicity and consistency. A screen is not a lot of real estate so we need to use the space wisely. A horizontal format, balance, and consistency will result in good composition. Using a flush-left alignment and a ragged-right edge is easy to layout and to read. A series of vertical axes can be used for the left alignment, thus keeping the frames from being too static. Establish a format for titles, subtitles, and bulleted points and adhere to it. There are some basic rules for text slides so that they do not become too crowded:

- one line—one thought,

- no more than six to eight lines per slide,

- no more than eight words per line,

- don't have the text tell everything.

Remember that the purpose of the slide is to prod the audience along; it's not a readout of what we are saying. The audience shouldn't be so busy reading what is on the screen that their attention is drawn away from what we are saying.

Fonts

The font chosen should be easy to read. Consistent use of a font, with some variation in size and style, along with consistent text placement is the key. Sans serif fonts tend to be the most readable and stand up well to projection. It is very easy to get caught up in trying a multitude of different fonts. Just don't put them all on the same slide or use different fonts throughout a presentation. Type is meant to be read and to communicate, so legibility is the number one priority when choosing a font. Whether to use all capital letters or a combination of upper and lower case is still debated by the experts. Choose one font and vary it by size, underlining, or boldness to add interest to your slides. Consistency is still the key.

Color

Color is a very subjective element. As with fonts, it is easy to get caught up in all the choices. A rule of thumb is to use color sparingly and with restraint; one or two colors on a consistent background is sufficient. Consider contrast and brightness when selecting colors for backgrounds and text elements. Graduated backgrounds are a way to add depth, and most software programs offer horizontal, vertical, or diagonal blending options. Keeping the background and text colors consistent on each slide lends continuity to the content. If you intend to project from a computer on to a screen, keep in mind that colors do not always look the same. What appears bright and readable on the monitor may look faded when projected on the screen. The type of projection device and the ability to control the lighting of the room will also be factors. If at all possible, check colors, font sizes, and continuity by projecting in a room similar to the one in which you will be teaching.

Graphics

Graphics can enhance the visual communication of our presentations. Most packages have clip art and drawing tools incorporated in them, but it is also possible to import images provided certain requirements are met. Software-provided templates will often provide enough graphical interest. The key question is, what does the graphic add to the content? It may be for visual interest, for humor, or to illustrate a point or complex relationship. One caution about using scanned or imported graphics, sound clips, or video clips is copyright implications. If in doubt, either secure necessary permissions or do not use them. Simplicity and consistency are also the rule with templates. The template should reflect the content, audience, and occasion.

Builds and Transitions

Lastly, we need to consider builds—the movement from point to point on a slide; and transitions—the movement from slide to slide. Choose a build for points and a transition for slide progressions and be consistent throughout the presentation. The fact that there are numerous build and transition choices does not mean we should incorporate a different one on each slide. They should be unobtrusive. We do not want our audience to be so interested in the next special effect that they lose interest in the content. The purpose of builds is to hold the students' attention. If all points are shown at once, students try to read the whole slide rather than concentrating on the point being made. By revealing one point at a time, the audience cannot jump ahead.

Delivering the Presentation

When delivering an electronic presentation, we need to be aware of posture and movement, eye contact, and speech. These are the same elements we are cognizant of when giving an instruction session that does not involve technology. Just as we should not hide behind the podium or anchor ourselves to it when delivering a talk, we should try not to hide behind the computer. Experiment with positioning equipment in such a way as to facilitate ease of movement and provide the audience with good sight lines. Consider using a remote mouse or one with a long cord. Some presenters prefer using the timed slide advance option offered by most software. For more formal presentations, you may wish to have a colleague advance the screens for you. Choose an option that allows you to move, use gestures, and retain the delivery style to which you are accustomed.

Eye contact with the audience is very important when delivering electronic presentations. An occasional glance at the computer monitor or projection screen is certainly appropriate and sometimes necessary, but remember who and where your audience is. By becoming comfortable with the hardware, software, and transitions of your presentation, you will be able to focus more on the audience and less on what is going on behind you.

Clear and articulate speech is something we strive for in any lecture we give. The use of presentation software does not change this nor the fact that we need to pace our delivery. There is a tendency to rush because we think all the information is on the screen. Keep in mind that what is on the screen is an outline that we must flesh out.

But how do we handle those things that are not an extension of a lecture-style presentation? A program that crashes in the middle of a presentation or before it even begins. An incompatibility with the software and computer on which the presentation was developed and the one from which it is being delivered. Keyboard strokes or swapping disks. These are things we have not had to deal with in the past. Preparation, anticipation, and a back-up presentation will give you the confidence needed to handle most situations.

Preparation means knowing that the development computer and software, including versions, are compatible with the delivery system. Preparation means practice, a dress rehearsal if you will, to work out the logistics of screen, projection device, and computer placement, practicing any needed keystrokes or disk swapping and becoming familiar with builds and transitions, all of which affect the flow of the presentation. In essence, preparation means being comfortable with the technology—hardware and software.

Anticipation means running through some "what if" scenarios. What if my computer crashes or freezes? There are a number of ways to handle this, depending on certain factors. If your initial comfort level with the technology is very low, you may wish to consider asking a colleague to attend your session and respond to any technological difficulties that arise. If you are comfortable with the technology, you may prefer to do your own troubleshooting. Time is probably the main factor to consider. If you have just started, you may wish to try rebooting. If there are only five to ten minutes left, you may not wish to lose the opportunity to summarize key points and answer questions. It becomes a judgment call if you are somewhere in the middle of the lecture.

It is for these situations that a back-up plan is essential: a handout, which you may have already distributed, a back-up disc of your presentation, transparencies, or the blackboard. The audience to whom the presentation is being made as well as the content of the presentation may dictate what type of back-up you have in place.

Common Pitfalls

Let's briefly summarize some of the common pitfalls that can weaken a design and hence a presentation:

- **Type that is too small and too light**—Begin with medium or bold type weights. Use type that's large enough to be read easily but small enough to fit a phrase on a single line.

- **Cluttered layout**—Use restraint when it comes to graphics. Open space really helps draw the eye to the element in it.

- **Backgrounds**—A clean, uncomplicated background is much more professional looking and effective than a cluttered one.

- **Color**—Color is a powerful design element that can have both negative and positive impact so use it judiciously.

- **Alignment**—Establish an alignment plan that will work for the whole presentation. Avoid centering each line of text or using left-right justification.

- **Emphasis**—Emphasis can be achieved with color, size, or capitalization. Chosen carefully, colors, type sizes, and use of uppercase letters will provide the emphasis needed for the points being made.

- **Cliché**—Just as there are verbal clichés, there are visual clichés; both can be boring. They are not necessarily bad ideas, just overworked.

Conclusion

As important as design and layout are, we need to remember that their purpose is to support our message. If the presentation does not meet the objectives of the instruction session, then we need to consider revising it so that it more clearly reflects our ideas. What we are striving for is a visual interpretation of ideas and information that will be understood and remembered by our students. Presentation software can truly enhance instruction sessions. Visually it provides a strong focal point for our students' attention. Instructionally it forces us to think critically about content, connections, and continuity. The key elements to remember are simplicity and continuity in preparation and practice and back-up for delivery.

SUGGESTED READING

Azarmsa, Reza. "Technology-Mediated Presentation in the Classroom." *Syllabus* 10:5 (January 1997): 10-11, 16.

Gribas, Cyndy, Lynn Sykes, and Nick Dorochoff. "Creating Great Overheads with Computers." *College Teaching* 44:2 (Spring 1996): 66-68.

Lindstrom, Robert L. *The Business Week Guide to Multimedia Presentations*. Berkeley, CA: McGraw-Hill, 1994.

Meilach, Dona Z. *Dynamics of Presentation*. Homewood, IL: Dow Jones-Irwin, 1990.

Raab, Margaret. *The Presentation Design Book: Tips, Techniques, and Advice for Creating Effective, Attractive slides, Overheads, Multimedia Presentations, Screen Shows and More,* 2d ed. Chapel Hill, NC: Ventana Press, 1993.

Rupp-Serrano, Karen, and Nancy Buchanan. "Using Presentation Software for Computerized Instruction." *Online* 16:2 (March 1992): 60-64.

Strasser, Dennis. "Tips for Good Electronic Presentations." *Online* 20:1 (January-February 1996): 78-81.

Designing and Implementing CLUE, an Interactive, Multimedia Instructional Program

Abigail Loomis and Lee Konrad

In Spring 1995, the General Library System of the University of Wisconsin-Madison (UW) received an Instructional Technology Support Grant to develop CLUE (Computerized Library User Education), an interactive, multimedia instruction program designed to teach basic information literacy skills to students enrolled in courses that meet a new, two-course undergraduate communication requirement on campus. This paper examines some of the pedagogical, technological, and administrative issues that librarians need to consider when planning a multimedia instructional package like CLUE.

As of Fall 1996, all incoming freshmen at UW-Madison (ca. 5,400 students) have been required to take a two-course sequence designed to teach communication skills. Both courses include information literacy components, the bulk of which are taught by campus teaching librarians. While the campus library user-education program welcomed this opportunity to teach library skills to students early on in their campus lives, the new program did make significant demands on resources that were already stretched thin.

Traditionally, for the freshman level of instruction, our program has done two library sessions for each class, both of which emphasize active learning by providing frequent opportunities for hands-on practice in our computer-equipped classrooms. But when we looked at the numbers involved in using such a model, we knew that we had a major resource challenge. Given our staff and facility resources, there was no way—even just for the first course of the requirement—that we would be able to do two sessions for some 240 new sections, while continuing to do the nearly 1,800 sessions that make up our regular program each year. After a lengthy investigation of our options, we decided to turn to CAI to help us address the needs of this new program. In particular, we decided to develop a multimedia, instructional package that would teach some of the basic skills that we traditionally teach in the two sessions of our introductory-level classes. Our hope was that this package, which we called CLUE, would enable us to cut back from two sessions per class to one. Students would be required to complete CLUE before coming to the library session, which then would build on the skills taught in CLUE and focus on the more conceptual aspects of the information-seeking process. The single class session would continue to emphasize active learning by giving students an opportunity during the last half of the class to practice the research process in a hands-on setting. In the past year, this has proven to be a workable plan.

While resource issues played a major role in our decision to develop a CAI package, there were also pedagogical reasons for our decision to go with a multi-media mode of instruction. First we hoped that a multimedia format would hold the interest of an MTV-raised generation of students whose learning styles seem to be shaped primarily by multimedia. By engaging students' interest, we hoped to be able to address the question of student motivation, an all-too-familiar

---

Konrad is electronic information services coordinator, College Library, University of Wisconsin-Madison, and *Loomis* is coordinator for library user education, General Library System, University of Wisconsin-Madison.

challenge in library instruction, particularly at the freshman level. We also thought that, because of its interactive nature, our tutorial would enable us to continue to use active learning techniques. Finally, we hoped that a CAI package would enable us to provide self-paced instruction at the point of need—two critical ingredients for successful library instruction. For the most part, these expectations have been realized. Students, with their varied range of library experience, have been especially appreciative of the self-paced nature of CLUE.

We decided to develop our own tutorial rather than go with an existing package for a number of reasons. First, at the time we began to plan this project, the CAI packages we looked at did not appear to meet the criteria we had identified as being critical to the success of such an endeavor (see below). Another important factor in this decision was the fact that the tutorial was being designed, not as a replacement for classroom instruction, but as one part of a two-part library module that included classroom teaching. We felt we could integrate the two components more fully by developing our own tutorial rather than by modifying our objectives to fit an existing package.

Though we were excited at the prospect of this project, we realized early on that, for planning purposes, it was important to explore fully the feasibility of putting together a major program like CLUE, especially in terms of the time and staff resources required. Toward that end, we conducted an extensive literature review through which we identified other CAI developers from whose experiences and accomplishments we might benefit. After contacting them and reviewing their programs, we realized that most of the then-existing packages reflected the state of technology at the time they were produced (i.e., the late 1980s and early nineties). Thus they were primarily electronic page turners, developed in black and white, with few, if any, graphics and little or no sound or video. After three months of review and campuswide discussions, we decided upon the following criteria for selecting our development software.

First, and foremost, we wanted CLUE to be highly interactive in order to engage students' interest and to give them control in navigating through the program. We wanted to keep students interested by offering them a variety of ways to respond and interact with the program (e.g., clicking on buttons, typing in answers, doing drag-and-drop exercises). While we couldn't produce a full-blown entertainment CD-ROM product such as Myst or DOOM, we needed to meet students who are used to playing such games halfway in terms of reducing the boredom factor inherent in many educational software programs.

The ability to network CLUE also was critical in order to provide the widest level of access and to allow for the collection of data for program assessment.

Another key consideration for us was cross-platform capability. Because the computing labs on the UW-Madison campus have a variety of Macintosh and Windows machines available for students to use, developing for both platforms would allow us to make CLUE available on more machines. This criterion eliminated from consideration many development tools that did not have such cross-platform capabilities.

Control over the programming of CLUE also was extremely important to us. We wanted to be able to do our own development since working with outside programmers would be costly and make us too dependent on their timelines and priorities. Since we did not have a programmer in house, we needed to find a multimedia authoring tool that would allow us to develop the in-house skills needed to prototype, modify, and revise CLUE according to our own needs and internal timelines.

Cost was another huge consideration. While some multimedia authoring systems, like HTML, are free, others can cost as much as $30,000. Needless to say, these were beyond our reach. There was a wide range of features in the authoring systems we looked at and an equally wide range of price tags. It also was important for us to balance cost with our need for long-term support. Thus, we wanted a system from a reputable vendor that we could expect to be around for awhile. While some systems are freeware and shareware programs, long-term support for them is not always a guarantee.

After analyzing various softwares in light of these criteria, we settled on three. We seriously considered using HTML but felt that its lack of flexibility in terms of design outweighed its attractiveness from a networking standpoint. We also considered using a mix of Asymetrix Toolbook for Windows and Apple's HyperCard but had concerns about the conversion utilities available for developing cross-platforms. Finally, we examined Macromedia Authorware, which we chose because it met all of our criteria. We were particularly impressed with its cross-platform capability. The Windows and Macintosh versions of Authorware are nearly identical and the program's internal conversion utility makes it possible to develop in either platform and port to the other.

A few comments about how CLUE was developed: CLUE was funded by a campus grant, the Instructional Technology Support Grant, for $23,000. This grant covered development equipment, student salaries, consultant fees, and supplies. However, it did not cover library staff time which was significant, especially for the two project directors, one of whom did all the programming for the package.

The development team was made up of the two project directors (the authors of this paper) and three teaching librarians. Also included on the development team was an instructional-design consultant from the campus computer center. His expertise in such things as screen design, computer graphics, and the creation of interactive exercises was critical since no one on the team had had any experience with CAI development prior to this. We also contracted with someone from the campus computer center to help assess the success of CLUE in the context of its contribution to the two-part library module as a whole. Finally, we had one or two students on the development team throughout the project. Their involvement proved to be critical for they provided us with feedback on what students like or dislike in such a tutorial, thereby helping us avoid many time-consuming errors in design.

In terms of design principles, the development team was fortunate in that it did not have to spend a lot of time developing instructional goals for the package. The UW-Madison campus libraries already had an instructional plan in place that clearly outlined the goals and objectives for freshman/sophomore levels of instruction, as well as for juniors, seniors, and graduate students. The team simply took its instructional content goals from the plan. However, we quickly realized that, while we could easily lift our objectives from an existing document, we would not be able to take one of our many freshman-level lesson plans and simply translate it into a multimedia tutorial. We discovered early on that the linear structure of a classroom script did not readily lend itself to an easy translation into this new, nonlinear, Web-like medium.

We also realized that we would need an overriding instructional model to work with in designing the structure of CLUE. After much discussion, we settled on a cognitive apprenticeship model of instruction, based on a model developed by the Educational Testing Services at Princeton. Sometimes called a scaffolding model, it consists of four stages of instruction. The first stage is the "modeling" phase in which students are given opportunities to observe effective writing, reading—or, in the case of library instruction, good information-seeking—skills in action. In the second stage, the "scaffolding" phase, students practice the observed skills but with a great deal of guidance, feedback, and support (i.e., scaffolding). In the next stage, the "fading" phase, the support is slowly taken away, giving the students more and more responsibility for their own learning. Finally, in the "monitoring" phase, most, if not all, of the scaffolding is removed and students are given a way to monitor or assess their own learning.

In the early stages of design, we spent several months trying to come up with a dominant metaphor for the information-seeking process that would carry across the tutorial and help make it understandable to new students. We explored a plethora of metaphors for the research process including a treasure hunt, the working of the brain, sailing, and taking a road trip. However, all these images seemed contrived and so, fearing that students would respond negatively, we abandoned our search for a dominant metaphor and returned to lecture-workshop-quiz structure implicit in the cognitive apprenticeship model.

The final design principle that the development team wanted to incorporate into CLUE was cognitive modelling. We decided to try, during the workshop segments of the modules, to actually model for students the thought process one goes through in doing a search. We hoped that such modelling would help students see the search as a series of decisions that involve critical thinking skills. By a stroke of luck, we decided to have students (with "off-screen" advice from a librarian) do the modelling instead of librarians, a feature that students have responded to with enthusiasm. The tutorial introduces CLUE users to four students who have real-life information needs. All four tell of trying to solve their problems by going to a campus library but, because they lack the skills and strategies covered in CLUE, they meet with failure. In the workshop segments of the tutorial, users assist the four CLUE students by applying what they have learned to the situation at hand.

During the second half of this LOEX presentation, segments from CLUE, including samples from the lecture, workshop, and quiz modes, were demonstrated and special features of the program were highlighted.[1]

By way of conclusion, we would like to discuss some of the lessons we have learned from this development process and indicate some of the changes that are being incorporated into the next revision of CLUE, scheduled to be available this fall.

First, we learned that it is vital to invest what may sometimes seem like a frivolously large amount of time establishing criteria for the package you want to develop. While you—and your administrators—may be anxious for you to move ahead quickly and purchase the software, the time invested in deciding exactly what you want your package to accomplish is critical for success down the road. The three months spent evaluating existing tutorials and authoring software and discussing what we wanted CLUE to teach and how proved to be well spent. Authorware has done what we wanted it to and the basic pedagogical structure of CLUE, including our scaffolding model and cognitive modelling components, has worked well.

We learned the hard way to expect the unexpected. Although we did a great deal of planning and testing, we had a few unpleasant surprises. For example, one of the last modules we developed contained several long (30 seconds) audio segments. We ran into trouble running these segments across the network as the sound would break up. To counter this, we rerecorded these as shorter, consecutive segments. Such unexpected occurrences are to be anticipated and need to be built into the planning timeline.

We also learned that student involvement in the development process, both on the development team and in periodic usability testing of the product as it is being developed, is critical. As noted earlier, it was because of strong student feedback that we changed our minds about lockstepping them through the program and opened it up so that students now can skim through and skip over parts of the program if they choose to do so. We also found out from students that the audio in CLUE, which for many of us in the over-40 age bracket was often an annoying distraction, actually enhanced their learning. Such feedback has been invaluable, both in designing the program and in "selling it" to the instructors who assign CLUE to their students. Of course, one must also be flexible enough and willing to make the changes the feedback calls for.

We also learned that peer-assisted learning is of great value, not just in the classroom but in an interactive, multimedia learning situation as well. Our decision to model the thought process that is involved in developing a search by having CLUE users help four students solve their real-life information needs has proven to be well liked by students.

We also have learned that networking multimedia is still dicey unless your campus has a great deal of bandwidth and low network traffic. For CLUE, we managed to run ten users simultaneously over a 150-node network but had trouble beyond that point. In the end, many labs installed CLUE on local hard drives wherever space permitted.

Another lesson learned involves building relationships with computer lab staff. If you are planning to run your program on machines you do not control, you need to understand and be able to explain the technical requirements of your program. You should not expect the lab to test your program for you or to help you work out its bugs. Be prepared to give an estimate of the total number of hours you expect lab computers will be in use for your program and to project peak periods of use so that lab managers can plan accordingly. Finally, if you plan to collect results for use in assessing your program, you will need write access to the server on which you plan to collect data. All of this needs to be worked out with your lab manager early on in the process. The more clearly you communicate your needs upfront, the more likely lab managers will be to help you anticipate and/or resolve problems that may come up.

One final lesson about access learned in this year of development: We discovered we could not always rely solely on the instructors to give students consistent and accurate verbal instructions about how to access the program. So we developed a handout that tells students where they can access the package, what they will need to have in order to access it (e.g., headphones), and where to go if they run into problems using the package. Instructors distribute these to students the first week of class.

As to CLUE's future, this past fall, we extensively evaluated both CLUE and its classroom counterpart in anticipation of getting feedback we could use in revising CLUE this summer. The 2,400 students enrolled in the communication course were surveyed, as were their instructors. Librarians who taught the library module participated in a focus group. Online comments collected from students as they completed CLUE were analyzed; so were the scores from the two quizzes and the final.

Among the findings from this extensive assessment, two stand out. First, a significant number of students thought it took too long to do CLUE. Part of this perception has to do with the pacing of CLUE, which is, admittedly, slow in parts, especially in the audio. But, interestingly, part of this perception seems to be related to the unrealistic expectations of many students regarding how long it takes to learn to use a library system. Even though students complained that CLUE took too long to do, 72 percent of those who responded to the fall survey indicated that it took them one to two hours to complete CLUE, which is exactly the time we estimated it would take. But some of the survey comments indicate that students expected to have to spend far less time learning the library. To help correct this misperception, this past spring, we included a paragraph addressing this problem in the CLUE handout and we asked instructors to talk about it with students when assigning CLUE to their students. We will see if these remedies have had any impact when we reassess the program again this fall.

A second finding from the fall assessment was that students who responded favorably to CLUE were less enthusiastic about the library classroom session and, vice versa, students who liked the class were less enthused about CLUE. Clearly this seems to indicate that our library module as a whole is addressing a range of different learning styles.

In terms of basic content and structure, version 2.0 will not change significantly. Feedback from the fall assessment does not indicate any major problems with either. But we are working to make major changes in other aspects of the program. An extensive, screen-by-screen review of the tutorial revealed a number of instances where there is dissonance between what appears on the screen and what is being said. This results in cognitive processing conflicts for the user who can become frustrated trying to process two different messages simultaneously. The upcoming revision will eliminate such conflicts. To enhance learning for field-dependent learners, menus within the modules are being reworked to include advance organizers that provide an overview of what will be covered in that module. The pacing issues raised by students also are being addressed in this version. Finally and most importantly in terms of the appearance of CLUE, both its audio and graphics components are being redone by professionals, enhancements we did not want to invest in until we were sure CLUE was solidly established.

An interactive, multimedia tutorial like CLUE can be an effective method for supplementing the teaching resources of an instruction program in order to meet the significant increase in demand that many programs are facing. However, careful planning for such a tutorial is needed and should be factored into the project's timeline. Not only do pedagogical and technological issues related to content need to be addressed, but "big picture" administrative issues related to allocating resources and to defining the role of the tutorial in relation to the program's traditional classroom instruction need to be considered well before actual development of the package begins.[2]

NOTES

1. To view the segments of CLUE that were demonstrated in this presentation, go to the following Web site: <144.92.96.89/college/loex/demo.htm>.

2. For information about the technical apsects of CLUE, contact Lee Konrad (e-mail: mrlee@macc.wisc.edu). For information about the pedagogical and/or administrative issues related to CLUE and its development, contact Abbie Loomis (e-mail: loomis@macc.wisc.edu).

Of Course the Library Is Important! Getting Library Instruction Included in a Freshman Experience Course

Marsha A. Miller

PART 1: FROM LSC 100 TO UNIV 101

Indiana State University (ISU), like many universities, allows a certain number of conditionally admitted students (CAs) to its first-year, or freshman, class. The average freshman class numbers approximately 2,300 to 2,500 students. Until and including the Fall 1995 semester, all conditionally admitted students were required to enroll in a Learning Skills Center course (LSC 100: "Study Skills") administered by student academic services. Students remained in the course throughout their first semesters, or until their grade point averages reached acceptable levels. Meanwhile these students were also enrolled in the usual sorts of first-year classes, such as "Freshman Writing" and "Introduction to Speech Communication." Motivation for conditionally admitted students ran the gamut among people who were truly interested in trying their hands at higher education, young people who were not sure what they wanted to do in life but thought they'd give college a try, and students whose parents were determined that their children would attend college, regardless of whether it was the best place for them. Resentment, confusion, and a number of other emotions associated with having to be placed in LSC 100 created an unusual teaching atmosphere, both for the instructors and for library instruction contact.

LSC 100 instructors consisted of student academic services, residential life, or student life staff. Often they were unfamiliar with the need to improve students' library skills, as well as the extent of the students' lack of recognition that library skills are an essential part of the higher education package. Mental preparation of the students to attend library instruction sessions was often lacking. However, this is not unique to this course, as instruction librarians well know.

The Library Instruction Program and LSC 100

Each fall semester, 18 sections of LSC 100 were offered. An average of 25 students took each class, with spring semesters offering three to five sections. Some sections were designated athletes-only, and one or two sessions were promoted for adult learners. The coordinator of LSC 100 regularly scheduled all sections to attend a library instruction session, regardless of the inclinations of the individual instructors. Initially, content was similar to that received by students in freshman composition; thus many students received two almost identical library sessions in one semester. The library sequence began with a required self-paced tour of the library. The tour booklet and exercise allowed students to interact with the online catalog and introduced them to areas of the library that they would need later on. Students required to take the tour in other classes could receive credit so that they wouldn't have to go through the exercise several times in the same semester.

Over time, the library instructional staff worked to make the LSC content different from the freshman composition content, on the assumption that a majority of the LSC students would have received or would be receiving both contacts at some time during the same

---

Miller is instruction librarian, Indiana State University, Terre Haute, Indiana.

(or next) semester. Since other instruction available to them involved detailed demonstrations of the library's online resources, LSC lecture content evolved into a more general discussion of basic research techniques, keyword search strategies, and so on.

Evolving from Freshman to First Year

In Spring 1993, a campus advisory committee for the student academic services center was activated. While the library was not included in the initial committee structure, the library proactively moved to become part of it. As the dean of library services wrote to the vice president for academic affairs, "since the library does a considerable amount of library instruction with students from the Learning Skills Center...it might be appropriate to have a library faculty member on this committee."

A subcommittee structure focused on a number of issues, including student-athlete support programs, open preference advisement, conditional admissions advisement, tutoring, learning disabled and handicapped services, curriculum development, grants and special programs, and upward bound programs. The library representative (this author) would logically have been included in the curriculum-development subcommittee; however, she served only on the overall steering committee.

By late 1993, this group evolved into the Steering Committee on the First-Year Experience, co-chaired by the director of student academic services and the director of admissions. The committee was asked to implement a coordinated program in stages, beginning with the Fall 1994 entering class.

Subcommittees worked on what have become standard components of First-Year Experience efforts: freshman interest groups, supplemental instruction, and a new course: University (Univ) 101, "Learning in the Academic Community." Other committees worked on freshman priority scheduling, the New Student Advisement and Registration Program (NSARP), activities for the "First Three Days," peer leaders, and development of "General Education in Action." LSC 100 students were to be subsumed within Univ 101, and the Spring 1995 semester found the LSC 100 students (fewer than ten sections) being used as a pilot group to test the program. During that time, the library instruction component remained similar to that in the past.

A full-fledged "Freshman Year Experience" course (Univ 101, "Learning in the University Community") was approved by the Curriculum and Academic Affairs Committee of the faculty senate, the faculty senate, and the university administration in the Spring 1995, and inaugurated in Fall 1995. Thirty sections (25 filled) were offered as an elective; however, 18 of those remained cloistered for the conditional admits. Five hundred seventy students entered Univ 101 (43 withdrew). Seventy-six (15.4 percent) failed the course.

Univ 101 instructors were a mixture of faculty, emeritus faculty, and full-time administrators with a minimum of a master's degree and at least three years of employment. There were problems finding instructors. There was discussion about the possibility of having a summer workshop sponsored by the Center for Teaching and Learning that would expand the half-day workshop conducted by Cathy Baker into at least a day. It was noted that the University of South Carolina had a week-long workshop that was also used to screen prospective instructors.

University 101 used as its basic text *Study Skills for Today's College Student*, by Jerold Apps (McGraw-Hill, Inc. College Custom Series, 1990. ISBN 0070055963). After examining several such texts, the steering committee chose Apps. Additional information specific to Indiana State University was added at the end of the generic text.

Chapter 15 of Apps, "Using the Library," was the first chapter in the section, "Resources for Learning." The computer center was given a paragraph in chapter 16, "Finding Learning Resources/Sources of Information and Help on Campus." After examination by several librarians, this chapter was expanded by adding an ISU Library section (see appendix 1) to the supplemental text. ISU contributed 131 pages to the basic Apps text; the library section added 19 pages.

Unfortunately, the library section was never included in the table of contents for the supplemental section of Apps; thus some instructors forgot about it. There was confusion about the inclusion of the self-paced tour in the text. Instructors were supposed to tell their students to use the tour in the text, partly as a means of saving paper, and partly to be sure they were aware of the library section. Students were supposed to come to the library, pick up an exercise sheet from the check-out desk, and then follow the tour in the text. Another problem, as with all commitments to text, was that the tour became slightly obsolete after two semesters' use. So, the Fall 1996 instructors were informed not to use the text-based tour. Even though explicit instructions were given, some students showed up at the check-out desk and some at the door of library instruction and orientation, looking for the exercise.

I Know I'm Talking; I Can Feel My Lips Moving

The library continued to have problems communicating its need for a role in this process. After the original ten (later nine) objectives appeared in the 21

March *1994 Interim Report from the Steering Committee on the First Year Experience*, the assistant dean for library services wrote to the committee chairs, pointing out that four of the objectives supported the need for first-year students to know how to access and utilize library electronic [and print] information resources, namely,

- "To help student develop academic skills;

- To help student develop critical thinking skills;

- To introduce students to the resources and services of the University and the local community; and

- To help students develop an appreciation for diversity and a multicultural perspective."

The assistant dean went on to reiterate, "It is clear to me that library information search skills strongly support the development of each student's academic skills, critical thinking skills, important introduction to the library resources and services of which almost all students avail themselves and, finally, the vitally important ability/skill to access database (via Internet training/instruction) to learn about cultures throughout the world through electronic access. In short, our students can ill afford not to have these important information search skills in their first-year experience; indeed they should be required."

At the 29 April 1994 steering committee meeting, the author distributed a "Rationale for a Library Component in the First Year Experience Course" (see appendix 2). The library instruction computer lab was in the development stage at this point, and the author indicated that it might be incorporated into the library's FYE program. Also at this meeting, one of the committee co-chairs spoke about the boring LSC 100 library classes she had experienced; indeed, she had fallen asleep during one of them. However another committee member, from the English department, spoke in the library's defense. Unfortunately this was the last committee for the semester, so the "Rationale" was distributed, never discussed, and misunderstandings about the level and type of library involvement continued to surface in such areas as the course syllabus.

By the 11 November 1994 steering committee meeting, the Univ 101 course proposal had been given to the provost. Meanwhile it was becoming obvious to some of the librarians that the library component of the course needed to be expanded. On 2 December 1994, Scott Davis, head of library information services, wrote to the chair of the steering committee, the assistant dean, and the director for academic computing/networking services. In his letter he stated:

After taking a look at the proposal, it looks like things are moving along nicely. However, it occurred to me that a lot has happened campus-wide since discussions and work began on the development of this course. I am referring to events over the past year to six months that I think impact the way in which the Library and Library Services should be integrated into the Univ. 101 course content...specifically the President and Provost's development of the Information Services Division and also the implementation of the CORAL student server. With this in mind, I would strongly suggest that you and the Univ. 101 Committee consider an "Information Services" unit as opposed to a more narrowly focused "Library" unit. Ideally, the course might include 3 sessions and/or activities revolving around the Information Services concept that has emerged on campus. Off the top of my head, an initial session could provide an overview of the networked computing environment on campus, with emphasis on information access. It would be during this session that we could emphasize the basics of the CORAL server (i.e. what it is, what its extreme practical value is and will be, how to activate your account, Pegasus mail, etc.). A second session could focus on LUIS III and the CD network, incorporating appropriate hands-on exercises, the self-paced tour, etc. The third and final session could focus on the Internet and basic concepts like gopher, UseNet news, etc., since our recent experience with all levels of students is that they love the 'Net. One thing we could subtly emphasize in the final session is the issue of the Internet as a tool for promoting cultural diversity and diversity in general. We could also introduce the students to the general idea of what the National Information Infrastructure is and how it relates to them personally as students on this campus. In terms of who would provide the instruction for these sessions, that would still fall within our bailiwick given the cooperative/collaborative training roles of Academic Computing and the Library that have come about as a result of the Information Services Division being developed.

Hope these suggestions make sense and that the Univ. 101 committee realizes their relevance to a course such as this. Broadening the originally proposed Library content to something more consistent with the Information Services philosophy that is strongly supported by the top administration is logical (and also, I think, politically wise).

In February 1995 the author attended a meeting of the curriculum subcommittee, which discussed the previous semester's syllabus and the proposed syllabus.

The agenda included, as part of "Part IV: Learning about University Services and Resources," a listing, "Libraries," and, separately, "Computing Services." The author requested that those two listings be changed to one; "Information Literacy Skills," reiterating that the library component should take three days of the Univ 101 syllabus, but this change was not made.

During these same years (1993 onwards), the need to improve students' computer literacy skills became a campus imperative. The library already was involved in this, offering, as part of the New Student Advisement and Registration Programs, sessions about e-mail and the Internet that became the most-attended sessions (Fall 1995 onwards). Univ 101 was the logical place to expand upon general computer (and other information) literacy skills.

Freshman (or, now, First-Year) Experience courses are designed to attract and retain students by giving them a clear picture of what is in store for them as college students. Library research skills are recognized as a necessary component; however, it was hard to "steal" time from the course. The syllabus was overwhelming and the decision to schedule a library instruction session was subject to the whim of the individual instructor. When it became clear that instructors often were not willing or able to "allow" the library its two sessions, library instruction conceded the point, even to offering either the basic library skills lecture or the e-mail/Internet lecture.

Current Program

The Office of Library Instruction and Orientation (LI&O) requests and receives the list of instructors for the semester. It is now up to each instructor to contact LI&O to schedule instruction (most do). Or rather, it has become LI&O's responsibility to contact all Univ 101 instructors to let them know their options. Those Univ 101 instructors who choose to use LI&O tend to schedule the library skills content; the athlete sections combine library and computer skills.

One Univ 101 library instruction scenario is as follows. Introductory remarks are built around putting these words on the board:

ACCESS
SERVICES
RESOURCES
TECHNIQUES

and explaining that everything they need to know about using the library fits into these categories.

Materials ordered for the class tend to duplicate what the students already have in their textbooks: instructions on accessing the library network; a three-page handout on *Keyword/Boolean Searching*; a handout outlining a *Basic Research Strategy*; *LUIS III: A Brief Guide* (the online catalog); and a handout explaining how to access the World Wide Web. Rather than distribute the handouts, students are responsible for deciding which handouts they will pick up on their way out.

The Internet/e-mail sessions utilize a booklet, *Cyberspace, E-mail and You*, originally developed for the NSARP sessions. At present, lab time for Univ 101 is rarely scheduled due to time constraints but this may change, especially as instructional materials are added to the Web.

Instructors' perceptions of instructional content continue to evolve. For example, during Fall 1996, one instructor, the Univ 101 coordinator, requested, for her classes, a "traditional" presentation, keyword searching (truncation), research methods, accessing the Internet, and the reliability of Internet sources. A new handout, *Evaluating the 'Net*, was distributed and several "fake" Internet sites were visited, such as <http://www.whitehouse.org> and the City of Mankato's page <http://lme.mankato.msus.edu/mankato/mankato.html>. The students loved it!

Another successful in-class activity has been to pass out pieces of scrap paper without explanation. Then as the class begins, talk about the attempt to avoid overlap between this and other library instruction sessions they might have had or will have. Have them use the papers to write down a question about library resources. At an appropriate point after other introductory remarks, collect the papers and separate them out (they will divided into the usual sorts of questions). If feasible, a cluster of certain kinds of questions can be used to decide on the structure of the remainder of the class. Be sure to answer as many as possible. Encourage e-mail follow-up.

Problems with the classes have been general attitude (especially since so many sections are still designated for the CAs), getting teachers to have the students complete the self-paced tour exercise and turn the exercises in to the LI&O office for correction, teachers forgetting to order tours, and teachers forgetting that the students are to have completed the library tour before they come to the class session. Other problems are similar to those with other courses: late scheduling, no-shows, teacher input or lack thereof. Some of the sections are geared toward specific disciplines; it would be nice to work with the teachers to gear the sessions towards those disciplines. The Univ 101 coordinator tried, during Fall 1996, to set up a special session on the Internet and e-mail, since she only would give up one class period. But the students expected extra credit and weren't going to receive it; only one student came.

Table 1: University 101 Enrollment and Persistence,
Compared with All First-Year Students*

	Fall 1994 enrolled (LSC 100)	passed course	enrolled for Spring 1995	Fall 1995 enrolled (Univ 101)	completed	enrolled for Spring 1996	Fall 1996 enrolled (Univ 101)	completed	enrolled for Spring 1997
Conditional Admits (CA)	393	80 percent	79 percent	358	80 percent	71 percent	417	80 percent (369)	76 percent (197)
All LSC 100/Univ 100 students	475	n/a	79 percent	513	85 percent	70 percent	631	83 percent	
All first-year students			82.9 percent		85 percent				82 percent

[*Statistics from various reports and annual summaries prepared by the LSC 100/Univ 101 Coordinator for the Steering Committee or from the Office of the Registrar; some numbers do not add up properly or some data are missing as similar tables from different reports gave different figures; hence the comment above about the evolution of statistics]

Future Instructional Plans

The concept of learning communities is moving onto campus; this could have a very positive effect, especially if the library is involved from the beginning. Other plans include Web-based materials and more information transmitted via PowerPoint presentations. The instruction librarian will attempt to keep in touch via e-mail with the instructors throughout the semester, both before and after their library sessions (or even if they don't schedule sessions) with little tidbits of information, to get them thinking and, in turn, getting their students thinking more in terms of information literacy skills. The supplemental text developed for Apps has become out-of-date and difficult to update and include in recent editions. LI&O's best option may be Web access, as long as teachers will use it. LI&O needs to become even more proactive, including getting the syllabus changed: instead of *What is scholarship?*, change to *What is research?* or *What is information literacy?*

Other recent events have affected the evolution of the First Year Experience program. Since 1994, ISU's academic advising program has been given a lot of needed attention and has been redesigned. It is hoped that advisors will point their advisees in the direction of the Univ 101 course, especially open-preference and conditionally admitted students.

Most recently, in Spring 1997 the Eli Lilly Foundation (an Indiana-based corporation) gave ISU $50,000 to write a $2 million grant proposal for further Eli Lilly moneys, with a five-year plan of action. The focus of this grant coincided with FYE activities. An e-mail message to the ISU campus from the provost (24 March 1997) noted, "Thirty-six percent of freshmen enrolled in fall 1995 did not return in the fall of 1996, or 720 of the approximately 2,000 freshmen. Recent research and nationwide trends present overwhelming evidence that students' experiences during their first year of college largely determine their academic success in subsequent years and the likelihood of their remaining in school to complete their degrees." On 8 April John Gardner, executive director of the National Resource Center for the Freshmen Year Experience at the University of South Carolina, came to ISU to discuss the special needs of first-year students. Following his presentation (and day-long meetings with various campus groups), David Hopkins, assistant vice president for academic affairs, presented the university's grant proposal to the academic community.

PART 2: IS UNIV 101 MAKING A DIFFERENCE?

The quick answer to this, as far as Indiana State University is concerned, is, maybe a little bit so far, but we can't be sure yet. Statistics are being gathered by various university units, but are not always linked analytically, nor are the same statistics reported exactly the same way. One factor is the number of students who complete Univ 101, but more important factors are such signs of success as improving their general grade point averages, enrolling for the subsequent semester, and determining whether or not Univ 101 had a direct impact (see table 1). In addition to more esoteric considerations, retaining the first-year student is of vital interest to the university from a financial point of view. Overall, ISU's student population, like many other universities, has been declining. A comparison of Fall 1995 and Fall 1996 statistics shows the number of entering freshmen declining from 2,060 (Fall 1995) to 1,921 (Fall 1996). ISU draws the majority of its student from the following areas: The average high school class rank 59-60 percentile; average grade point average 2.84. The percent of students ranking in the top quarter rose from 30 percent to 31 percent and those in the top ten percent from nine percent to 11 percent. The average SAT combined score (recentered total) rose from 934 to 942. In both 1995 and 1996, 33 percent of first-year students had parents who never attended college. Many applied only to ISU (36 percent 1995; 40 percent 1996). Fifty-eight percent of new freshmen (1996) lived within 100 miles of Indiana State University (56 percent 1995). Fifty-four percent came from towns of less than 25,000 population.

First semester grade point average improvement for CAs climbed from 1.80 (Fall 1994) to 2.01 (Fall 1995) to 2.08 (Fall 1996). Between 1995 and 1996, the first-year persistence rate rose from 63 percent to 64 percent. The four-year graduate rate for ISU is not good; however, the five-, six-, and even seven-year are better. The six-year graduate rate increased from 36 percent to 38 percent, with the rate for African Americans increasing from 16 percent to 26 percent and the rate for those admitted conditionally improving from 20 percent to 26 percent. Many ISU students have to slow down their matriculation due to financial or other personal reasons. The efforts of the university towards *retention* (or, now *persistence*) of its freshmen students have refocused the attention given to Univ 101.

Student evaluations of the course were interesting in several ways, including student perceptions of their performances (higher than actual). Students felt that study skills, more discussion, group work, college information, and material to help make the transition were the topics that made Univ 101 most beneficial to them. The most beneficial aspects of the course included study skills, time management, Apps material, writing, college information, and transitional material. Least beneficial included reading a book entitled *Staying Put*, too much writing, history of Terre Haute, and ISU history.

Instructors were also given an opportunity to evaluate the course; however, few did (six of 20). Among their comments specific to the library:

- "students' responsibility" [to do what?],

- "fine, but not all students went to the library" [why not?],

- "an organized library workshop would be good" [for students, instructors, both?].

When asked, "What have you learned from teaching CA students?," instructors responded,

- "I have learned that these students require ongoing assistance."

- "They are open to learning and making a commitment if given a chance. Many are under-prepared and under-motivated."

- "They need guidance, motivation and a longer amount of time to adjust to college. They need someone (this course) to make them get into college..."

- "Writing skills are awful, but most are willing to work hard."

- "I appreciated the good work done by your office...and the library. I would like more critical thinking exercises..."

Selected statistics below give only a partial (in some cases, confused) picture of the various sorts of analyses being attempted. Between 1988 and 1993, the average withdrawal rate for CAs (in their first semester) was six percent. Of the 519 CAs who completed the Fall 1995 semester, 70 percent returned for the Spring 1996 semester. Average for all freshmen fell from 85 percent to 82 percent. Spring persistence rate for CA freshmen who entered Fall 1994 was 79 percent but fell to 76 percent. Only 48 percent of the Fall 1994 group re-entered Fall 1995.

During the Fall 1996 semester, approximately 52 percent of the CAs achieved A or B, 18 percent more than in 1995. Seventeen percent received C or C+ and seven percent were in the D range. The overall GPA for University 101 for Fall 1996 was 2.47, a .06 percent increase from Fall 1995. The good standing rate was 15 percent higher than the 1995 group. The percentage of students who achieved 2.0 or better rose 15 percent from 1994 and one percent from 1995. The athletic group also improved.

For Fall 1997, all Open Preference first-year students will take Univ 101. This will be a leap in the number of students taking the class (from 600 to 2,000?) and the number of sessions offered (from 30 to 80, if average 25 students per section) and could impact significantly on the entire library-instruction program (thus spurring consideration of more Web-based instructional contact).

PART 3: RECOMMENDATIONS AND OBSERVATIONS

Some universities, colleges, and community colleges have had freshman seminars in place for decades; some are just starting or haven't started yet. This focus on first-year students impacts on a number of other issues that librarians are concerned with, such as information literacy core competencies. Librarians on many campuses continue to have to work proactively to make university personnel understand (and appreciate) the role that librarians and libraries play in the research process. In addition, many faculty expect their students to have levels of technical expertise with electronic information retrieval but do not perceive it as a basic skill that might have to be addressed in a first-year program.

It impacts on the ongoing (haven't we said enough yet?) discussions on the need to incorporate critical-thinking skills into the 50-minute, one-stop lectures. The following are in non-prioritized order:

- Work intensely with individual instructors.

- With e-mail becoming a regular part of the communication process in the course, work out a system of pre-lecture contact among the instructor, the students, and the librarian assigned to teach the section.

- Pre-assess.

- Assume no prior relationship with libraries, reading, computers, and so on and move beyond that.

- Assume the students' need to take responsibility for their share of the learning and teaching process.

- Take nothing personally.

- Become proactive, or even more proactive about a campuswide recognition of the concept of information competencies and how the library and computing must play a role.

- If feasible, have one or more librarians teach or team-teach a Univ 101 section.

- Keep the dialogue focused on "information literacy," not library research skills. People have a gut reaction to the phrase, think of orientation to the physical structure, and can't focus on the real issues.

- If your campus doesn't have a required information technology course or doesn't pre-assess students' incoming technology needs, librarians will continue to have to include the teaching of such basic technical skills as using a mouse and printing, not to mention other computer skills that we have used along the way. Yet we also have to keep telling students not to let the technology get in the way of the process, even as we are lecturing exactly that (while at the same time teaching critical-thinking skills and everything else).

- Senior-Year Experience: It's never too late?? ISU is still investigating Senior-Year Experiences. The sub-committee surveyed academic departments to see what was already in place and also posted queries to an Internet discussion group to get ideas. It could be useful to survey them about their library experiences and what library use their professors required of them.

- Attend/present at National FYE conferences.

- Attend/present at Annual National Student Success conferences; the Tenth Annual National Student Success Conference was held 13-15 March 1997, in Wichita, Kansas.

- Attend/present at international conferences on the First-Year Experience; the ninth was held at St. Andrews, Scotland, United Kingdom, 15-19 July 1996.

PART 4: THE NATIONAL PERSPECTIVE

John Gardner (University of South Carolina) is the guru of the first-year experience, thus his invitation to visit the ISU campus and make a special presentation on 8 April 1997, during which he made a number of recommendations in a report entitled *Recommended Structural Changes to Enhance First-Year Student Learning, Success, and Retention*, including

- Give more emphasis to writing, speaking, and library work across the curriculum.

- Give more attention and resources to faculty training and development initiatives to help faculty learn what they did not learn in graduate school about becoming college teachers.

Table 2: Types of Freshman Seminar Programs*

Extended Orientation Seminar	520 or 72 percent	43 percent require the seminar
Academic Seminar with common content across sections	81 or 11 percent	this is what Gardner and USC offers, and includes 'a lot of library work'; this is where ISU is at right now
Academic Seminars on various topics	56 or 8 percent	
Professional Seminar	160	'hottest trend'
Basic Study Skills Seminar	37 or 6 percent	where ISU started, with its LSC 100 course
Other	18	mixture of above or whatever...

From The Freshman Seminar: A Flexible Fixture in American Higher Education

- A comment: "Shame on ISU" for not requiring orientation, especially with so many first-generation students.

Gardner utilized materials from the many publications of the National Resource Center for the Freshman Year Experience and Students in Transition at the University of South Carolina, including:

- from *Basic Principles of Student Retention*—points on the critical role of the freshman seminar, the critical role of orientation, use of resources/services, importance of teaching learning/study skills;

- from *Critical Skills Sought by Employers of College Graduates: Use of Technology* [unclear if this includes library/information literacy?]—effective writing skills, critical thinking, problem solving, time management, goal setting, desire and ability to learn;

- from *Current Topics for Freshman Programs*, presented in descending order of popularity within the following subheadings, from B. Barefoot and P. Fidler, *The 1994 National Survey of Freshman Seminar Programs: Continuing Innovations in the Collegiate Curriculum* (monograph no. 20). National Resource Center for the Freshman Year Experience and Students in Transition, University of South Carolina, 1996: "Academic Skills," "Skills for Living," and "Knowledge about the Institution and about Higher Education."

Under "Academic Skills":

1) Academic Skills (note-taking, test-taking, studying, reading, research)

2) Time Management

3) Writing and speaking

4) Critical Thinking

5) Using the Library

6) Learning Styles

7) Understanding Faculty

8) Computer Skills

Under "Knowledge about the Institution and Higher Education":

1) Campus Resources and Facilities

2) The Library

3) College Policies, Procedures and Regulation

4) History, Traditions, and Purpose of Higher Education and Institution

5) Liberal Arts, Disciplines and Interdisciplinarity

6) The Value of Involvement

- from *The Freshman Seminar: A Flexible Fixture in American Higher Education* (data from 1994 National Survey of Freshman Seminar Programs, Betsy Barefoot and Paul P. Fidler); survey done every three years so another one due in 1997. The 1994 survey was sent to 2,460 institutions—1,001 responded (40.7 percent; see figure 2).

- from *Nine Characteristics of Successful* First-Year Seminars* [*successful = one that enjoys strong, broad-based institutional support and long life]; from the 1994 survey; Third on list: *include academic content—often extra—or interdisciplinary content that is woven into essential process elements such as study skills, library use, and writing.*

PART 5: RESOURCES

Electronic

National Resource Center for the Freshman Year Experience and Students in Transition at the University of South Carolina
1728 College Street, University of South Carolina, Columbia, SC 29208
voice: (803) 777-6029
fax: 803-777-4699
e-mail: fyeconf@ss1.csd.sc.edu
Publishes the *Journal of the Freshman Year Experience*, a newsletter; series of monographs, conference proceedings) <http://web.csd.sc.edu/fye/>

Additional Freshman Seminar Web Sites—updated 15 October 1996 as listed at <http://web.csd.sc.edu/fye/moreweb.html>; to add freshman seminar World Wide Web links, please contact Ilana Myerson at ilanam@gwm.sc.edu. Project Renaissance <http://www.albany.edu/cetl/ programs/prfaq.html>
Trudi Jacobson (tj662@cnsvax.albany.edu) and others presented at ACRL (April 1997). Project Renaissance brings together 200 first-year students with teams of faculty, librarians, computer specialists, and student assistants in a shared academic and living community. The panel discussed how to integrate library instruction into the freshman experience.

Northwest Missouri State University Library home page: <http://www.nwmissouri.edu/www_root/northwest/admissions/library/index.html>
Connie Ury, coordinator of library use education and freshman seminar instructor
<CJURY@ACAD.NWMISSOURI.EDU>
Presented at 16th FYE conference, "Collaborative Learning, Peer Assessment and Technology in the Freshman Seminar Curriculum" (FYE program is 13-years old);

Utah State University
library home page: <http://www.usu.edu/~library>
Betty Dance, coordinator for library instruction, and others presented at 16th FYE Conference, USU's "Freshman Survival Class: Connections to the Library" <http://www.usu.edu/~acaserv/survive.html>

Indiana State University's Web version of "Transforming the First Year Experience; a model for fortifying student resolve to succeed"
<http://web.indstate.edu/oirt/firstyear.html>

Conferences and Events for The National Resource Center for the Freshman Year Experience and Students in Transition
<http://web.csd.sc.edu/fye/ conferences.html>

Conferences

Third National Conference on Students in Transition, Oak Brook (Chicago area), Illinois, 5-8 November 1997.

Ninth National Conference on Student Retention, New York (1995).

National Conference on Student Success—the 1998 conference will be in Kansas City, Missouri, on 1-3 April at the Adams-Mark Hotel. Contact Janelle Darr (janelle_darr@sa.gw.twsu.edu), who is in charge of the conference (Web site forthcoming). Look for a "Call for Papers" sometime during August; it'll be posted to BI-L.

Tenth International Conference on the First-Year Experience, Warwick, England, *International Dimensions of Student Success in Higher Education,* 21-25 July 1997, University of Warwick <http://web.csd.sc.edu/fye/ifyecfp.html>.

Journals

Journal of the Freshman Year Experience (see above); indexed by ERIC

E-lists

First-Year Experience List: To subscribe to the FYE-List electronic listserv, send your message to *listserv@vm.sc.edu* and use as your message "*SUB FYE-LIST firstname lastname* [searchable archives 1994-1997]."

Senior-Year Experience List: To subscribe to the SYE-List electronic listserv, send your message to *listserv@vm.sc.edu* and use as your message "*SUB SYE-LIST firstname lastname.*" Or simply request to be subscribed sending your e-mail address and first and last name to *fyeconf@ss1.csd.sc.edu*.

Books and Articles

Previous LOEX Proceedings, generally.

FYE course texts/materials authored by John Gardner include: *College Is Only the Beginning* (1985; 1989); *Step by Step to College Success* (1987); *Your College*

Experience; Strategies for Success (1992, 1993, 1995, 1996, 1997) with A. Jerome Jewler; *Ready for the Real World* (1994) with William Hartel and Associates.

Recommended by John Gardner: Tinto, Vincent. *Leaving College: Rethinking the Causes and Cures of Student Attrition* (Chicago: University of Chicago Press, 1987).

Alexander, Linda B. "LIBS 1000: A Credit Course in Library Skills at East Carolina University." 1994. [The course is required of all new students and is designed to introduce them to the academic library.] ED376818.

Apps, Jerold W. *Study Skills for Today's College Student* (New York: McGraw-Hill, 1990).

Arnold, Judith, Jo Ann Ellingson, and Ursula Zyzik. "The Unexpected Impact of a College Retention Program on Bibliographic Instruction." *Illinois Libraries* 72 (1990): 608-610.

Becker, Karen A. "Individual Library Research Clinics for College Freshmen." *Research Strategies* 11 (1993): 202-210. EJ479759.

Bush, Renee B., and Margaret R. Wells. "Bibliographic Instruction for Honors Students: The University at Buffalo Experience." *Research Strategies* 8 (1990): 137-143. EJ418685.

Erickson, Bette LaSere, and Diane Weltner Strommer. *Teaching College Freshmen* (San Francisco: Jossey-Bass Publishers, 1991).

Fenske, Rachel F., and Susan E. Clark. "Incorporating Library Instruction in a General Education Program for College Freshmen." *Reference Services Review* 23 (1995): 69-74. EJ506993.

Gammill, Linda, et al. "Linked Courses: A Method to Reinforce Basic Skills." *Journal of Education for Business* 67 (1992): 358-60. EJ449572.

Coordinated assignments required undergraduates to use skills in three linked introductory courses: computer science, library research, and economics. First-year students achieved the same levels of mastery as students in traditional sections of the courses, and they felt the courses enhanced learning.

Gardner, John, et al. *Guidelines for Evaluating the Freshman Year Experience*. 1990 [ED334885].

Gardner, John N., and A. Jerome Jewler, eds. *Your College Experience: Strategies for Success. The Freshman Year Experience Series*. 1992 [Chapter Eight, "An Information Age Introduction to the Library," discusses how to deal with information problems.] ED343469 [Document not available from EDRS].

George, Mary W. "What Do College Librarians Want Freshmen to Know? My Wish List." *Research Strategies* 6 (1988): 189. EJ385783.

Hooks, James D. *Teaching Library Skills to Academically Unprepared College Freshmen*. 1986. ED296740.

Krentz, Roger F., and Donald E. Gerlach. *Library Literacy of Incoming College Freshmen*. 1989. ED346866.

Leighton, Gordon B., and Marsha C. Markman. "Attitudes of College Freshmen toward Bibliographic Instruction." *College and Research Libraries News* 52 (1991): 36-38. EJ423288.

Lent, John. *Libraries and Librarians as Depicted in Freshmen English Textbooks: An Update*. M.A. thesis, Kent State University, 1991. ED352962.

Lungu, Charles B.M. "Educating Library Users at the Copperbelt University." *Information Development* 6 (1990): 210-214. EJ423276.

Describes a library user education program for first-year students at Zambia's Copperbelt University that is designed to increase student awareness of available resources; improve their skills in independent learning; and enhance the presentation of their coursework. Planning user education programs in conjunction with faculty and other considerations for implementing such a program are assessed.

Matenje, Flossie Alinawo. "Library Orientation at the University of Malawi." *Information Development* 11 (1995): 42-45. EJ503430.

Astin, Alexander, et al. *Perspectives on the Freshman Year: Selected Major Addresses from Freshman Year Experience Conferences: Views on the Critical First Year*. Columbia, SC: National Resource Center for the Freshman Year Experience, University of South Carolina, 1991. Monograph series no. 2.

Simmons, George, et. al. "The Effects of a Freshman Seminar on At-Risk Under-, Over-, and Low Achievers." *NACADA Journal* 15 (1995): 8-14. EJ516475.

Thompson, Dot S., and James A. Van Fleet. "Developing a Model of Library User Education for Freshman

Science Students." *Research Strategies* 10 (1992): 122-128. EJ456228.

Tiefel, Virginia. "Evaluating a Library User Education Program: A Decade of Experience." *College and Research Libraries* 50 (1989): 249-259. EJ395518.

Upcraft, M. Lee, John N. Gardner, and associates. *The Freshman Year Experience: Helping Students Survive and Succeed in College.* San Francisco, CA: Jossey-Bass Publishers, 1989). ED310664 [Document not available from EDRS].

Upcraft, M. Lee., and John N. Gardner. *The Freshman Year Experience. Helping Students Survive and Succeed in College.* San Francisco, CA: Jossey-Bass, 1989.

Ury, Connie J., and Terry L. King. "Reinforcement of Library Orientation Instruction for Freshman Seminar Students." *Research Strategies* 13 (1995): 153-164. EJ515010. [Note: Ury presented at 16th FYE, see earlier listing].

APPENDIX 1: THE INDIANA STATE UNIVERSITY
SECTION OF APPS; EXCERPTS OF LIBRARY PORTION:
INTRODUCTORY PAGE AND TABLE OF CONTENTS

LIBRARY—INFORMATION—RESEARCH—INFORMATION—INTERNET—LIBNET—LUIS—INDEXES—E-mail—INFORMATION LITERACY

Libraries are complex entities that require skill, training, and experience to be used well. Occasional, inexperienced and experienced users alike need assistance in order to extract maximum utility from a library's resources—S. Michael Malinconico, Technology and the Academic Workplace, **Library Administration & Management** 5 (Winter 1991) 27

Contents of this section

- Introduction

- Information Skills **Pre-Test**

- Self-Paced Library Tour plus **Exercise**

- Library Locations by Floor

- Getting Help

- ISU's Primary Information Systems & Points of Access, Summer 1995

- Basic Research Strategy

- Hypothetical Topics for Library Research (how to narrow your topics)

- The Type of Research You Do May Depend on the Type of Paper You Are Writing

- Library Research Paper Planner

- **Post-Test**

- The Internet

- Pre-test scale

This section supplements **Chapter 15** in your text, and is meant to give you additional general information on the use of libraries as well as information specific to helping you use **ISU Libraries** more efficiently. By more efficiently, we mean, helping you develop the skills and knowledge necessary to use the most appropriate library materials in the most efficient way. You will then be able to avoid spending unnecessary amounts of time becoming very frustrated and not getting the materials you need to continue on with your library projects and research assignments.

> **Instructions: Read these introductory paragraphs, then take the Information Skills Pre-test.**
> **You will also take a self-paced tour of the library (included in this section) and complete an exercise sheet (not included... keep reading). You will attend one or more library instruction sessions, read the rest of this section, and finish up with a post-test (included) that you will turn in to your teacher.**

Many books published each year tell college students how to succeed in college. Most include some information about the role the library will play, but usually it's not a lot of information or it's slightly out-of-date or it's too general or it's not quite right. Why is that? Possibly it stems from a belief that libraries are easy to use without assistance or instruction.

How many term/research papers are you going to write in the *real world*? That depends on your job, your interests, your needs, and the definition of *term paper*. But one thing you will always need to know: how to find out something [who, what, where, when, how, how much, etc.]. You'd be surprised how much of that information is readily available in the library and how few people even think to ask.

So, while it may be hard to visualize beyond your library/information needs for one class, one college degree, etc., remember, it all boils down to one thing: INFORMATION. (We'll deal with information overload later.) *For the rest of your life, you'll have to select and gather information on any number of topics. You'll have available more information than you can assimilate...You must learn basic information-gathering skills: (1) defining the question; (2) deciding upon subject headings to begin the search; and (3) browsing to select appropriate materials* (paraphrased from Barbara K. Stripling, *Library Research Skills Workbook*, page 6)

If you're in a course such as freshman composition, the *process* of writing the research paper is the real emphasis, so that you learn the skills that you'll need further up the academic ladder. If you're writing papers within a subject area, then it is the *information* contained within the paper on which the professor will be concentrating. But you'll also be graded to some extent on those same basic skills of writing and researching you learned earlier. Sometimes the purpose of writing the paper is to allow you practice in finding the typical sorts of library materials you will routinely use. Sometimes a library assignment consists of a lot of questions, with no clue as to what type of resource or what specific resource you are supposed to use to answer the questions. This last type of library assignment (often called a scavenger or trivia hunt) is discouraged by librarians because it doesn't teach you anything. Scavenger hunts that ask a question and then give you one source (or just a few choices) and the call number and location for that source, can be slightly more useful. Sometimes this is a good way to find out what is available within an academic discipline. But generally, if this sort of assignment is given out, check with *Library Information Desk* staff before you get started.

> *Information literacy involves: recognizing a need for information, identifying what is needed, locating it, evaluating it, organizing it, and using it effectively.*[1]

> *Information literacy has four components: (1) an attitude that appreciates the value and power of information, (2) an awareness of the diversity of information forms and formats, (3) an understanding that information is not necessarily knowledge until it has been analyzed, questioned, and integrated into the existing body of knowledge, and (4) a process to access and assess information critically and effectively.*[2]

> *The bewildering array of new information services will make libraries more useful and their services more effective, but it will also make them more difficult to use. It can be expected that modern technologies will cause users to become more, rather than less, dependent on librarians...For years we have sought to maintain the unsupportable fantasy that libraries are self-service operations and as a consequence diminished the role and importance of librarians.*[3]

NOTES

1. Minnesota State University System, 1991, p A-14, quoted in Linda Bunnell Jones, "Linking Undergraduate Education and Libraries: Minnesota's Approach," in *New Directions for Higher Education*, no. 78 (Summer 1992): 27-35.

2. B. Gratch, "Information Literacy," in *Information Literacy*, comp. by C. Doyle, 193 (Towson, MD: National Forum on Information Literacy, 1991); and Michael Malinconico, "Technology and the Academic Workplace," *Library Administration & Management* 5 (Winter 1991): 27.

3. Malinconico.

APPENDIX 2: RATIONALE FOR A LIBRARY COMPONENT IN THE FIRST YEAR EXPERIENCE COURSE

H. Scott Davis

At Indiana State University (ISU), there is currently no general education course required of all ISU undergraduate students, which consistently includes the *teaching* of basic research/information-access skills. Many faculty assume that students are being taught research mechanics in the first-year English composition classes; this, however, is not the case. There is considerable variation in what information access skills, if any, are effectively incorporated into undergraduate courses. Further, some faculty assume that undergraduate students know how to do basic library research as a function of their high school experiences; again, while some might, this is generally not the case. While the library staff would love to provide on-demand individualized attention and instruction to every ISU student, this is no more possible or practical than classroom faculty trying to provide individualized instruction to each of their students instead of meeting in a classroom setting.

A general observation regarding the impact of electronic information technologies on higher education curricula has to do with the cognitive and hands-on skills associated with locating information as part of the undergraduate term paper/research paper process. These skills have changed drastically over the past 20 years. A manual research process of gathering needed information that might have taken a student several hours or days to complete ten years ago can now be accomplished, literally, within a matter of minutes or seconds *if* the student is equipped with the skills necessary to do so. Students lacking such skills become frustrated quickly and spend an unnecessary amount of time simply trying to locate materials. The library and the research processes become negative experiences.

Electronic information access skills such as Boolean logic and understanding database structure are inherent to the modern research process, but not fully apparent to the average library user without some basic explanation and instruction. Some library users are able to achieve minimal levels of competence from being self-taught; however, the depth and breadth of self-taught skills are almost always grossly overestimated. The end result is that many students are not using information systems efficiently and are giving no consideration to information *quality* (i.e., they are not intelligent information consumers). It would seem that this scenario is the antithesis of what our educational goals should be in an information/knowledge-based society. When basic electronic information access skills are present and effectively integrated into the curriculum, an institution has done much to refine the meaning of being "college educated" today. Certainly, as the United States moves toward the development of a new National Information Infrastructure (NII) that will be funded by taxpayers' dollars, ISU students, as future taxpayers, should know what they are paying for and understand NII's importance in terms of how they can use it for themselves. Inclusion of a library component in the First Year Experience course could do much to provide students with important "information survival skills" at the outset of their undergraduate educations.

Proposed Goals for a Library Component in the First Year Experience Course

- **Primary instructional goal**—Students will begin the process of developing self-reliance and self-sufficiency in information access in a highly automated academic environment; and will understand, be able to apply their understanding, and appreciate today's modern information environment.
- **Cognitive goal**—Students will understand the logical structure of organized information and will be able to assess the appropriateness of different resources as they relate to a particular information need.

- **Psychomotor goal**—Students will be able to apply their understanding of information structure by conducting a variety of information searches, both in traditional print and electronic resources.

- **Affective goal**—Students will view the information search process with less anxiety; become more self-reliant; and will appreciate the wide array of resources available in the modern information environment.

Possible Key Content Areas

1. ISU's current information environment in relation to the global information environment; emphasis on information as an essential "academic commodity;" juxtaposition of traditional print resources and electronic information resources; "diversity" of information from cultural and individual-differences perspectives.

2. Major characteristics of electronic database structure, including field structure.

3. Keyword/Boolean logic as applied to electronic database searching, including logical and positional operators, limiting, nesting, and truncation.

4. Basic familiarity with major ISU information systems (e.g., LUIS III, LIBNET, gopher, UseNet News, electronic mail).

5. Conceptual framework for understanding the Internet; emphasis on the three major Internet applications and gopher.

6. Selection of appropriate resources based on information need; evaluation of relative strengths and weaknesses of an information resource in terms of a specific information need.

7. Understanding of the continuing importance of traditional print resources.

8. Miscellaneous information factors related to the research process (e.g., lag time in publishing and indexing, bias, propaganda, point of view in publishing)

Davis is head, library information systems, Indiana State University. This article is written expressly for the committee.

Training Course Instructors to Teach Library Instruction

Pixey Anne Mosley

This instructive session article describes the theory and practice of a program instituted by Evans Library at Texas A&M University for the purpose of training instructors of freshman English courses to teach library instruction. Material detailing the initiation of course instructor training is presented from a theoretical perspective. Other portions of this article relate to experience gained during redesign of the program, or the "Practice" aspect of the conference theme.

Site Background

The student body at Texas A&M University is traditional in that a large percentage of students have recently completed high school and are entering college for the first time. Generally, they are unfamiliar with research methods and information resources in the academic library setting. The university does not have a mandatory library instruction course; however, one section of an elective class on library skills is offered through the humanities department. The primary instructional contact with students occurs during course-related, single-shot sessions, usually lasting 50 minutes or the equivalent of one class meeting.

Among the user groups utilizing library resources, the Freshman Writing Program in the English department is one of the largest. Freshman English courses have been included as part of the university's core curriculum since the mid-1980s. Course instructors

Mosley is coordinator of instructional services, Sterling C. Evans Library, Texas A&M University, College Station, Texas.

were full-time lecturers with teaching experience. Instructor-led library orientations were implemented during the late 1980s and predate current instructional services personnel. Relevant library resources consisted of a card catalog, microfiche serials list, and the *Reader's Guide to Periodical Literature*. Over a ten-year period, miscommunications regarding educational objectives and practices had resulted in a lack of cooperation between the library and the English department's Freshman Writing Program. Today, most sections of English 104 are taught by masters and doctoral degree candidates from within the English department. In addition, the library has changed to include an online catalog, electronic periodical indexes, new branches, and expanded services. By the 1995 fall semester, episodes of misinformation during library orientation tours occurred frequently. In addition, the reference staff experienced repeated problems with class assignments and scavenger hunts. An obvious solution would be for the library staff to assume responsibility for the library instruction segment of the freshman writing program. However, this approach would not address the issue of problematic assignments, nor was it feasible given staff workloads.

There are 50 to 70 sections of English 104 scheduled during each fall semester. The instruction session for each class lasts 50 minutes and includes an introduction to the online catalog and Wilson periodical indexes and a basic orientation to the 12 main service point/collection groupings around the library.

Typically, instructors request that library instruction classes be held between the second and fifth weeks of the semester, the peak period for campuswide library instructional activities. To address the problems of instructor inexperience, misinformation, class assignments, scavenger hunts, and workload constraints, an approach had to be developed to improve the quality of instruction being provided to the students.

Confronting the Issues

Whether initiating a program or redesigning a program with problems, the basic process is the same. This process includes obtaining participation and support (i.e., buy-in) from involved parties, designing and implementing a plan, and assessing the results to determine the success of the effort. When initiating a program, it is not necessary to deal with the emotional baggage of those who have made an investment in a program (i.e., "the way it has always been done"). However, with a program redesign, there is the advantage of being able to draw upon experience to reinforce the need for procedural change. Program redesign was the approach adopted at Texas A&M University, Evans Library.

Faculty Buy-In

Any successful program requires the support of the administrators and participants. The first phase of this program required library staff to interact with the English department faculty to gain their support or buy-in. "Faculty" refers to those persons in authority with a vested interest in the course. Faculty buy-in is crucial to the success of this program and was accomplished through a series of steps. The first step reinforced the need for students to receive library instruction. The second step explored the realities of library staff limitations and workloads. The third step documented specific examples of inappropriate resource referrals and problem assignments from instructors unfamiliar with library services. Only when mutually beneficial interdepartmental dialogue has been established is it possible to proceed with corrective measures.

Assignments

This next phase of implementation addressed class assignments. It introduced faculty and instructors to the concept that library instruction should support the class assignment. It was also an opportunity to interact with both faculty and instructors in a non-confrontational manner while exposing them to potential problems and misunderstandings about library resources. Faculty are less likely to take offense at comments about "the assignment" than comments about "your assignment" or "your class." In working with faculty and instructors to create an accurate, effective assignment, avoid the following assumptions:

- Faculty have used the library recently.

- Graduate students are knowledgeable about library resources.

- Instructors are being closely monitored and advised by departmental administration.

Instructor Training

The third phase of implementation required that a librarian develop and present a formal training program for course instructors. This training must be customized to individual library settings and university courses. The training development at Texas A&M University for the English 104 instructors can serve as a guide or example of an appropriate training session. The basic structure of the training included

- scheduling procedures,

- effective teaching tips,

- detailed tour outline,

- audiovideo equipment,

- rules and limits, and

- optional tour (required for new student).

Scheduling procedures covered the who, when, and why instructors were to call to schedule class time in the library, including the phone number and e-mail addresses of the appropriate instructional services personnel. Additionally, instructors were provided information detailing availability of services and facilities.

Effective teaching tips addressed common problems often observed by library service desk staff. Examples might include an instructor's erroneous assumption that students had prior knowledge of the library, selection of a poorly defined research project, and student procrastination. Instructors were reminded that novice library users may be found at any college level from freshman to graduating senior, and would almost certainly include transfer students. Instructors should not assume that students will be familiar with terminology or the process of literature research. Regarding poorly defined research topics, a few examples are worth many words. Providing some examples of too broad or too narrow topic definition serves to improve understanding. Additionally the librarian should remind the instructor that if scholarly sources are a requirement in the bibliography, then the research topic must reflect this requirement. Obviously, there may be a lack of such material regarding a favorite hobby or movie star. Finally, the librarian should encourage instructors to establish "milestones" or incremental assignment due dates throughout the semester to prevent student procrastination, unforeseen problems with topics, and last minute panic.

The instructors were provided a detailed tour outline (see appendix 1) that should be adhered to when conducting library orientation. The tour outline serves several functions:

- It provides sequenced stops at relevant service points and collections.

- It provides good online catalog examples.

- It defines specific material of interest to novice library users.

- It limits information so that students are not overloaded.

Instructors should be told explicitly not to add material to the outline.

The introduction of audiovisual equipment for use by the course instructor represented a major change in tour procedures. In the past, classes would cluster around a terminal in the OPAC area during demonstrations of the online catalog and tape-loaded Wilson periodical indexes. At one time, the demonstration equipment had been used by librarians, but improvements in technology had relegated it to a dusty corner of a closet. A Compaq XT computer was reconfigured as a terminal connection to the online catalog and connected to a passive-matrix LXS panel. Equipment setup and tear down in the instructional facilities was handled by library staff. Instructors less comfortable with the equipment were encouraged to request additional one-on-one training prior to their class demonstrations. Approximately five instructors per semester requested additional orientation with the equipment. The use of audiovisual equipment served to reiterate the need to schedule class orientations.

The next portion of the training dealt with rules imposed by the library. These rules were included in the program after the first semester that training was implemented. The presentation of this material depends upon the degree of support being provided by academic program administrators, as well as the comfort level of the individual librarians. The first rule prohibited unscheduled, disruptive, or uncontrolled tours. The second rule stated that classes would not be allowed to clump around a terminal in the general online catalog area. The third rule established that trivia-heavy, scavenger hunt assignments would not be tolerated. Individuals who refused to follow these basic rules were reported to the writing program administrators

The last part of the training was an optional walking tour. The tour was required for all new instructors. It was required that experienced instructors participate a minimum of every other year. The tour covered the same material presented on the tour outline. Less-experienced instructors or individuals new to the university were encouraged to use the library's audio-cassette tour or the Virtual Tour on the World Wide Web.

Assessment

The overall time required to implement the redesigned program was four semesters over a period of two calendar years. Table 1 provides statistics showing the increase in instructor participation. Generally, more experienced instructors with positive course evaluations were chosen as spring semester instructors. Problems were addressed and corrected as they developed. By the second year, the number of mistakes observed by the library staff averaged two to three per semester. This is contrasted with the 15 to 20 mistakes per semester observed prior to implementation of the training program. In addition, positive written feedback was received from the administrator of the writing program.

In order to inform instructors of changes in the library orientations for English 104, it was necessary to have the training sessions included as part of the required orientation for all instructors. During the first semester, instructor attendance at the training sessions was encouraged by the writing program administrators, but was not required. Unfortunately only the new instructors took advantage of the opportunity. The more-experienced instructors ignored the training and continued to pass along erroneous information. The next semester, program administrators scheduled the training session as a part of the instructor's two-day departmental teaching orientation and mandated attendance. The instructional services librarian focused on gaining their support for the changes. This was accomplished most effectively by explaining the benefits. These included access to audio video demonstration equipment, improved assignments from students, and an increased awareness of library resources. There will still be the occasional instructor who resists the "new way." Fortunately, graduate students are required to implement changes mandated by university faculty and program administrators. How-

SEMESTER	TOTAL SECTIONS	CONDUCTED TOURS
Fall 1995	62	30 (48%)
Spring 1996	22	21 (95%)
Fall 1996	60	47 (78%)
Spring 1997	19	18 (95%)

Table 1: Number of English 104 Sections Incorporating Library Instruction

ever, librarians will have to accept that when a faculty member refuses to participate, options are limited to working around the uncooperative individual.

Several issues were addressed after the first semester of program implementation. One problem developed when instructors added to the tour outline, resulting in confusion and misinformation. Some instructors were uncomfortable with computer demonstrations and projection hardware. This was resolved by providing additional one-on-one training. In a few rare cases, an instructional services librarian taught the computer-related portion of the orientation, with the English 104 instructor then leading the walking tour. Occasionally, an instructor refused to cooperate with library personnel. Rather than confronting the instructor, librarians went through appropriate channels and reported the instructor's behavior to the writing program administrators. Often the instructor would return to the library, apologize, and request training.

This emphasizes the importance of academic departmental administrative support and interdepartmental communication.

Conclusion

Implementation of a training program for course instructors is an ongoing process. New instructors are constantly being added as others leave or graduate. If a library is changing dramatically, material will need to be updated and experienced instructors will need to attend frequent "refresher" courses. As success is achieved in one course area, it may be appropriate to customize the material and extend the methodology into other areas with proportionately large numbers or students or courses. These might include speech communications classes or introductory classes in a subject discipline.

APPENDIX 1: SAMPLE WALKING TOUR OUTLINE

Evans Library Tour Outline.
Structure of the libraries on the campus
    Evans—Main Library
    West Campus—Supports Colleges of Business Admin. and Life Sciences/Agricul
        (Branch library, same use/circulation policies)
    Medical Sciences Library—Supports Colleges of Medicine & Veterinary Medicine (extends access/circulation to students, but some restrictions on study area usage)
Food and Drink Policy
    Emphasize that Food and Drink are not allowed in the Library
    Vending machines are located outside, on the concourse, for snacks and beverages
NOTIS Demo in Bibliographic Area
    CAT<ENTER> (mention other catalog options) <ENTER>
    T=Aggieland
    Emphasize that STACKS refers to shelving areas on floors 3-6
    HOL—Give brief explanation and encourage them to contact info desk for assistance
    Type STA

    Explain Wilson Indexes Database
    Type INDX
    Go into WILS
    K=CRIME AND COMPUTER

    Find article entitled "Crime in cyberspace: the digital underworld" and enter this number
    Point out citation information
    Type HOL to get call number and location
    Type STOP to exit NOTIS
    Turn off overhead projector (switch or bar on front)*

Now take group on walk-thru
Circulation
    Check-out periods vary depending on the item and individual University status
    Any ID validation problems should be referred to this desk
    Recall requests processed (to retrieve an item that someone else has checked out)
Information Desk
    General handouts available
    Assistance with NOTIS/WILS
    Answers to general library questions
Reference Area
    Index tables—Print indexes grouped by subject
    Reference Stacks—tall shelves, these books do not circulate, typical books include subject encyclopedias, handbooks, directories
    Reference Desk—librarians and experienced staff members; there to help you locate materials for your research; some high use items that require an ID for use in library
Library 110 (Do not take group into this area—stop outside door and point)
    Electronic resources (tend to be subject specific)
    Most are networked and can be accessed from various locations, others are on stand-alone setups (one machine/one database)
    Online resources: Dialog and Lexis/Nexis (library absorbs cost for class assignment related searching)
    Some products have printing limits. Encourage bringing a 3 ½" diskette for download
Now head back to hallway and move to CPD. On the way point out new book shelves, copy center, and phones.
CPD
    Most recent unbound issues
    "Current" definition dependant on bindery schedule may be 6 months to 2 years.
        Remind that NOTIS will tell you which issues are in CPD.
    Arranged in call order with a few high usage items (TIME, Newsweek, at desk)
    Newspapers also kept in this area
Reserves
    Materials that professors have placed for class usage
    Limited circulation periods as defined by the professor
    Strict overdue fines policy so make sure you return materials on schedule
Government Documents/Microtext
    Service desks: Reference for questions on locating materials, Circulation for checking out materials and assistance using readers/copiers. Microform materials can be checked out along with portable readers.
    Point out some specific resources: College Catalogs, Standards materials, Index shelves and tables, terminals (both LAN and standalone)
    Mention use of special call number system for Gov Docs—SuDocs (includes colons and slashes).
    Library collects State and US documents, not international or United Nations. Material on microformat includes old journal issues, old newspapers, technical reports, patents, ERIC education documents.
    (Move back toward the front of building)
Cushing Library Collection (special collections and archives)
    Rare books, manuscripts, and University archival materials
    Department hours limited (Open Monday - Friday 8-5)
    These materials must be used in the reading room, they cannot be checked out
Interlibrary Services
    Can acquire materials that we don't have in the library.
    Available to all students (graduates and undergraduates).
    Need to allow at least 10 days lead time to get books or articles this route.

There is no cost involved (except for copying dissertations in some cases) thanks to the students' Library Use Fee.

Map Library

Include all types of maps in book and sheet format. These include topographical maps, nautical maps, geological maps, atlases, and road maps.

Many of the sheet maps are not in NOTIS

Map materials can be checked out at the Map Library service desk.

Otherwise discuss this area from the 2nd floor elevator lobby.

5th and 6th floors only accessible from the front stairs/elevators

NOTIS terminals and copiers are available by the front elevator lobbies

Library layout maps are located near each bank of elevators

Group study rooms available on the 3rd & 4th floors. For reservation of Group Study Rooms contact Library Administration on 6th floor (845-8111).

Most materials arranged in call number order on the floors, exceptions include

TAMU Theses & Dissertations—3rd floor

Dewey Decimal books (old)—3rd floor

Curriculum Collection—4th floor

Books being reshelved (reshelving areas are indicated on the maps)

The Old Cushing area of the library has been closed off for construction & renovation. NO materials are located in this area.

Learning Resources Department (do not go up to the 6th floor)

Located on the 6th floor

Houses all multimedia (audio and video materials) and equipment for listening/viewing

Computer facilities with word processing/spreadsheet packages

Reinventing Bibliographic Instruction: The BGSU Experience

Julia K. Nims

Introduction

What do Madonna and the Chrysler Corporation have in common? If Mick Jagger and Wal-Mart join this group, does their commonality become clearer? They have all reinvented themselves. Madonna reinvents herself frequently. In fact, she creates a new persona just when the public starts becoming comfortable with her image. Chrysler Corporation has succeeded in maneuvering itself back into the top of the car manufacturers after a long and difficult slump. Both the entertainment world and corporate America recognize the necessity of reviewing operations and assumptions and then discarding those they deem outdated and adopting new ones. To the public, new companies and people seem to emerge overnight, and it surprises us to realize that these entities have been around for quite some time.

Although studying Madonna and Mick Jagger may be far more fascinating than Chrysler or Wal-Mart, we looked to the business world for a model for reinventing an existing bibliographic instruction program. A quick search of our library catalog retrieved many results to help explain this phenomenon. In short, businesses have found it necessary to reinvent themselves to thrive, or even to survive, in the late twentieth century. Michael Hammer and James Champy formulated a formal definition of "reinventing" in their book *Reengineering the Corporation: A Manifesto for Business Revolution*. They state that to reengineer, or

---

Nims is coordinator, library user education, Bowling Green State University, Bowling Green, Ohio.

reinvent, itself, a corporation needs to do "fundamental rethinking and radical redesign of business processes to achieve dramatic improvements in critical, contemporary measures of performance, such as cost, quality, service, and speed."[1] They go on to discuss four key concepts of the definition: *fundamental*, to start questioning all assumptions and "givens"; *radical*, to go beyond superficial changes and get to the root of things; *dramatic*, to make changes in leaps rather than steps; and *processes*, the activities that result in a desired outcome.[2]

They explain how the business environment is different now than it was even 20 years ago. Hammer and Champy identify three forces behind the new environment, what they call the three Cs: customers, competition, and change. Customers, they state, have the upper hand. Not only are customer bases more diverse as our population changes, but they have increased expectations. Second, competition has intensified. Corporations must deal with new competitors and niche markets. Finally, change has become the norm, and is happening at an accelerating rate.[3]

We realized that Hammer and Champy's three Cs exist at Bowling Green State University. Our students, indeed the entire academic community, have changed considerably since the mid-1970s. We do not consider our students and other users customers, but undoubtedly our user base is shifting. Our students are more diverse, with more minorities and adult learners in the library. Like business customers, the students and the faculty have increased expectations about what we should offer and how we can assist them. Competition comes from previously unlikely arenas: the

Internet, where students believe they can find all information without librarian assistance, commercial services such as UnCover or outsourcing agencies, and university computer services, which offers training in Internet navigation. Finally, we are experiencing change as well. Library resources, our technology, our profession are in a state of transformation. While our mission and goals are quite different from a corporation's, we could take their model of reinventing and apply it to our own situation. Although the reinvention of BGSU's bibliographic instruction program is not nearly as flamboyant as Madonna's most recent persona or as massive as the new Chrysler corporation, it is still a new program all the same.

The BGSU Library Environment

Bowling Green State University (BGSU) is located in the small town of Bowling Green in northwest Ohio. Originally founded as a teacher-training college, BGSU has evolved into a mid-sized four-year institution with a range of nationally recognized programs and a diverse population. In 1995-1996, more than 18,000 students were enrolled at BGSU, including over 2,500 graduate students. Although most students are from Ohio, all other states as well as 54 countries are represented in our student body.

The primary research facility for the university is BGSU's Libraries and Learning Resources (LLR). LLR consists of a large main library housing materials in the humanities and social sciences, and six special collections, Ogg Math/Science Library, the government documents collection, a curriculum resource center, the music library/sound recordings archive, the popular culture library, and the career resource center. Additionally, the library system includes instructional media services, the Popular Press, the Center for Archival Collections, and the Historical Collections of the Great Lakes. Fifteen miles north of the campus is the Northwest Regional Book Depository, shared by BGSU, the University of Toledo, and the Medical College of Ohio.

The entire library system holds nearly two million volumes, and one million sound recordings. Besides print resources, microformats, and other media, the library provides access to 56 research databases, including the library catalog and the OhioLINK statewide catalog, and the Internet. Students, faculty, and staff can access BGLink, the library system, from any of the 27 computer laboratories on campus, from their department offices and residence hall rooms, and off campus. BGSU is fully networked, and computers capable of accessing the World Wide Web and other Internet services are scattered throughout the buildings, including LLR.

LLR has had a formal bibliographic instruction program in place since the mid-1970s. At BGSU, we use the term "library user education," or LUE, instead of bibliographic instruction. By 1996 when Julia K. Nims became the library user education coordinator, BGSU had several successful program components already firmly established. At BGSU, library user education is part of the broad area of information services. Within information services, five of the 11 full-time librarians in information services (Kelly Broughton, Stefanie Dennis, Julia Nims, Linda Rich, and Mary Wrighten) have LUE responsibilities in addition to reference and collection development duties. The other six librarians' primary duties focus on collection development or reference. Although the information services LUE librarians do work with librarians in our special collections and other departments, we focused BGSU's "reinventing" activities on those components that involved the five information services librarians with LUE responsibilities.

The Old LUE Program

As mentioned earlier, BGSU's library user education program has had a tremendously successful history. The existing LUE components fell into five broad categories: course-integrated instruction, course associated instruction, non-course-associated instruction, library orientation activities, and instructional publications. We had course-integrated instruction in our introductory English class, "Varieties of Writing" (ENG 112). Modeled after the University of Pennsylvania's innovative English composition bibliographic instruction program, the 3,000 students enrolled in this course are required to each successfully complete a library packet. The packet consists of three units that walk them though the research process, including determining a topic focus, finding information in the library system, and integrating their library research into their final papers. The library has always tied instruction to course work. To facilitate this, we assign the information services librarians liaison responsibilities in specific departments. Most of the LUE librarians have eight to ten different departments to which they provide instruction. All the LUE librarians in information services share some departments that request a great deal of instruction, such as the English department.

In addition to this course-associated and course-integrated instruction, we offered open instructional sessions tied to no specific course:

- PERCS, BGSU's PErsonalized Research Consultation Service, which provides long-term, individual instruction to students in the final stages of masters' or Ph.D. programs;

- Sixty-minute seminars where graduate students and faculty members receive hands-on, discipline-based instruction on our research databases;

- Internet seminars where students, faculty, and staff learn how to use Pine e-mail and navigate the World Wide Web with Netscape Navigator;

- Residence hall computer lab drop-in sessions, where librarians go to residence hall labs to provide research assistance;

- In-depth research consultations with library user education liaisons when requested;

- Graduate college professional development program sessions the week before the beginning of fall semester that introduce new graduate students to library services and research; and

- Instructional sessions geared to our multicultural students, including hands-on orientation sessions.

We also provided library orientation services during Pre-View days when prospective students visited the university, and during pre-registration activities for incoming first-year students and transfer students. These activities included demonstrations of our online catalog and research databases, brief tours of the library, and manning information booths with other campus services. Eventually, library orientation expanded to include tours and instructional sessions to outside groups, such as high school classes.

Finally, we had a series of instructional publications designed to help students use our resources. *Research Aids*, what we call pathfinders, *Guides* to library services and collections, and *How-to-Use Aids* for some of our more difficult research databases and print reference sources provided assistance to our users while they were in the building.

Additionally, each LUE librarian fully participated in instruction at the reference desk for 12 to 15 hours a week.

Why Reinvent?

Our program was broad-based and inclusive. It had something for everyone, and it kept all of the information services librarians incredibly busy, an easy, but inaccurate sign of success. We were constantly thinking, What else can we do?, instead of considering; What do our users need? We had all taken some sorts of management courses in library school, where most of us learned that it is poor management practice to initiate a new service without stopping one if you want to continue to provide quality service with no additional resources, such as money or people. However, it took a semester of unusually long hours, dozens of instructional sessions, and a vague sense of dissatisfaction to open our eyes to the quandary in which we found ourselves.

First, we realized that some of our LUE components were no longer working. In previous years, library users had virtually flocked to our 60-minute seminars and Internet seminars. Two years ago, we noticed that attendance at these sessions was falling. Instead of 20 people in a session, we had three or four. At first, we thought that we were doing something wrong; we were not promoting them efficiently, or we had scheduled them at inconvenient times in the semester, or they needed to be longer, 90-minute seminars instead of 60-minute seminars. So we continued them for another semester, but this time we increased the number of seminars and their length, and we doubled our promotional efforts. Attendance continued to be poor, and we had to rethink the component.

The residence hall drop-in clinics failed. We believed that by going to the students, we would be providing research assistance when they needed it, when they were doing their research. We promoted the clinics in the residence halls, over the campus radio station, and in cafeterias. In an attempt to increase participation by the residents, we advertized prizes to people who asked questions. We had spent weeks soliciting donations from local businesses. In the end, we had dozens of coupons for free video rentals, free pizzas and other food, and free copying services, and donations from local car washes, movie theaters, and tanning salons. We distributed a total of seven prizes. Not counting the preparation time, the drop-in clinics used approximately 20 hours of librarians' time. Although this experience was disappointing, we did learn that BGSU students are not doing research in the residence hall computer labs.

Second, we saw that we were starting down the path toward librarian burnout. Planning library instruction demands incredible amounts of time and energy. When these sessions failed to live up to our expectations, our sense of discouragement increased. Librarians at BGSU have faculty status, and are required to do research and publish and to serve on various committees. We did not have time to fulfill all our professional obligations and provide all the services we offered. We found that we were doing instruction without planning a focused program. With all these demands, none of us felt that we were providing the best service we could.

Last October, after an unbelievably busy month of course-associated instruction, Internet seminars and 60-minute seminars, and high school tours, the library user education librarians in information services decided that enough was enough. It was time to fix our program.

Process of Reinventing

Our first step in reinventing the program was to decide what our ideal library user education program would look like. Although library user education is only one program within the greater library organization, we decided to take Hammer and Champy's advice and think of making fundamental and radical changes. We decided to disregard our constraints of tradition and lack of resources at this stage, and focus on what we would like our user education program to become. What should our priorities be? What types of instruction did our users need? When did they need it? How could we provide this instruction?

We began our search for answers to these questions by reading library literature. (An abbreviated list of sources we examined is included.) Not all of us read all these articles. Instead we broke them down into groups, read them, and discussed them in meetings. We focused our research on literature that discussed programs that had succeeded, paying particular attention to why they succeeded. Not all successful activities would work in our environment, but if we could learn why they worked, we could create new services at BGSU that would be equally successful. We also talked and brainstormed among ourselves. What activities had we offered that were popular and productive? What made them so?

This happened quickly. Later in the semester, we created the Library User Education Statement of Priorities. Preceding the outline of the priorities, we stated that "BGSU Libraries and Learning Resources Library User Education Program exists to promote the mission of LLR (Libraries and Learning Resources) and support the College's goals and objectives." To fulfill its mission, the library user education (LUE) librarians determined the following priorities to focus the activities of the LUE program, and to guide us in the allocation of our resources, including staff expertise and time.

Our top priorities became the provision of instruction when it was most effective, which meant when it was tied to specific class assignments and projects, and the promotion of information literacy skills in all our instruction. The next level of priorities included instruction that is not directly associated with a course or job assignment or project. Preferably, these services would be provided by point-of-need/point-of-use instruction. Finally, we decided that those activities that are primarily outreach in nature and cannot be classified as library user education would no longer be a priority.

Deciding these priorities and then ranking them in this order is not a groundbreaking process. In fact, it makes perfect sense, and it became obvious to us once we started really thinking about what type of program we wanted. However, when we compared these priorities with our previous activities, it became apparent that the time and energy we devoted to LUE activities did not reflect these priorities. In our attempts to provide as many services as possible to as many people as possible, we treated all our activities with the same priority: something needed to be done immediately.

Once we selected our priorities, we went on to the next step: developing specific LUE activities to meet our priorities. We started this process by looking at the services we already had in place. Not surprisingly, many of them fit in perfectly with our "ideal" program. First, we decided to maintain our liaison system with the academic departments. Assigning one librarian to each department allows the liaisons to become knowledgeable with the resources the students and faculty use and need, but also lets us cultivate relationships with the teaching faculty, who control their class assignments and who are responsible for requesting course-associated library instruction.

We also decided to keep our course-integrated instruction in the English 112 course. While we plan to change the format of the instruction from a printed packet of activities to online, interactive activities sometime in the next two years, we believe that the system we have in place serves the needs of these students for the time being.

The librarian-written instruction publications, *Research Aids*, *Guides*, and *How-to-Use Aids*, were excellent point-of-need assistance. Previous library user education coordinators had worked with graduate students in BGSU's technical writing program to develop effective publications. Copies of all these publications are kept at the reference desk and some are also placed at other services desks. We did decide to make these publications available over the World Wide Web so library users could access them when researching outside the library.

We also kept our PERCS program for graduate students. Our research showed that individual consultations on specific research problems were most beneficial for the students, and, therefore, a priority for us. Originally, they designed PERCS for graduate students in the last stretch of their program. PERCS graduate students enjoyed subsidized online searching and dissertation purchases. Since these elements of the PERCS service have been phased out with the increase in our research databases that students can search for no charge, and our ongoing grappling with an ever-decreasing budget, we have opened PERCS to all graduate students, regardless of where they are in their programs. The name PERCS was recognized around campus, and we chose to keep it as the name for graduate consultations.

GCPDP, Graduate College Professional Development Program, remains part of our program, as does in-depth reference consultations on an as-needed basis. The in-depth reference consultations, although infrequent, give us the opportunity to work with students on a one-on-one basis. Also, since the students seek out the appointments, they usually come with specific research problems that need solving. GCPDP is a unique situation. Since it occurs before classes even start, it is clearly not tied to any assignment or project. However, the graduate students are required to attend our sessions, giving us a "captive" audience. We have changed our focus of these sessions from providing detailed instructions on how to use many of our resources, to giving information on basic library services and research sources graduate students will need to know for their upcoming research.

Our multicultural students still require special assistance with library resources. Mary Wrighten, BGSU's multicultural services librarian, continually revises the library orientations and instructional sessions to meet the needs of these users.

Next, we looked at our existing services, and decided which ones to cease. A quick decision was to discontinue those activities that we considered more orientation than instruction. These activities included Pre-View Day, pre-registration days, and tours to outside groups. While these services certainly have merit, we could not devote valuable and finite library user education time and energy to them. Library administration created a new outreach team devoted to recruiting new students and promoting library resources to outside groups.

We also ceased our "cattle call" activities, the 60-minute seminars and the Internet seminars, which are not associated with any specific credit courses and are open to all BGSU community members. These activities were difficult to divest. Previous LUE coordinators had initiated them when the BGSU catalog became automated and when we joined OhioLINK in the early 1990s. Not long after, BGSU introduced BGNet, the university network, which allows users to connect to the Internet. With a BGNet account, which is freely available to all members of the BGSU community, users can access not only e-mail and other Internet services, but the library system as well. Library staff had to introduce thousands of users to a new system and acquaint them with all the different ways they could access it. Understandably, five years ago, these seminars were extremely popular and necessary. However, over time, our users became more comfortable with the system and able to transfer the skills necessary to search one database to other databases. Also, we suspect that some users simply could not wait for our seminars to learn how to use e-mail or search the Web. Out of necessity, they sought help from other sources, such as the reference desk, their friends, and their instructors. A combination of our newer projects now covers information previously covered in the 60-minute seminars, and we rely on commercially produced videos to provide instruction on e-mail and navigating the World Wide Web. Currently, we are searching for online tutorials we can make available over our Web page, which will allow our users to access these services outside the library.

Obviously, we were not left as full a slate of traditional program components. However, we did have time and energy to start implementing new projects. Our top priority was to focus on providing in-depth, meaningful instruction. The first project we began working on was developing the library credit course, "Research in the Electronic Library." A 200-level course, "Research in the Electronic Library," focuses on the research process, common database features, conducting research on the Internet, and exploring issues such as copyright. Currently, we offer one section of this course each semester to the general student body, and hope to have the resources to offer more sections per term soon. In the spring of 1998, we will offer a new course, "Living in the Information Age," which will cover more information access issues in greater depth.

Since we wanted to tie our instruction activities to class assignments, we chose to concentrate on class-associated activities. Based on our literature reviews, our experience, and our common sense, strengthening our relationships with teaching faculty appears to hold the most promise in getting students into the library when they have assignments where our resources are required or beneficial. We have also started creating Web pages for individual classes, so students can access customized assistance with specific projects whenever they require it.

Our second main priority, providing point-of-need assistance, required more creativity. We anticipate that the World Wide Web will become a primary vehicle for providing instruction, and we have developed as many of our point-of-need/point-of-use services as feasible to delivery via the Web.

Although we were re-inventing our library user education program, we were not prepared to reinvent the proverbial bibliographic instruction wheel, so we looked at other successful bibliographic instruction programs and projects and modified them to match our users' needs. For graduate students and faculty, we developed "Research Database Fundamentals," an e-mail seminar. Participants sign up for a mail distribution list, and receive 12 weekly messages from a librarian, giving step-by-step instructions on how to use a particular database. This method of instruction is not new. In fact, we got the idea from the well-known "Bck2SkOL" e-mail seminar created by at the University of South Carolina. Many librarians in the information services department had signed up for the e-mail seminar in previous semesters, and found it immensely helpful in learning the Internet. We believed that our users would like to have succinct database instructions delivered to their e-mail accounts for them to read immediately or save for later. This method of instruction met our point-of-need priority perfectly. One of the LUE librarians, Linda Rich, chose to create the mailing list, update the lessons, and generally manage the program. At the end of the semester, we posted all the Research Database Fundamentals lessons to the LUE Web page.

Because the PERCS project had proven successful with graduate students, we wanted to provide a parallel service for our undergraduate students. After considerable discussion, we decided to offer term paper clinics. BGSU had never offered these individual consultations with students in the past, but other schools, such as Indiana University in Bloomington, have had great success with them. By offering individualized assistance on a specific assignment, we feel we have the student's attention, and the creation of a learnable moment. We made one minor modification to the term paper clinics—we decided to call them "Research Project Clinics," and possibly entice participation from some students who had projects that didn't fall under the heading "term paper." We have offered these "Research Project Clinics" for two semesters, and will continue them in the future. Our undergraduate students have responded positively to this individual instruction, and give the librarians at BGSU undue credit for creating this program.

We still had the interminable problem of how to provide basic instruction to lower-level undergraduate students, and so *PILLAR* (Partners Introducing Library Literacy And Resources) was born. *PILLAR* is a version of "instructing the instructors." When we decided to train instructors to introduce our library resources, our first step was to determine what classes we envisioned using this, what the classes were usually taught about library resources, and how to provide instruction and materials to the teachers. The obvious solution to the first part of the equation was to substitute *PILLAR* for in-person instruction in the basic "University Success" classes, which normally has no library assignment associated with them, and the introductory English sequence, English 110 ("Developmental Writing") and English 111 ("Introductory Writing"), whose students needed to learn how to find periodical and newspaper articles. All of these courses required instruction on the most basic research strategies, such as keyword searching, screen interpretation, and locating the item in the library. Our solution was to create a hypertext canned presentation for our catalog and two of our general research databases. We also created exercises for instructors to assign if they wanted, a brief outline of a library tour, and sections on library research basics, such as evaluating information, and on research assignment strategies. These materials are currently available over the Web, and will be integrated into classes in Fall 1998.

Our final new project is FALCON, an interactive tutorial introducing the BGSU Libraries Web-based catalog created by Stefanie Dennis. Designed for students to use at their own pace, FALCON walks the student through numerous searches, including known-item searches and keyword searches. If a participant selects an incorrect answer on the tutorial, FALCON will explain the mistake and then guide the student to the correct answer. At the end of the tutorial, the student is asked to register so that documentation stating that the student has successfully completed the assignment can be sent to the instructor. We envision integrating this tutorial into our ENG 112 library instruction component, and using it as a basic instruction tool at the reference desk.

The third and final step, which we still are working on, is the introduction of our new program to the rest of the library and the university as a whole. To announce our new priorities to the rest of the library, and to document our policies and procedures, we wrote an LUE manual that covers everything from our statement of LUE liaison responsibilities to our criteria for including materials on our *Research Aids*. Paper copies are available in offices and at various public desks around the library. Eventually, the manual was marked up in HTML, and placed on the Web for all library staff members to access at will. We introduced our new services, the *Research Project Clinics*, *PILLAR*, FALCON, and *Research Database Fundamentals*, to appropriate audiences through campuswide listservs, the campus newspaper, flyers and tabletents, and visits to teaching departments. While we never publicly announced that we were ending certain services, such as the 60-minute seminars and the Internet seminars, we have not heard any questions or complaints about their absence.

Overall, library staff and the university community have embraced the new LUE program. New programs, such as the "Research Database Fundamentals" e-mail seminar for faculty and graduate students, and the "Research Project Clinics" for undergraduate students, have been greeted with tremendous approval and appreciation. Librarians and library staff feel that they have more time to devote to preparing for course-associated and course-integrated instruction, and for planning new services that fit in with our new priorities.

Problems

Changing BGSU's library user education program has not been without some difficulties. The major problem has been letting go of programs that have been successful in the past, such as the 60-minute seminars and the Internet seminars. We are tempted, at times, to try a new version of these open sessions, believing that our users still want these services. Eventually, we remind ourselves that we had a valid reason for discontinuing these services. Still, parting with previous success has been hard.

A less obvious, but just as real, problem stems from the paring down of our programs. When we decided to focus on instruction for formal classes or on instruction somehow tied to discrete assignments, we shed library user education activities that library staff with M.L.S. degrees could participate in. Library tours, pre-registration, and Pre-View Days activities were extremely popular with library staff who do not generally conduct library user education sessions. People from our technical services and access services units participated in a very public aspect of LLR's services. The creation of an outreach team to take over the activities no longer part of the LUE program has proven a successful outlet for library staff who do not have library school training. Our library staff have experience and talent to offer our users. More important, they have a desire to interact with our users, and share their skills and knowledge with them.

Finally, we have the recurring problem of saying, "no" to people who request instruction that no longer falls within our LUE program. Declining to provide a tour to a high school group, or giving a hands-on session on our OPAC to students in a "University Success" class is not easy. Not only is it at times uncomfortable to try to explain why we no longer offer instruction as we did previously, saying "no" is contrary to our service ethic. Saying "no" is frightening and risky. When all of academe is under fire to justify their contributions to higher education, the library, usually considered a support service, and librarians, as support staff, can quickly come under scrutiny. If and when we do face this inspection, we must have the documentation to support our claims that quantity of services does not directly correlate to quality of services. It is a struggle to balance our desire to provide every possible service to the BGSU community with our ambition to provide excellent education of research skills and techniques. Our experience showed that we could not do both.

Conclusion

The reinventing of BGSU's library user education program has proven a positive experience. All the LUE librarians feel the program has a focus and provides optimal assistance to our users. Additionally, the librarians have the time and energy to devote to more advanced instruction and to devise new services to meet the changing needs of our user population. We anticipate that our program will need continual evaluation, and that our priorities and services will change over time.

To those librarians seeking to revitalize their own bibliographic instruction programs, we offer the following suggestions:

- Read literature about successful bibliographic instruction services and projects. Even if the model library in the article is larger or smaller than yours, or has additional resources, the reasons behind their success can provide ideas for programs that can be tailored to any specific library's situation.

- Start the process by establishing your priorities and creating your "ideal" library instruction program. If your first step is to decide which current services to keep, you may find that you are clinging to activities because of tradition, and not because they achieve the results you want.

- Remember Hammer and Champy's definition of reengineering: the change needs to be radical, dramatic, and fundamental. Creating our library user education program was not a piecemeal process extended over several months. We needed the changes to be real and introduced as quickly as possible.

- Gain the support of the library administration. Without the approval and blessing of our head of information services and the dean of libraries, we could not have taken such risks in discontinuing old services.

Despite a seemingly successful revitalization of our program, the BGSU LUE librarians will not rest on their laurels. Our next steps are to focus on staff development, to make sure that we have the skills and resources to develop effective services, and to implement an assessment program to document students' learning successes within the framework of this new program. We believe in the strength of our program, the correctness of our priorities, and the process we went through to develop the program. Now, we will need to prove its success to the rest of our academic community.

(To visit our LUE Web site, jump to <http://www.bgsu.edu/colleges/library/infosrv/lue/luehome.html>. The LUE staff page, with the LUE manual is available at <http://www.bgsu.edu/colleges/library/infosrv/lue/staff/staff.html>)

While planning our new program, we relied heavily on the experiences of our colleagues at other institutions. We would like to thank these authors for sharing their knowledge. Below is a very selective list of reading we found particularly enlightening and helpful.

SELECT BIBLIOGRAPHY

Arp, Lori. " Structures of Bibliographic Instruction Programs: A Continuum for Planning." *The Reference Librarian* 24 (1989): 25-34.

Barr, Robert B. "From Teaching to Learning—A New Paradigm for Undergraduate Education." *Change* 27 (November/December 1995): 12-25.

Becker, Karen A. "The Characteristics of Bibliographic Instruction in Relation to the Causes and Symptoms of Burnout." *RQ* 32 (Spring 1993): 346-357.

BI-L (Bibliographic Instruction Discussion List). Discussions related to "Re: Managing Library Instruction Workload" and "Re: Library Instruction and Everything Else." November 1996. Subscription address: listserv@bingvmb.cc.binghamton.edu. Archived.

Carter, Thomas L. "The Human Touch in Bibliographic Instruction: At Loyola Marymount University." *Catholic Library World* 65 (January-March 1995): 14-16.

Dusenbury, Carolyn. "The Future of Instruction." *Journal of Library Administration* 20 (1995): 97-117.

Eadie, Tom. "Immodest Proposals: User Instruction for Students Does Not Work: A Former User Education Librarian Challenges a Basic Belief." *Library Journal* 115 (15 October 1990): 42-45.

Hammer, Michael, and James Champy. *Reengineering the Corporation: A Manifesto for Business Revolution.* New York: Harper Business, 1993.

Hardesty, Larry L. "Faculty Culture and Bibliographic Instruction: An Exploratory Analysis." *Library Trends* 44 (Fall 1995): 339-367.

Hardesty, Larry L., Jamie Hastreiter, and David Henderson, eds. *Bibliographic Instruction in Practice: A Tribute to the Legacy of Evan Ira Farber.* Ann Arbor, MI: Pierian Press, 1993.

Kohl, David F. As Time Goes By...: Revisiting Fundamentals of Library Instruction." *Library Trends* 44 (Fall 1995): 423-429.

LaGuardia, Cheryl, Stella Bentley, and Janet Martorana, eds. *The Upside of Downsizing: Using Library Instruction to Cope.* New York: Neal-Schuman, 1995.

Leckie, Gloria J. "Desperately Seeking Citations: Uncovering Faculty Assumptions about the Undergraduate Research Process." *The Journal of Academic Librarianship* 22 (May 1996): 201-208.

Lee, Catherine A. "Teaching Generation X: Six Guidelines for Developing More Appropriate BI Programs." *Research Strategies* 14 (Winter 1996): 56-59.

McCool, Donna L. "Staffing for Bibliographic Instruction: Issues and Strategies for New and Expanding Programs." *The Reference Librarian* 24 (1989): 17-24.

Patterson, Charles D. "Library User Education: Assessing the Attitudes of Those Who Teach." *RQ* 29 (Summer 1990): 513-523.

Rebaza, Claudia. "Enough Is Enough: Electronic Overload and Information Literacy." Paper presented at the 22d Annual Conference of the Academic Library Association of Ohio, Columbus, Ohio, 1 November 1996.

Rettig, James R. "The Convergence of the Twain or Titanic Collision? BI and Reference in the 1990s' Sea of Change." *Reference Services Review* 23 (1995): 7-20.

Stoffle, Carla J., and Karen Williams. "The Instructional Program and Responsibilities of the Teaching Library." *New Directions for Higher Education* 90 (Summer 1995): 63-75.

Turner, Diane J. "Viewpoint: What's the Point of Bibliographic Instruction, Point-of-Use Guides, and In-House Bibliographies?" *Wilson Library Bulletin* 67 (January 1993): 64-67.

NOTES

1. Michael Hammer and James Champy, *Reengineering the Corporation: A Manifesto for Business Revolution* (New York: Harper Business, 1993), 32.

2. Hammer and Champy, 32-36.

3. Hammer and Champy, 18-24.

APPENDIX 1: LUE STATEMENT OF PRIORITIES AS IT APPEARS IN THE LUE MANUAL

Library User Education
Statement of Priorities

BGSU Libraries and Learning Resources' Library User Education Program exists to promote the mission of Libraries and Learning Resources and to support the College's goals and objectives.

To fulfill its mission, the Library User Education (LUE) Librarians determined the following priorities to focus the activities of the Program, and to guide in the allocation of resources, including staff expertise and time.

TOP PRIORITIES

- Based on a review of library literature and our own experiences, we have decided that library education is most effective when tied to specific class assignments or projects. We also endeavor to promote information literacy skills for lifelong learning.

    Examples: Educating students on the research process and in the use of information resources available to them here at BGSU.

SECONDARY PRIORITIES

- Library education that is not directly associated with a course (or job) assignment or project.

    Examples: Instruction on broader information skills, such as Internet navigation. Instructional sessions that are not tied to course requirements.

NON-PRIORITIES

- Activities that are outreach or promotional in nature and cannot be classified as library user education related will become the responsibility of the LLR Outreach Team.

    Examples: Instruction/orientation to non-BGSU affiliated groups. Participation in BGSU Pre-View and Pre-Registration activities.

Adopted 12/96

Presentation Basics: Skills, Techniques, and Learning Styles

Jan Orf and Marianne Hageman

Introduction

When designing a presentation, the librarian needs to consider what information, resources, and techniques need to be included to make the session memorable and part of the learning experience. There are many different presentation skills and techniques that the librarian can use in developing an instruction session. "Active learning" can also be included in designing the session and as methods of evaluating the presentation without taking a lot of time away from instruction. By examining adult learning styles and combining that knowledge with the presentation techniques that are most comfortable for the presenter, the instruction session can be interesting and retain the attention of the attendees.

Designing the Presentation

There are several basic actions that should be considered during the preparatory stages when designing a presentation. The librarian should begin by setting goals and objectives for the session. The goals and objectives identify what he or she is attempting to achieve in the instruction session. Once these are set, the librarian should outline or flowchart the presentation. Either method is acceptable and depends on the learning style of the presenter (i.e., an outline for those who are text-based learners and the flowchart for those who are visual learners).

The next step is to develop the opening and the closing. Some instructors write the opening first to define what information will be covered. Others prefer to start with the closing, which identifies the direction the presentation should take by showing where the session will end. The librarian should start with whichever he or she prefers and with which he or she is most comfortable. As part of the opening, the instructor should consider possible icebreakers to get the attention of the students and to make them more comfortable. Asking questions about their experiences on the resources to be covered, introducing themselves to the rest of the class, and brainstorming a "wish list" of what the students would like to have covered in the session are examples of possible icebreakers.

Methods of assessing the presentation should also be examined at this stage. The librarian should have some means by which to evaluate whether the students are grasping the concepts covered in the session. There are several methods of assessing during the session which will be discussed later in this paper. Further, the instructor can also assess the audience. Using icebreaker questions both at the beginning of the presentation, and at different times during the session, the librarian can discover at which level the students are and either adjust the instruction or make use of more experienced students who could help others who need additional assistance.

The next strategy in designing a presentation would be to break up the session into "teachable chunks." The average attention span of the adult learner

---

Orf is reference librarian and *Hageman* is acting reference coordinator, University of St. Thomas, St. Paul, Minnesota.

is 20 minutes. That means that each "chunk" should be a maximum of 20 minutes. Unfortunately, the average attention span of the traditional-age college student is only about seven minutes, so within each "chunk," the librarian should include different activities and presentation styles to keep the attention of all of the students in the class.[1] Within each "teachable chunk," there should be repetition in order to reinforce the major points. The librarian should 1) tell them what you are going to tell them; 2) tell them; and 3) tell them what you told them. The instructor should give an overview of the information to be covered in that section, then cover the material, and, last, review the main points that were covered within each "chunk."

The librarian also needs to consider what canNOT be covered in an instruction session. Because librarians frequently are given a limited time period to cover the material, there is often not enough time to cover everything that they would like. Therefore, the instructor must pick what he or she cannot teach and find ways to compensate. This may be done in several ways, including: 1) provide reference material or a bibliography that emphasizes the uncovered material; 2) give a phone number at which students can obtain additional help, or where they can schedule appointments for assistance; 3) try to give a brief overview of the information for which in-depth coverage cannot be provided; 4) find a way to follow-up the session with additional consultations or a session outside of class time; 5) attempt to sneak in an example of the uncovered material; 6) offer two sessions (or a series of sessions) if that can be arranged; 7) state up-front time needs so that the students are aware that there is still information available, which cannot be covered in the time allotted.

As previously stated, the librarian should begin designing the presentation by developing basic information like goals and objectives, outlining the session, creating the opening and closing, and reviewing possible icebreakers and assessment tools. Probably the most important factor to consider is the attention span of the students and therefore information should be presented in "teachable chunks," which provide an overview, detailed information, and a review of material within a time period not to exceed 20 minutes. The librarian also needs to consider what cannot be covered and consider ways in which the information can be included without exceeding the time limit of the class.

ACTIVITIES

Once the design basics have been completed, consider including different activities in the presentation. Why? Activities can reinforce learning and make it meaningful; they also can help get people involved. This incorporates "active learning": what one hears, sees, discusses, and does, allows one to acquire knowledge and skill.[2]

Plan activities carefully, to make them meaningful. Activities should be based on the presentation objectives. State the purpose of the activity, then give clear instructions and ask for questions to make sure people understand what they are to do. Monitor the participants during the activity, to see how they are doing and to see if questions have come up. Then "debrief" or discuss the activity; the librarian can review or summarize what has been covered, or can see if they have understood what was intended. One exercise we use for undergraduate marketing students has them break into small groups to discuss basic marketing questions and types of information needed (company, industry, and demographic information.) We come back together as a large group to review answers they have, and to discuss different options.

In planning activities, the instructor needs to consider different adult learning styles. People learn in different ways, and being aware of this causes the instructor to think about ways to reach the individuals in the audience in appropriate ways. In the literature of adult learning different labels are sometimes used, but we will use the terms *activists, reflectors, theorists*, and *pragmatists*.[3] *Activists* are people who enjoy the here and now; they learn from new experiences and are extroverts. *Reflectors* tend to observe and analyze information at their own pace; they may mentally "step back" to think about things. They are good at collecting and analyzing data. *Theorists* value logic and rationality; they like concepts, models, and theories, and they like to explore the interrelationships between things. *Pragmatists* are practical and down-to-earth. They look for relevance and ask, how can I use this? (We all tend to be like this sometimes.) Many people are combinations of more than one learning style. Plan to have some of each of these in your audience.

There are various types of activities that can be included in a session. One of our favorites (that isn't too expensive) is stickers, which participants can use to highlight key points, or the instructor can hand out as a reward. Candy is another inexpensive option. Icebreakers have already been mentioned in beginning a session; they can also be used within a session for brainstorming, for polling participants, or for socializing. Exercises can be used to present materials instead of a lecture, or to check and see if people understand what has been covered.

Videotapes can also be used as an activity. They are useful to tell a story and to stimulate discussion. Remember to keep your video clip short; don't let it *be* the presentation. Popular games such as "Jeopardy" or "Monopoly" can be used to repeat information and skills, to reinforce learning, and to get people to participate. Games can also involve more than one of the senses, another way to encourage learning. They can be planned as board games, pen and pencil, on a flip chart, or e-mail. Be careful with games done via e-mail if not everyone has equal access to an e-mail account, or if people only use their e-mail at certain times of the day.

As mentioned, activities can and should reinforce learning, so plan them carefully. Remember the four kinds of adult learning styles, and incorporate several types of activities into the sessions to accommodate them.

PRESENTATION SKILLS

There are many skills that can be included in a presentation which are easy to add to the instructor's repertoire and can keep the students interested so that they will learn. The instructor can influence the students by using an unusual entrance, giving some background through which the students recognize that he or she also had to learn the material, relating the material to something that the students can understand, or even just getting them up and moving them around the room. The use of several different formats to present the information, as well as different types of resources frequently will keep and hold the attention of the attendees.

There is a scene near the beginning of the Robin Williams film *Dead Poets Society* that nicely demonstrates a variety of presentation skills. In the film Williams portrays an unorthodox instructor at a private boys' school in the 1950s. On his first day as their new English instructor, he gets his students out of their chairs and into the hallway, starts to learn their names, and encourages them to "seize the day" and make their lives meaningful (he does this by having them look at photographs of former students and, while he has them lean in towards the display cases, whispers to them as if he were the voice of those past students.) It's an interesting scene to watch and see the various techniques his character uses to engage his audience, catch their attention, and get them involved (such things as whispering, identifying them as individuals, getting them moving, and using humor).

When working on presentation skills, study the subject or otherwise review the materials. The more the presenter knows the material, the more confident he or she will feel.

In developing a presentation, a useful first step is to state the purpose or central idea in one or two sentences. Some people find it helpful to put it in writing. This can be the "touchstone" as the librarian considers what to include, and how something relates to the purpose. When preparing the closing, think of it as the destination. Restate the key points in the closing; students will remember what they hear last.

An opening should catch the audience's attention in some way. One of the most effective openings I've ever experienced was at a workshop on disaster planning and recovery that I attended some years ago. The presenter brought us into the basement of a new art museum, into an interior storage area, and then turned out the lights. It was pitch dark. She said, "Okay, you're at work, and the power just went out in your building. What would you do?" As it turned out, only the presenter and one of my co-workers had small flashlights on their keychains. This definitely caught our attention and was directly related to the theme of disaster planning.[4]

In the opening, acknowledge the expertise of the students, since all will bring some "life experiences" to the session. Let the students know that their time will be well spent, and be prepared to show them "what's in it for me?"

An instructor can use the *Know-Feel-Do* principles to develop the key points in a presentation. Ask what the students need to *know*, how they should *feel*, and what they should *do*, as a result of the presentation. Use "real-life" examples and anecdotes to support key points as an aid to remembering.

Develop visuals (flip charts, videotapes, overhead transparencies) to enhance learning and increase attention. It's been said that 75 percent of what we know comes from the visual.[5] In general, the presenter should use visuals to highlight key points, should not overuse them, and use that with which he or she is comfortable. Flip charts are good for recording information, for listing instructions, and for brainstorming. Try not to start writing at the very top: filling that large blank area can be intimidating. Start writing partway down the page; write on the top if necessary to fill up the page, then judge if it should be continued on another sheet. Practice writing on the flip chart from the side while facing the audience; turning your back to them while writing should be avoided.

In the literature useful tips for overhead transparencies can be found. Try to have each transparency cover a single idea. It's recommended that there should be no more than six lines per visual and no more than six words per line: the "six-by-six rule."[6] While I like to use 18- or 24-point letters (or larger), a nice tip to check if the letters are large enough is to print out a page and throw it on the floor. If it can be read at one's feet while standing up, it is large enough.

For videos and presentation software, remember that these should enhance the presentation. If not comfortable using them yet, the librarian should give some time to pick up those skills and use what works for him or her. Know the equipment, and double check things (if possible) before presenting. More than once we've experienced things like the mystery of missing bullet points on our slides!

One last tip: always have a "Plan B." I recently had to do a hands-on computer workshop—except that the computers weren't working. Nor could we find the backup overheads we'd made. Luckily, we had copies of the slides as a handout, and the students agreed to do the "lecture" part with me and the "hands-on" part on their own. Sometimes I've brought a blank overhead and a marker as backup. And some years ago at ALA I heard a speaker describe his experiences in presenting in parts of the world where there was no electricity![7]

When developing the presentation, be clear on the purpose. Create memorable closings and openings, and use the "Know-Feel-Do" principles to develop your key points. Use real-life examples to aid remembering, and use visuals to enhance learning.

EVALUATING THE PRESENTATION

There are many reasons why a librarian would choose or not choose to evaluate a presentation. The most common reason to choose NOT to evaluate is the lack of time. Most library sessions are given limited class time and many librarians decide to cover more information rather than spend time handing out a questionnaire, providing time to fill it out, and collecting the finished surveys. However, there are many ways in which an instructor can evaluate during a session which take little time away from the purpose of the presentation. The librarian needs to decide at which level he or she wants to evaluate the session, and then find a method to do so.

Before deciding what level of evaluation need to be assessed, the librarian should realize that there WILL be negative evaluations that may be hard on the ego. The librarian needs to emphasize the average evaluation and try to ignore the extremes (although it is entirely acceptable to concentrate on the most positive ones). There are four levels of evaluation as identified by Donald L. Kirkpatrick.[8] The first level evaluates reaction: did they like it? If the students did not like the session, that interferes with the learning process. This can be as easy as noticing that half the class is falling asleep, or being thanked and complimented as people leave the classroom.

The second level evaluates learning: did they learn? This is usually the level at which most librarians evaluate their sessions. The third level evaluates behavior: will they use it? This level takes more time as it means that the instructor needs to follow-up the session with an additional evaluation. Sometimes this can be done by sending a questionnaire to the instructor of the class after the library-related assignment has been completed. Unfortunately, this frequently does not work, since the instructor may ignore the request to evaluate his or her students, or the students may not return the evaluation forms.

The fourth level evaluates results: did it make a difference? This is almost impossible for the librarian to evaluate since it measures the cost of the session versus the cost of not providing the information. It involves compiling the hidden costs that are extremely difficult to identify.

There are several methods of evaluating during the instructional session. The first method is the *T-chart* which prompts the students to identify the pros and cons of a topic. In order to use the *Apple Tree*, the students are given a paper apple (or apple blossom if it is spring!) and asked to identify one thing apiece that they have learned, or comment on how the instructor has accomplished his or her goals, or what they liked best and what they liked least about the instruction. They then tape the apples to drawn trees that are posted on the walls as they leave the room. *Post-It Notes* can be used in the same way. The objectives of the class could be posted around the room, and students could be requested to identify what was done to accomplish each objective, and then attach the post-it notes under each objective.

Another method of evaluation uses *index cards*. The students each receive a card and can be asked to identify what they liked best about the class on one side, and what they liked least on the other. A *wish list* can be used at the beginning of a session to identify what the students would like to cover, and the session could then be adapted on the spot to include those topics. If some topics are difficult to merge into the session, a question-and-answer time toward the end of the presentation could be included to cover the topics. The expertise of the students could be called upon to help answer the problems which the students wanted to cover.

One method that expands to cover the behavior level of evaluation is called *"Dear Instructor."* The students are given cards or pieces of paper and asked to write down what they would STOP doing because of what they learned in the session, what they would START doing because of what was mentioned, and what they would CONTINUE to do because the session reinforced the ideas or methods that they already were using. This requires follow-up, however. The librarian then needs to contact students, after an assignment has been completed, in a week, in a month, or even three months later, and find out if they actually did STOP, START, and CONTINUE to do the things that they said they would.

Contests, games, and puzzles can be used in the session, not only as learning tools, but also as evaluating tools to find out if the students did learn anything. *Discussion groups* also can be used as a combination learning and evaluating method. While the groups are discussing their topics, the instructor can wander around the room and eavesdrop. This is a good method to use to see if the students understood what they were to do in their groups, as well as to see if they understood the material covered in the session.

If the instructor/librarian does decide to use a more lengthy evaluation form, there are several things that he or she should include. Some of the questions should be based on the objectives of the session. No questionnaire should consist of only open-ended questions or only ranking questions. A combination of these types of questions should be included in every questionnaire. A sample survey is included in the appendix to show how this can be done.

Evaluation of a presentation is essential to the improvement of the instruction, and is frequently needed for the personal evaluation of the presenter. Due to time limits and lack of cooperation with the course instructor, the librarian often does not have the time to include a formal questionnaire during or after the instructional session. Frequently, other methods can be used, which require little time and/or are part of the instructional session. When questionnaires are feasible or necessary, they should include a variety of types of questions, and some questions should be based on the objectives of the session.

CONCLUSION

When creating an instructional session, an instructor should begin by setting goals and objectives for the presentation, followed by developing the opening and closing, examining methods of assessing the session, and breaking up the presentation into "teachable chunks." The librarian should then consider different activities that could be included, like icebreakers, games, and exercises, in order to address the different learning styles of the students. Several techniques that can be included in the presentation—such as openings that catch and keep the students' attention, using the Know-Feel-Do principles, and making effective use of visuals—can make the session more effective for the students. Finally, the instructor can make use of numerous methods of evaluating the session at different levels, using both methods that take little time away from the learning experience, and questionnaires, including different types of questions which rank the presentation and provide detailed feedback from open-ended questions.

In this paper, we shared presentation skills and techniques, examined adult learning styles and using "teachable chunks," discussed how "active learning" can be included in designing a session, and considered different methods of evaluating the session as part of the instruction session. A variety of methods should be incorporated in any presentation in order to attract and hold the attention of the students. The librarian should add new techniques and formats as he or she becomes comfortable using them.

NOTES

1. Linda Halverson, "Train the Trainer: Design Basics," a workshop by Linda Halverson, University of St. Thomas, 1995.

2. Mel Silberman, *20 Active Training Programs* (San Diego, CA: Pfeiffer & Co., 1994), 16.

3. Tony Pont, *Developing Effective Training Skills* (New York: McGraw-Hill, 1991, 54); and Halverson, "Activities."

4. Barbara Roberts, "Disaster Recovery Planning Conference," sponsored by the Upper Midwest Conservation Association at the Weisman Museum, University of Minnesota, 6 May 1994.

5. Linda Halverson, "Train the Trainer: Presentation Skills," a workshop by Linda Halverson, University of St. Thomas, 1995.

6. Halverson, "Presentation."

7. Michael Molenda, "Class Act: Producing and Presenting Library Instruction," a presentation at the American Library Association Conference, Chicago, IL, 25 June 1995.

8. Donald L. Kirkpatrick, *Evaluating Training Programs: Presentation Skills for Consultants, Trainers, and Teachers* (New York: John Wiley and Sons, 1993).

SUGGESTIONS FOR FURTHER READING

Bender, Peter Urs. *Secrets of Power Presentations*. Rev. ed. Willowdale, Ontario: Firefly Books, 1995.

Bodi, Sonia. "Teaching Effectiveness and Bibliographic Instruction: The Relevance of Learning Styles." *College and Research Libraries* 51 (March 1990): 113-119.

Branch, Katherine, and Carolyn Dusenbury, eds. *Sourcebook for Bibliographic Instruction*. Chicago: ALA, Association of College and Research Libraries, Bibliographic Instruction Section, 1993.

Brookfield, S.D. *Developing Critical Thinkers: Challenging Adults to Explore Alternative Ways of Thinking and Acting*. San Francisco: Jossey-Bass, 1987.

Butler, Kathleen A. *Learning and Teaching Style: In Theory and Practice*. 2d ed. Columbia, CT: The Learner's Dimension, 1987.

Dead Poets Society. 128 min. Touchstone-Silver Screen Partners IV/BV, 1989.

Gardner, Howard. *Frames of Mind: The Theory of Multiple Intelligences*. New York: Basic Books, 1983.

Guild, Pat Burke, and Stephen Garger. *Marching to Different Drummers*. Alexandria, VA: Association for Supervision and Curriculum Development, 1985.

Halverson, Linda. "Train the Trainer: Activities," a workshop by Linda Halverson, University of St. Thomas, 1995.

Halverson, Linda. "Train the Trainer: Design Basics," a workshop by Linda Halverson, University of St. Thomas, 1995.

Halverson, Linda. "Train the Trainer: Presentation Skills," a workshop by Linda Halverson, University of St. Thomas, 1995.

Heinich, Robert, et al. *Instructional Media and Technologies for Learning*. 5th ed. Englewood Cliffs, NJ: Merrill, 1996.

Hoff, Ron. *I Can See You Naked*. Kansas City, MO: Andrews and McMeel, 1992.

Information Literacy: Learning How to Learn (a collection of articles from *School Library Media Quarterly*). Chicago: American Library Association, 1991.

Jolles, Robert L. *How to Run Seminars and Workshops: Presentation Skills for Consultants, Trainers, and Teachers*. New York: John Wiley and Sons, 1993.

Kirkpatrick, Donald L. *Evaluating Training Programs: The Four Levels*. San Francisco: Berrett-Koehler, distributed by Group West, 1994.

Kolb, D.A. *Experiential Learning: Experience as the Source of Learning and Development*. Englewood Cliffs, New Jersey: Prentice-Hall, 1984.

Lee, Catherine A. "Teaching Generation X." *Research Strategies* (Winter 1996): 56-59.

Molenda, Michael. "Class Act" Producing and Presenting Library Instruction," a presentation at the American Library Association Conference, Chicago, IL, 25 June 1995.

Newstrom, John W., and Edward E. Scannell. *Games Trainers Play: Experiential Learning Exercises*. New York: McGraw-Hill, 1980.

Pont, Tony. *Developing Effective Training Skills*. New York: McGraw-Hill, 1991.

Rader, Hannelore. "Information Literacy: A Revolution in the Library." *RQ* 31 (Fall 1991): 25-29.

Rader, Hannelore. "Information Literacy: One Response to the New Decade." In *The Evolving Educational Mission of the Library*. Ed. by Betsy Baker and M.E. Litzinger. Chicago: Association of College and Research Libraries, 1992.

Reichel, Mary. "Refocusing and Library Instruction." (Library Literacy column.) *RQ* 31 (Fall 1991): 497-501.

Ridgeway, Trish. "Information Literacy: An Introductory Reading List." *College & Research Libraries News* 51:7 (1990): 645-648.

Roberts, Barbara. "Disaster Recovery Planning Conference," sponsored by the Upper Midwest Conservation Association at the Weisman Museum, University of Minnesota, 6 May 1994.

Silberman, Mel. *20 Active Training Programs*. San Diego, CA: Pfeiffer & Co., 1994.

APPENDIX 1

UST Libraries
Electronic Resources Workshop Feedback

Name of workshop: Date:

Your feedback helps us constantly improve our training services to you. Please respond below. Thank you.

1. Please name two things you understand better or will do differently as a result of this training experience.

    1)
    2)

2. How would you rate this program?

1	2	3	4	5
Not Valuable		Somewhat Valuable		Very Valuable

3. Please rate the effectiveness of the following workshop objectives:

    a. To consider when to use the Web for research.

1	2	3	4	5
Ineffective		Effective		Very Effective

    b. To learn search strategies and techniques.

1	2	3	4	5
Ineffective		Effective		Very Effective

    c. To explore Web search systems.

1	2	3	4	5
Ineffective		Effective		Very Effective

    d. To find Web resources on specific topics.

1	2	3	4	5
Ineffective		Effective		Very Effective

4. How appropriate was

   program length:

	Too Long	Perfect	Too Short

   program pacing:

	Too Long	Perfect	Too Short

5. Please rate your interest level.

1	2	3	4	5
Little Interest		Interested		High Interest

6. Please rate the usefulness of information provided.

1	2	3	4	5
Not Useful		Useful		Very Useful

7. What specifically did you like about the program?

8. What specifically did you like about the instructors' performance?

9. What would make this a better program?

10. What would improve the instructors' performance?

11. What other programs, workshops, sessions would be useful to you?

Please return to: Jan Orf, Mail No. 5004

Constructing Web Pages for Course-Related Library Instruction: A Business and Government Information Perspective

Patrick Ragains

The introduction of graphical Internet browsers has in recent years greatly widened the vistas of information available to college and university students in the United States. A collateral benefit is the availability of the World Wide Web as an instructional medium, which may be used to disseminate textual materials such as syllabi and library user guides and also to guide students to specific Internet sites via the linking capability of Netscape and other Web browsers. This paper focuses on integrating Web-based information sources into library instruction for business and government information. Several examples of instructional Web pages are also reproduced.[1] As an instructional librarian, I recognize that traditional information-gathering strategies based on bibliographic research must now be modified to incorporate searching for and evaluating information found on the Internet. Unfortunately, the familiar model of one-shot, course-related BI is often an unsatisfactory setting for such instruction. I myself am subject to the limitations of the one-hour stand, because I provide much of my group instruction in that setting. I have used course-specific and reference-related Web pages to minimize these limitations, but it is often unclear if students are using the Web pages to optimal effect. So, what I will discuss here is not in any sense a finished program, but instead a representation of my current practice. The paper will conclude with comments about my plans to create more course-related instructional Web pages in the near future.

Ragains is business and government information librarian, University of Nevada, Reno, Nevada.

I first included Internet-based sources in my instructional sessions in 1993 when I presented a session on federal legislative and regulatory processes for a course on public policy and the delivery of social services. At that time, the *Federal Register* was one of the few legal information sources freely available online, and it was the only non-print source I listed on my handout for the course. Other information sources such as congressional bills, hearings, and reports, were available in print or on microfiche in my library's depository collection. It was particularly relevant for students of human services policy to know about free or low-cost *online* information sources announcing the availability of federal grants and other public funds, since such funds are typically available on a competitive basis and for limited periods of time, making rapid access to information quite important. The response of the course instructor was quite positive, as she indicated the session "seemed to desensitize students of their tremendous fear of government documents."

Several times since, I have made similar presentations on the legislative/regulatory process and I converted the handout I was using into a Web page with links to *GPO Access* for congressional bills, documents, public laws and the *United States Code* (see figure 1). *GPO Access* provides the full text of these sources, with files such as the *Federal Register*, *Congressional Bills*, and *Congressional Record* being updated daily. On this Web page, all information sources, whether print- or Internet-based, are listed in appropriate subject categories. This page has been quite useful in delivering library instruction in several other public policy-focused courses.

UNIVERSITY LIBRARIES
University of Nevada, Reno

U.S. Legislative Process & Related Publications

U.S. LEGISLATIVE & REGULATORY INFORMATION AVAILABLE ON THE WORLD WIDE WEB AND IN THE UNR LIBRARIES

The Internet-based **GPO Access** service provides Congressional Bills (all versions), Public Laws, History of Bills, the Congressional Record, Congressional Record Index, Congressional Documents and Reports, the House and Senate Calendars, and the Federal Register, from 1994 to the present. The United States Code is also searchable on GPO Access.

BILLS: GPO Access includes the full text of Congressional bills and public laws from 1994 to the present. The UNR Libraries has congressional bills from 1933 to the present in microfiche format. Bills are located in the Business and Government Information Center, 2nd floor.

PUBLIC LAWS:

Public Laws..............................GPO Access, 1994-present

Statutes at Large......................BGIC Legal Alcove AE 2.111:
Chronological record of all federal laws, public and private. Laws passed from 1994 to the present are included in GPO Access (i.e., Public Laws and Congressional Bills databases).

United States Code..............................GPO Access or BGIC Legal Alcove Y 1.2/5:
The U.S. Code is a compilation of all current federal statutory law, arranged by subject. Revisions or other changes in federal laws are identified in the U.S. Code.

FEDERAL REGULATIONS:

Code of Federal Regulations(CFR).......BGIC Legal Alcove AE 2.106/3:
Compilation of current rules and regulations issued by federal executive agencies. Also available via the U.S. House of Representatives Internet Law Library is a **web-based version of the CFR**.

Federal Register......................GPO Access & BGIC Legal Alcove AE 2.106:
Daily record of new and proposed regulations, announcements of availability of federal funds, scheduled meetings, presidential proclamations and executive orders. Available via GPO Access from 1994 to the present.

INDEXES & FINDING AIDS TO CONGRESSIONAL BILLS AND PUBLIC LAWS:

Congressional Index................. BGIC Legal Alcove J69.C6

Congressional Record.............................GPO Access & BGIC Legal Alcove X/A
Daily verbatim record of activity of the U.S. Congress (excluding committees).

Congressional Record Index..................GPO Access & BGIC Legal Alcove X/A

CIS Index................................BGIC Legal Alcove
Gives legislative histories for all bills passed into law. Bill numbers are also given in abstracts of congressional committee hearings and reports.

Figure 1: Handout on U.S. Legislative Process

> History of Bills..GPO Access, 1994-present
>
> Public Laws...GPO Access, 1994-present
>
> **CONGRESSIONAL DOCUMENTS, COMMITTEE HEARINGS & REPORTS:**
>
> Congressional Documents........................GPO Access, 1994-present
>
> Congressional Reports............................GPO Access, 1994-present
>
> Print and microfiche copies of selected hearings and reports are held by the library. To find these, use the following:
>
> **CIS Index**...BGIC Legal Alcove
>
> <u>GPO Access Federal Locator Services</u>....http://www.access.gpo.gov/su_docs/dpos/adpos400.html
> Records from the **Monthly Catalog of U.S. Government Publications** from 1994 to the present, linked to selection profiles of federal depository libraries.
>
> **U.S. Government Documents Index**.......BGIC Local Area Network terminals (LAN)
> CD-ROM equivalent of the **Monthly Catalog of U.S. Government Publications**, covering 1976 to the present. Location: **BGIC Reference shelf, Y 1.1/7:101-139**.
>
> **BACKGROUND INFORMATION ON LEGISLATION & ACTIVITIES OF THE CONGRESS:**
>
> **Congressional Quarterly Weekly Report**..BGIC Legal Alcove JK1.C15 1989-present
> News and analysis from current issues of **CQ Weekly Report** are avalable on the Internet at
> <u>gopher://gopher.cqalert.com</u>.
>
> **This home page was created and is maintained by:**
> Patrick Ragains
> Business and Government Information Librarian
> <u>ragains@unr.edu</u>
> (702) 784-6500, ext. 309
>
> url: http://gordo.library.unr.edu/~ragains/bill_law.html
> Last modified January 23, 1997
>
> [Main Menu] Return to the UNR Libraries' main menu

Figure 1: Handout on U.S. Legislative Process (continued)

More recently I've developed both course- and discipline-related Web pages, treating Internet sources as supplemental to locally available printed information. My handouts list both selected print and Internet sources, including the URL, or uniform resource locator, for the Web page I've created for the course. Figures 2 and 3 reproduce a course handout I created listing print, CD-ROM, and Internet sources, and the corresponding Web page.

I began to create these course-specific and reference Web pages before my library had officially launched its Web site. The University of Nevada, Reno (UNR) Libraries' NEON Web site was made public in the fall of 1996, although at the time of this writing it lacks a high-level link to any instructional pages. Subject-based links appear under a category titled "Information Resources by Subject," which links to a group of pages for each subject area to which the

HDFS 740: Family Economics and Management
Selected Library Resources

Demographic and Economic Data

ACCRA Cost of Living Index   **Current Periodicals Display**
     Compares costs in 325 urban areas.

CPI Detailed Report (Consumer Price Index)   **L 2.38/3:**
     Monthly retail price index, reporting changes for the nation, regions and selected metropolitan areas. Current issues are available on the Current Periodicals Display. This publication is also available on the Internet-based *Economic Bulletin Board* on the day of its release.

Economic Indicators   **Y 4.EC 7/ (year & no.)**
     This monthly publication presents current and historical data on the nation's output, income, spending, employment, wages, production, business activity, prices and finance. Current issues are available on the BGIC Current Periodicals Display. This publication is also available on the World Wide Web-based *GPO Access* service on the day of release each month.

Employment and Earnings   **L 2.41/2:**
     Current national, state, and metropolitan area data on employment and wages. Current issues are available on the Current Periodicals Display.

Geographical Mobility   **C 3.186/3:(year)**
     Annual report of the Census Bureau providing detailed statistics on the geographical mobility of U.S. residents.

Household and Family Characteristics   **C 3.186/17:(year)**
     Annual report providing information on household size composition, family type, race and Hispanic origin.

Income, Poverty, and Valuation of Noncash Benefits   **C 3.186: P-60/ (number)**
     Annual report describing income and poverty status of households, families, and persons.

Individual Income Tax Returns   **T 22.35/8:(year)**
     Compiled statistics from tax returns filed, including detailed explanation of terms.

Marital Status and Living Arrangements   **C 3.186/6: (year)**
     This report analyzes marital status and living arrangements in U.S. households.

Money Income in the United States   **C 3.186:P-60/(number)**
     This annual publication contains detailed income tables compiled for the nation as a whole. Also reports median income of households by state.

SOI Bulletin (Statistics of Income)   **T 22.35/4:**
     This report provides the earliest published annual financial statements from tax and information returns filed with the Internal Revenue Service. Also included is information from periodic or special analytical studies on the tax systems of the United States and other countries.

Indexes to statistics, articles and other publications:

Dissertation Abstracts   NEON First Search
Expanded Academic Index   NEON Infotrac

Figure 2: Course handout for print, CD-ROM, and Internet sources

Indexes to statistics, articles and other publications (cont.):

Monthly Catalog of U.S. Government Publications	Local Area Network
PAIS Decade (*Public Affairs Information Service*)	NEON First Search
Statistical Masterfile	Local Area Network
U.S. Government Periodicals Index	Local Area Network

World Wide Web Resources for Family Economics:

Census Bureau Definitions of Income and Poverty Terms
        http://www.census.gov/ftp/pub/hhes/income/defs/def.html

Consumer and Textile Sciences: Web Resources by Topic
        http://www.hec.ohio-state.edu/cts/osue/topic.htm

Consumer Price Index -- All Urban Consumers: 1946 to present
        http://www.agribiz.com/economy/histcpi.html

Dissertation Abstracts Online   Available from UNR Campus Network only

Expanded Academic Index   Available from UNR Campus Network only

Family Economics and Policy Web Resources
        http://www.hec.ohio-state.edu/cts/osue/famecon.htm

Family Resource Online   http://www.familyresource.org/content.html

Government Information Sharing Project
        http://govinfo.kerr.orst.edu/
  Data from the U.S. Census Bureau and other federal agencies

GPO Access Databases   http://www.access.gpo.gov/su_docs/aces/aaces002.html
  Congressional Bills, Federal Register, the U.S. Code and other federal databases

Kiplinger Online   http://kiplinger.com/
  Information on personal and family finance

PAIS - Public Affairs Information Service Decade
        Available from UNR Campus Network only

UNICEF Home Page   http://www.unicef.org/
  Includes the report *The State of the World's Children*

Yahoo! - Society and Culture: Families
        http://www.yahoo.com/Society_and_Culture/Families/

A World Wide Web home page providing links to the above-listed resources in family economics has been created for this course and is available at the following address: **http://www.library.unr.edu/~ragains/hdfs740.html**

(3/97,pr)

Figure 2: Course handout for print, CD-ROM, and Internet sources (continued)

library has assigned a fund from its collection development budget. Each librarian is assigned to manage one or more of these funds and act as a liaison to the respective academic department, which includes providing library instruction. My assigned funds include business, government publications (which does not correspond to an academic department), and political science. Mainly because of my involvement with government information, I do a fair amount of instruction for departments outside my assigned subject areas. The grouping of Web pages by funded subject areas managed by individual librarians doesn't work as well in these circumstances. For example, historic preservation courses are taught at the university, but there is no collection development fund for it. So, for the time being, students can reach my Web pages for these courses either by typing in the entire URL on a computer that is connected to the Web, or by following a succession of links to reach my personal home page or my department's page. I don't think either of these alternatives is entirely satisfactory, and would like our introductory Web pages to provide more direct links to these. That said, I consider it only a mild criticism, since our Web site is still very much in the early stages of its development.

I also am responsible for developing the political science-related links on the library's Web site. These are really a group of links related to political science, public administration, and government. The initial political science page (see figure 4) provides links to relevant FirstSearch and Infotrac databases to which the library subscribes, GPO Access, and some pages I've created gathering important gateway sites and electronic journals. There are also links to my own instructional guides, covering topics like the federal legislative and regulatory process and citing government information sources. I cover these pages in the drop-in sessions I now offer several times each semester on using the Internet to find information by and about governments. The drop-in sessions consist of two separate hour-long classes, offered on consecutive days. During the first session I cover some of the links on the UNR Libraries' political science pages. I devote the second hour to looking at my own collection of government information and social science bookmarks, and copy the bookmarks file for anyone who wants it (and most of those who attend do ask for it). The bookmarks are also available as a Web page.[2]

Perhaps we should ask, from a pedagogical viewpoint, what good are these instructional and subject-based Web pages? Such an assessment includes the following considerations:

1) Do students have access to an adequate number of workstations equipped with Netscape or another graphical Web browser? Ideally, a sufficient number of these should be located in the library, where we can most easily assist students.

2) Is the available Web-based content appropriate for the students' level of interest? For example, students in an international marketing course, assigned to develop an export strategy, may be more interested in getting their hands on the information sources actually used by exporters, in preference to finding magazine and journal articles about international marketing.

Assuming these basic criteria are met, instructional Web pages offer several advantages. First, they are available to guide students interactively as they begin to search for information in their particular subject. I've long believed that library and information users want to do as much on their own as possible. Customized Web pages, including those that are course-specific, offer students non-intrusive gateways into their subjects. This can be an important service to users, since such a guide may not threaten their self-sufficiency in the same way as does approaching the reference desk with a question. In other words, I believe these kinds of Web pages are helpful to students in ways not met either by browsing or a reference interaction. For me, this has been confirmed anecdotally by faculty whose students have used the pages and by students themselves. Of course, I don't discourage anyone from asking a reference question or browsing; the Web page simply is meant to give the student more options by providing some structure to his or her information seeking.

Another advantage is that Web-based instruction allows me more direct access to students, which a colleague of mine once termed "librarian-initiated instruction." This may or may not mean that I have more direct communication with students, but a Web page is accessible to students even if I am not asked to provide library instruction for a particular class. Here's where the broad, subject-focused pages, such as my political science pages, are intended to meet existing but unstated needs for instruction. I also consider these pages as a springboard for a more aggressive outreach effort I plan to launch in the coming academic year.

In my current position I am the bibliographer and department liaison for political science. However, the political science faculty at my institution are not prone to request library instruction. This seems due to the accumulated history of my predecessors and their interactions with that department. Relations are cordial and productive in matters relating to collection development and reference service, but there is no tradition

UNIVERSITY LIBRARIES
University of Nevada, Reno

HDFS 740: Family Economics: Web Resources

- Census Bureau Definitions of Income and Poverty Terms
- Consumer and Textile Sciences: Web Resources by Topic
- Consumer Price Index -- All Urban Consumers: 1946 to present
- Dissertation Abstracts Online [available from UNR Campus Network only]
- Expanded Academic Index [available from UNR Campus Network only]
- Family Economics and Policy Web Resources
- Family Resource Online
- Government Information Sharing Project: data from the U.S. Census Bureau and other federal agencies
- GPO Access Databases: Congressional Bills, *Federal Register*, the *U.S. Code* and other federal databases
- Kiplinger Online: information on personal and family finance
- PAIS - Public Affairs Information Service Decade [available from UNR Campus Network only]
- UNICEF Home Page: including the report *The State of the World's Children*
- Yahoo! - Society and Culture:Families

Main Menu   Return to the UNR Libraries' main menu
Please direct questions to: Patrick Ragains, Bibliographer
URL of this document: http://www.library.unr.edu/~ragains/hdfs740.html
Last modified: March 3, 1997

Figure 3: Corresponding Web page for HDFS 740 course handout

of group library instruction. Also, only a few political science students and faculty have attended my drop-in sessions. As mentioned above, I believe there is an unstated need for library instruction for students in this department. It is an area in need of development and one for which conditions seem favorable.

In preparation for the Fall 1997 semester, I plan to develop a series of resource pages for courses in that department. There will be links to the broader pages we looked at, but I will tailor these for the department's course offerings in American government, comparative politics, public administration, political philosophy, international affairs, and other areas of emphasis, staying in touch with faculty concerning the best information sources for their courses and keeping them apprised of Web pages as I make them available. If the availability of these pages results in increased requests for course-related presentations, so much the better. If not, I will not need to come to class in order to reach these students. Instead, I'll continue to offer my two-part drop-in sessions, and may offer both basic and advanced presentations if warranted by increased attendance. This, briefly, is my strategic plan to provide more librarian-initiated instruction to this department.

Finally, it is worth noting that shifting the focus of library instruction to Internet-based sources has caused me to change my presentation style in a number of ways. Overall, I think I'm doing more of the talking than when I used active learning techniques in some of my instructional sessions. The main problem with this is that I'm less sure that students are really engaged with the topic when I'm lecturing, as opposed to giving them a task requiring them to think about relevant

Resources for Political Science

- **NEON Databases** including citations, abstracts, some full text [available from UNR Campus Network Only]
  - PAIS - Public Affairs Information Service Decade
  - WorldCat
  - Expanded Academic Index
  - Article1st
  - PapersFirst
  - FastDoc
  - ProceedingsFirst
  - Dissertation Abstracts Online
  - Biography Index

- Electronic Journals
- UNR Libraries Collection Highlights
- GPO Access
   Cong. Bills, Public Laws, U.S. Code, Federal Register, GAO Reports, 1996 Plum Book, etc.
- Selected Internet Resources for Political Science, Public Administration, and Government
- Reference and Instructional Guides

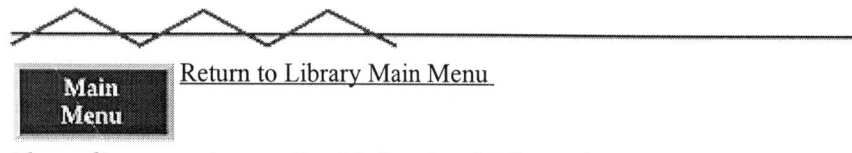
Return to Library Main Menu

Please direct questions to: Patrick Ragains, Bibliographer
URL of this document: http://www.library.unr.edu/SUBJECTS/political.html
Last modified: January 23, 1997

Figure 4: Political science Web page

information sources and search techniques. I sometimes used to divide classes into groups, asking each to examine one or more information sources in a particular topical subset of the broader subject; for example, marketing students would look at information sources on companies, industries, and consumers; or geology students would examine indexes, abstracts, handbooks, and subject encyclopedias. I came to favor these interactive exercises because they often seemed to reveal quite effectively what students needed to know and gave me the chance to answer questions and clear up misunderstandings they had about the catalog, library services, or reference sources. Such experiences are still desirable but, in preparing any one-shot session, choices must be made about the essential sources and processes to cover in a single class period. Currently, the more urgent need seems to be to introduce students to new sources, old sources with new Web interfaces, and tell them why, how, and sometimes even where to use them.

Although I have less time in class for group work or active learning exercises (a problem compounded by the lack of any student workstations in the UNR Libraries' two instruction rooms), some of my instructional Web pages address the issue of evaluating sources, and I can at least point these out in passing to students. That's actually another problem related to compressing my instruction that I would like to solve, since reading a guide about critical thinking is pretty passive (even presuming students *will* read it), compared to giving them some guided experience in locating and evaluating information. The effectiveness of this type of teaching may come at the expense of in-person group instruction, which is a precious commodity to instructional librarians. It has been argued (wisely, I think) that instructional multimedia do not represent very well the dialogue that is often integral to learning.[3] So, I don't think we should use Web pages to replace in-person instruction, but instead use the technology as a tool to enhance our instructional sessions *and* to reach students in courses for which there is no group library instruction.[4]

As we teach students the techniques of searching the World Wide Web, we should also address the need to evaluate the information one finds there. The media has recently devoted much attention to strongly biased, offensive and inflammatory information and images on the Internet. However, we must recognize (and help others to do so) that the Internet is somewhat of a hybrid form of communication, combining the casual nature of speech with the seeming authority afforded by publication and at least some of the attractiveness of television. As librarians we cannot, in many cases, expect an increase in the amount of time allowed for face-to-face group instruction, during which we might discuss in more depth the evaluation of general and discipline-specific information sources. For me, the current solution is to present to students what I believe are the best sources, and to qualify the rest. Marsha Tate and Jan Alexander of Widener University's Wolfgram Memorial Library have defined a number of useful criteria for evaluating World Wide Web-based information, as have several librarians at Cornell University and Richard Terrass of Massachusetts General Hospital.[5] I believe we should address the need to evaluate information sources whether the instruction we provide is brief or extended, in-person or virtual.

What I have presented here is very much a "work in progress." In fact, I'm very interested to know what others are doing to provide Web-based instruction. To provide instruction this way seems to be a natural progression, and certainly the Web is a medium of communication we can easily exploit. The primary barrier seems to be bringing the information to users in the library, their computing labs, homes and dormitory rooms. As this is accomplished, it also will become possible to improve library services in support of distance education, and course-related Web pages can include links to document delivery and reserve services as well as having a link to a reference librarian some pages I've seen already provide this). The goal, of course, is that this will become a standard for library service that is more seamless and removes some of the current barriers between students, ourselves, and the information they need.

NOTES

1. Some Web pages reproduced here have been shortened for publication. The author's complete instructional Web pages are listed at <http://www.library.unr.edu/~ragains/index.html>.

2. Patrick Ragains, "Government Information and Social Science Bookmarks," <http://www.library.unr.edu/~ragains/govmarks.html>.

3. Martyn Wild, "Perspectives on the Place of Educational Theory in Multimedia," in *Learning Technologies: Prospects and Pathways. Selected Papers from EdTech '96 Biennial Conference of the Australian Society for Educational Technology*, ed. by John G. Hedberg (Melbourne, Australia, 7-10 July 1996), p. 171. ERIC Document ED 396 718.

4. Some efficiencies inherent in Web-based instruction are addressed in Ronald D. Owston, "The World Wide Web: A Technology to Enhance Teaching and Learning?," *Educational Researcher* 26:2 (March 1997): 31-33.

5. Marsha Tate and Jan Alexander, "Teaching Critical Evaluation Skills for World Wide Web Resources," *Computers in Libraries* 16:10 (November-December 1996): 49-55 <http://www.science.widener.edu/~withers/Webeval.htm>; Joan Ormondroyd, Michael Engle, and Tony Cosgrave, "Critically Analyzing Information" (Ithaca: Cornell University Libraries, 1996): <http://www.library.cornell.edu/okuref/research/skill26.htm>; and Richard Terrass, "Evaluating Internet Resources" (Cambridge: Massachusetts General Hospital, 1997), <http://Web.wn.net/ricter/Web/valid.html>. The preceding Web sites were viewed 27 April 1997.

Teaching Library Users to Evaluate WWW Resources

Dena Siegel and Susan Levendosky

Introduction

Library users today find the fast resource gathering that the Internet has to offer very appealing. As librarians know, however, the Internet abounds with non-specific, unconfirmed, and often erroneous information. Teaching library users to critically evaluate Internet information is a crucial role of the instruction librarian today.

The library instruction program at Ball State University has incorporated instruction in the evaluation of Web resources in several different ways, from briefly mentioning to a class the need for evaluation to conducting full-fledged workshops on the topic. This paper will cover how evaluation of World Wide Web (WWW) resources is integrated into instruction sessions offered at the Ball State University Libraries, give specifics on evaluation criteria used for WWW resources, and include tips on making this type of instruction more memorable for students by adding collaborative exercises and facilitating hands-on time with the Internet.

Instruction at Ball State University

The library instruction program at Ball State University instructs over 16,000 people each school year, from high school students, to freshmen college students, to graduate students and faculty. Sessions are

---

Siegel is automation services librarian and *Levendosky* is instruction librarian, Alexander M. Bracken Library, Ball State University, Muncie, Indiana.

taught in an electronic classroom used only for library instruction. The classroom is equipped with 26 student terminals that have access to the University Libraries' catalog, CD-ROMs, online databases, and the World Wide Web. The instructor's station allows demonstration of library resources and control of the student terminals using the LINK system by Applied Computer Systems. The student desks have recessed monitors, permitting an unobstructed view between the instructor and the audience.

The format varies widely between classes. Freshmen are required to come to the library for two instructive sessions with their English classes. These sessions are fairly structured, with little room for additions since they are required to complete an established research proficiency assignment. Professors from many other departments schedule library instruction as well, however, and there is considerable variety among them, in subject matter, student ability, and time permitted. Increasingly the instructors have been asking that an introduction to searching the Web be included. For some professors this is an afterthought tacked on to the usual list of print sources and CD-ROMs they want us to cover; however, some professors wish to devote entire class periods to Web instruction.

When an instructor calls to schedule a class for instruction which will cover the Web, we ask what he or she would like us to cover, often suggesting a format when the instructor is unsure. The format might begin with going over the basics of how a Web browser works, followed by navigating the Web, and searching using subject archives and search engines. Finally we

Evaluating World Wide Web Information

Scope

　　Subject: What is it about?
　　Depth: How detailed is it?
　　Coverage: Is the subject limited to certain time periods?
　　Comprehensiveness: Is this *everything* on the topic?
　　Does the information accurately portray the subject, or is there information missing?
　　Format: Are only certain resources included, i.e. only WWW sites, only telnet, newsgroups, etc?

Audience

　　For whom is the page written? Children? Adults? Scholars?
　　Is the content appropriate for the intended audience?

Authority

　　Who wrote the page?
　　What are their credentials? Are they experts?

Currency

　　Is the information up to date?
　　Is it consistently being updated?
　　Is timeliness important to the subject area?

Accuracy

　　Is there a bias present? Is it stated or not?
　　Is the information correct?
　　What is the source of this information?

Purpose

　　What is the purpose of the resource? To Entertain? Inform? Teach?
　　Is the purpose stated?
　　Does the resource fulfill its purpose?

Organization, Structure, and Design

　　Is the page easy to understand and use?
　　Is it organized in a way appropriate for the content and purpose?
　　　　Are the graphics meaningful? Do they need to be?
　　Are there too many graphics, making it difficult to load?

Figure 1: Evaluation criteria handout

would suggest including a section on the evaluation of Web resources. Naturally the length of time allotted for Web instruction determines to what extent we can cover evaluation. Unfortunately, evaluation is necessarily the last point covered and sometimes is neglected because of it.

Evaluation Criteria

As an introduction to the evaluation criteria in an instructive session, one might cover why evaluating Internet resources is important at all. Many users of Internet information have never considered this. Unfortunately, many people assume that if it is on the Web, someone intelligent put it there. To illustrate why we need to evaluate Internet information, start by demonstrating an obvious example of a questionable site. In addition to fraudulent or questionable information, try to find an example that "looks smart" with attractive graphics. This helps to stress that "all that glitters isn't gold" on the Internet. The 1996 presidential election provided many Web sites of this nature.

If an entire workshop is allotted to evaluating Web sites, then more in-depth introduction is possible. For these, contrast the differences between library and Internet information. Discuss the nature of Internet information and why it is particularly pertinent for evaluation. Issues such as its non-static, constantly changing information, varied authorship, and lack of an editorial process are issues that make Internet information very different from traditional library resources. Particularly for an audience that is involved in research already (like faculty or graduate students), these are useful comparisons because they are already familiar with the library environment.

Figure 1 illustrates a set of criteria that we have assembled. Each librarian has his or her own set of evaluation criteria, varying slightly from each other in categorization and terminology. To develop your own set of criteria, consult other librarians' work. Figure 2 includes several URLs, which list other evaluation criteria lists. Here each criterion is explained briefly, followed by its application on the Internet.

Sites which list evaluation criteria:

The Web as a Research Tool: Evaluation Techniques
(Widener University)
http://www.science.widener.edu/~withers/evalout.htm

Thinking Critically about World Wide Web Resources
(UCLA College Library)
http://www.library.ucla.edu/libraries/college/instruct/critical.htm

Evaluating Internet Resources: A checklist
(Berkeley)
http://infopeople.berkeley.edu:8000/bkmk/select.html

Evaluating information found on the Internet
(Elizabeth E. Kirk, Milton S. Eisenhower Library, The Johns Hopkins University)
http://milton.mse.jhu.edu:8001/research/education/net.html

Evaluating World Wide Web Information
(The Libraries of Purdue University)
http://thorplus.lib.purdue.edu/library_info/instruction/gs175/3gs175/evaluation.html

General Criteria for Internet Resource Evaluation
(University of Detroit at Mercy)
http://www.udmercy.edu/htmls/Academics/library/webpage#criteria

How to Critically Analyze Information Sources
(Cornell University)
http://urisref.library.cornell.edu/skill26.htm

Figure 2: URLs which list evaluation criteria

- **Scope**—Scope refers to the subject of the material, including its treatment and exhaustiveness. What is the Web page about? To what level of detail does it go? Is the subject limited to certain time periods? Is it comprehensive, including everything on the topic, or is there information missing? The treatment of subject matter on the Internet is evaluated essentially the same as other information sources; however, when considering comprehensiveness, you need to consider whether the site includes other electronic resources, like telnet sites, ftp archives, gophers, listservs, and newsgroups. To get an idea of the scope of a Web site, look at the section headings on the home page. Some Web sites will quickly reveal the scope of their contents on a well organized home page, but others may require more browsing.

- **Authority**—Who are the authors of the information? What are their credentials and expertise in the subject matter? Although undoubtedly one of the most important evaluation criteria, authority is difficult to track on the Web. Usually author information is located at the bottom of the home page. Ideally, the authors include information about their education, occupation, and years of experience. Remind students that an e-mail address at the bottom of a WWW page does not necessarily signify authorship. Often, this address will be the person who put the information on the Internet but may not be responsible for its content. Time permitting, discuss domain name reading in order to understand with whom an author is affiliated. Then delve further into fingering e-mail addresses to find identity and searching for individuals on the Internet to identify background and expertise information.

- **Currency**—Is the information up-to-date as well as consistently being updated? Just because a Web page loads does not mean the information on it is current. Typically, the last revision date of the Web page should be listed at the bottom. Sometimes, a creation date as well as a revision date is included.

- **Accuracy**—Accuracy is one of the most difficult criteria to explain. Judging accuracy depends on one's familiarity with a particular field of study. Evaluate the information for its correctness. Is the information true and without errors? Beyond doing actual fact checking, compare the site in question with other sites on a similar subject. Does the information on the one site contradict or corroborate with information on other sites? Another concern is bias. Does the author have a political, ideological, or personal slant? Is this bias apparent or not? Consider if the information supporting the bias compromises the truth and validity of the facts presented.

- **Purpose**—The purpose of any work greatly affects the information contained within it. Web sites can have a variety of purposes. Is the purpose of the site to inform and educate, or to influence and sell a product? Users of the WWW will find that they come across similar marketing approaches used in other mass media venues. Web sites intended to sell products can be disguised behind an educational front. Oftentimes, the only area to find information about the authors of a Web site and the purpose behind the site is under the "About us" or "About this Web site" links that often appear on a Web site.

- **Audience**—Audience is one of the few criteria that is the same in both the print and online worlds. Consider for whom the Web page is written and whether the content is appropriate for that audience. Although this concept is obvious for the librarian, who regularly considers audience in the purchase of library materials, it is rarely considered by the end-user. Users should particularly consider the audience if the site is to be used for a scholarly endeavor.

- **Organization, structure, and design**—In the print world, those evaluating the structure and organization of a work would look at the table of contents, the chapter headings, and any index or bibliography accompanying the work. On the Web, evaluating the success of the organization, structure, and design of the site involves examining the menu choices and graphics. Do they help or hinder use of the site? Are the menu choices meaningful? Take also into consideration the time it takes for the page to load. Does a lengthy load time take away from its usability? Are any additional programs needed to use the site, like a PDF reader or Shockwave plug-in? These details will make a site either easy or impossible to use. Because more and more individuals are becoming information providers themselves, consideration of the organization, structure, and design of a Web site is essential for effective resource gathering.

In addition to the criteria, if time is permitted, one might also cover citing WWW resources. Always leave time for questions, comments, and discussion. If you are demonstrating Web sites as you speak of the criteria, there will most likely be many questions. In the setting of an electronic classroom, leave 15 to 20 minutes for hands-on time at the end.

Internet Examples

In addition to covering the evaluation criteria, it is best to show the class examples of WWW resources that exemplify a criterion. Show the students how you would evaluate a Web site. It is difficult to find one site that is a good example or a poor example of all of the criteria. Usually, you will have to be prepared with several sites to demonstrate.

- **Feline Reactions to Bearded Men**—Located at <http://www.improb.com/airchives/cat.html>, this site is a great example of how legitimate a site can appear. This is a good site with which to start because it looks like a serious research study that includes a review of the literature, and data apparently generated by the study, and finishes with a correctly cited bibliography. When used at the beginning of the class, this Web site prepares the students that everything is not as it appears on the Internet, and alerts them how important it is to look at online material with a critical eye.

- **Welcome to the White House**—Located at <http://www.whitehouse.net/>, this site is another example of how one cannot judge a Web site by its cover. Although this site looks exactly like the official White House Web site <http://www.whitehouse.gov>, it was actually created by a

Evaluation Sheet

Title of WWW page: _____

URL: _____

Scope: _____
_____
_____
_____

Audience: _____
_____

Authority:
    Author: _____
_____
    Expertise/credentials: _____
_____

Currency: _____
_____
    Last update: _____

Accuracy: _____
_____
_____

Purpose: _____
_____
_____
_____

Organization, Structure & Design: _____
_____
_____

Figure 3: Evaluation worksheet

> **Sites for help developing exercises:**
>
> *Teaching Students to Think Critically about Internet Resources* (University of Washington C&C/UWired Computer Training) [see Activities links]
> http://weber.u.washington.edu/~libr560/NETEVAL/index.html
>
> *Evaluating Web Pages: Links to Examples of Various Concepts*
> (Widener University)
> http://www.science.widener.edu/~withers/examples.htm
>
> *Dr. Nancy Everhart's Web Page Evaluation Worksheet*
> (St. John's University, Division of Library and Information Science)
> http://www.capecod.net/schrockguide/neeval.htm
>
> **For general information on evaluation:**
>
> *Evaluating Internet Resources*
> (The Medical Radiography Homepage)
> http://web.wn.net/~usr/ricter/web/valid.html
>
> *Bibliography on Evaluating Internet Resources*
> (Nicole Auer, Virginia Polytechnic Institute and State University)
> http://refserver.lib.vt.edu/libinst/critTHINK.HTM

Figure 4: URLs for developing exercises and general information

Web development design firm. Initially, one cannot tell the difference between the two sites, but upon closer inspection, there is evidence of questionable information. For example, under "Briefing section" it suggests that the president "prefers these to boxers." This site is an excellent example of how much information about a site can be gleaned from the "About us" sections. In this case, there is a link titled "Why?" It is under this section of the Web page that the authors state who they are and why they created this site. Only under this link do they offer this information.

Exercises

After some demonstration of how to evaluate several Web sites, it is valuable to use hands-on exercises to reinforce what has been discussed. A variety of formats are possible, including activities involving class participation, small groups, and individual exercises.

- **Large group collaborative exercise**—This activity is effective as a warm-up to be used after presenting the evaluation criteria. In preparation, two contrasting examples should be found for each evaluation criterion. During the exercise, the librarian presents a topic or scenario and asks which of the examples would be the more credible source, based on that one evaluation criterion. Students are then asked to "shout out" their answers, and could be grouped into teams, competing for points if desired.

    For example, in discussing the authority of a piece of information, consider presenting students with pictures of Howard Stern and George Bush side by side via presentation software (PowerPoint, Presentations). Ask them which would be more of an authority in the field of alternative music and why he would be considered an authority. Hopefully the students would not only find Howard Stern to be the authority in that arena, but would also volunteer that he could be considered so because he is a deejay at a radio station that plays alternative music. The librarian could then proceed to an example related to bias, asking students to consider the effect of reading the statement "Ninety percent of all Web pages are created on the Macintosh platform" on the Apple home page, and of reading that same statement on the PC Week Online home page. Progressing to examples from each of the other criteria will help to reinforce the criteria for the students. If graphics can be used in the form of pictures through presentation software, that helps to maintain student interest. Follow-up with class discussion.

- **Small group collaborative exercise**—Another exercise could ask students to work in pairs to evaluate a Web site. The site itself might be from a list suggested by the professor, or may be chosen by the librarian or the students themselves. A worksheet, prompting the pairs to look at each criterion, helps to give structure to the process. Figure 3 is the worksheet the authors have developed. The worksheet can also be completed by individuals working alone, depending on the circumstances. Class discussion, using open-ended questions, should follow. Figure 4 lists some URLs found useful in preparing exercises.

Facilitating Hands-on Time

At Ball State, we have the good fortune to have a classroom environment where the audience can get hands-on time, using the Internet and evaluating what they find. We have discovered a few techniques for making that time most effective.

First of all, when we have a full classroom of 26 participants, we have found that it is vital to have two librarians there during hands-on time, if at all possible. Inevitably there will be one or two students who may dominate one librarian's time with questions and problems. Having another librarian there to rove around ensures that the rest of the class does not get neglected.

Second, while circulating to help students, we find that they will ask your opinion of such issues as a site's authority, relevance, or currency. Refrain from answering them directly; rather, try asking open-ended questions to encourage them to think on their own.

The worksheets also help to guide the exploration and evaluation process. Figures 1 and 3 are the front and back, respectively, of the worksheet we have developed.

Finally, we suggest using collaborative assignments whenever possible, such as those suggested above. These group tasks help to enforce what the librarian has gone over in the demonstration, and collaborative work is a highly effective way for students to learn. Additionally, we have found that collaboration increases the level of interest in the classroom, to the extent that the students are genuinely excited about using what they are learning.

Pitfalls

One problem with teaching in a hands-on environment is the difficulty of keeping students on task when they're using the Internet. The temptation to stray from the assignment of evaluation, and to wander over to some more entertaining site, is difficult for students to fight. Other than warning them to keep to the project at hand, the librarian has little control over this situation.

If a presentation software is used with screenshots of examples from the Web, very large files can result. The librarian needs to be sure to have adequate hardware to accommodate files with large graphics.

On the other hand, including a live Web demonstration can also prove unsettling if the Web site which was the perfect example of poor construction and inaccuracy has improved since you last visited it. Check the examples before the session to reduce the chance of unwanted surprises during class.

Another pitfall to look for is librarian burnout. Especially if one person conducts the bulk of the workshops on evaluation and other Internet-related issues, the pressure can lead to fatigue and apathy. Involving more librarians eases the burden.

Conclusion

More and more people are considering the Internet and the World Wide Web as the ultimate information resource to consult. Particularly in academia, the Internet is becoming the preferred medium of accessing information and our patrons expect to find all information on the Internet. In addition, now that many of us are teaching the Nintendo generation, we are finding that this patron group assumes that information is delivered via computer, and they consider electronic information to be more authoritative than what is in print. This is the reverse of what was true a generation ago.

As librarians and information professionals, it is becoming paramount that we educate our patron populations as to the real nature of Internet information and how people can become more effective consumers of information. We can do this by teaching them the tools librarians have used for years—how to use evaluation criteria.

Life on the Information Super-Treadmill: Management Issues in Creating a Departmental Web Page for Reference and Bibliographic Instruction

Jeanie M. Welch

Introduction

The Internet provides a new medium for enhancing both reference service and bibliographic instruction. The printed brochures, user guides, and subject bibliographies that we have provided for years in print can become the foundation for a departmental Web site for both in-house and remote-access reference service and for bibliographic instruction. Reference departments can create Web sites that include these converted print sources, interactive features, and links to other sources of information on the Internet. This presentation is an overview of ideas for identifying issues and setting goals, implementing a departmental Web site, integrating Web pages into library instruction, and some of the "ugly realities" of such a project. You might also call it "If I Only Knew Then What I Know Now."

Identifying Issues and Setting Goals

Before undertaking such a major project, reference departments that provide library instruction need to have a departmental plan. Here are some of the issues and goals to consider.

Welch is reference unit head, Murrey Atkins Library, University of North Carolina at Charlotte.

- **Organizational issues**—The first issue to consider is a very basic one: the organizational framework of your parent organization (e.g., university, agency, or public library system). You need to assess its level of commitment to an Internet initiative. You also need to know the level of commitment of your library's administration. Measures of an institutional level of commitment include an understanding of and sympathy for the resources and time involved, the adoption of administrative polices and procedures in place for all library Web sites, training and technical support, and the adoption of guidelines and standards about Web page content and design (e.g., use of logos, arrangements of buttons). The second issue consists of technical concerns. These include the necessary connections, hardware, and software, an Internet provider, "clip art" pages for logos and gifs, and templates with basic codes and logos to assist with preparation.

- **Departmental issues**—Some of the same organizational issues also apply to reference and bibliographic instruction departments. There is a need for a departmental commitment to establishing a Web site and for agreement upon goals and objectives. There should also be a technical infrastructure for creating a departmental Web site.

Implementation of a Departmental Web Site

Once a reference or bibliographic instruction department decides to implement a Web site one of the first priorities is to set its purpose and scope. Accessing reference and bibliographic instruction Web sites at similar institutions may be a place to start. Most such Web sites fall into one of the four following categories.

- **Informational**—This Web site is similar to a departmental listing in a basic library brochure. It includes services available, personnel, hours, phone number, and a summary of resources. An informational Web site is usually a beginning for a department with limited resources in time and staffing.

- **Interactive**—This type of Web site includes the same features as an informational Web site but also includes hot links for direct contact via the Internet (e.g., mail links and form mail).

- **Gateway**—This type of Web site includes hot links to other useful Web sites, especially meta pages for Web crawlers (e.g., Yahoo! and Alta Vista) and electronic journals, indexes, and full-text sources.

- **Comprehensive**—This type of Web site includes all of the feature of the previous three types, plus subject- or course-specific Web sites and other Web-related information (e.g., how to evaluate Web sites, how to cite Web pages in bibliographies, and how to create their own Web pages). Most larger departments have this type of Web site.

The next step is the implementation of the type of Web site that your department has decided to mount. At this time the department needs to keep its institutional and departmental commitment, goals, and resources in mind as it deals with the next set of issues. These issues include:

- **Personnel issues**—Personnel issues include the assignment of overall and individual responsibility as departmental Webmaster. The responsibilities of the Webmaster could be given to the department head, to the electronic services coordinator, or to other departmental staff (including support staff) on either a permanent or rotating basis. This responsibility needs to be reflected in job descriptions, evaluations, and the assignment of workloads. Personnel issues also include territorial issues—who can change departmental Web pages other than their own.

- **Technical issues**—Technical issues include access to a computer with a browser, an HTML editor, and FTP (loading software), and the creation and arrangement of directories and subdirectories for testing and loading (including a "shared" directory for in-house viewing before loading). Other technical issues include training, and the access that departmental members have to the same level and amount of training, including training manuals. It needs to be determined if the institution will provide training or if it is a "do-it-yourself" project within the department. As new employees are added there need to be provisions for their training as well as training in new features and enhancements (e.g., Java applets and frames).

- **Maintenance issues**—A third set of issues belong to the category of maintaining existing Web sites. Either the institution or the department need to include standards for revising Web sites and each staff member's responsibilities for maintaining their knowledge of and technical competencies in browsers, crawlers, HTML, graphics, and ftp. There are both quantitative and qualitative methods to handle maintenance issues. The quantitative methods include Web site quality and usefulness. There is assessment software available for detection of spelling/syntax errors and dead links. As measures of a Web site's usefulness, the number of times a Web site has been accessed is one place to start. Either an on-screen counter that tracks the number of hits or reports generated from server statistics are two standard methods to measure access. Log file analysis software can do more sophisticated tracking of Web sites as well. Other quantitative methods include evidence of revision (revision date changes on the Web site), evidence of public relations (letters to faculty or announcements on listservs and in newsletters), and a record of number of Internet demonstrations in bibliographic instruction sessions. Qualitative methods include positive or negative e-mail, comments from end-users, or surveys done to gauge patron reaction and usage.

Integration into Bibliographic Instruction

Integrating a Web site into library instruction is dependent of several factors. These include:

- **Facilities and equipment**—The department needs to determine if its bibliographic instruction facility can be wired for Internet access. Standard configurations include a demonstration workstation and a computer projector for a demonstration or lecture format, a computer lab setting with enough workstations for individual hands-on training, or the ideal situation of a combination with both demonstration and hands-on capabilities. This opens up another set of issues as to the maintenance and training for additional types of equipment.

- **Types of instruction**—Another factor is the type of instruction that the department will offer. Types of instruction include the traditional lecture/demonstration as part of one session that also includes print and other electronic sources, a separate lecture session on the Internet, and a hands-on session in a computer lab setting.

- **Coordination with faculty members for course- or subject-specific Web sites**—Getting faculty cooperation is vital to a successful program in integrating the Internet into bibliographic instruction. Methods to gain faculty cooperation include giving faculty members demonstrations of useful Web sites and getting faculty cooperation for feedback and evaluation.

- **Evaluation**—A final consideration in integrating the Internet into bibliographic instruction is the evaluation of the effectiveness of your efforts. Traditional bibliographic instruction evaluation methods that bibliographic instruction librarians have used for years can be adapted to Web sites. These include pre- and post-tests of students' knowledge of Internet sources in subject area, evaluation forms at the end of the session, project, or class, and citation analysis of students' bibliographies to ascertain whether Web sites were used in their research.

Ugly Realities

The Internet is an additional responsibility. It is a never-ending, time-consuming, additional responsibility. We still provide all of the traditional reference and bibliographic instruction services such as reference desk staffing and collection development. The Internet is another "add-on." Administrators (who may not have Web pages themselves) need to realize this.

Variations exist in individual interests, abilities, and willingness to devote time to the Internet. Some staff members will take to Internet training and run with it. Others need more encouragement.

Conclusion

After doing all of this work you may wonder if it was all worth it, or your administration may question the merit of what you have done. There are quantitative ways to show that what your department has done is worthwhile. One way is to count the number of times your Web site has been accessed by patrons and compare your statistics to the rest of the library and to your in-house patron activity. Thanks to the Internet and the World Wide Web all libraries can provide their patrons with access to thousands of new sources of information. Even the smallest, most remote library can use the Internet just like the New York Public Library and MIT. We have found at UNC Charlotte that more people visit our various Web sites than contact us at the reference desk either in person or by telephone. However, the characteristics of the Internet require that reference and bibliographic instruction departments integrate an unorganized, unregulated, rapidly growing collection of data sets in an organized, rational manner on top of dealing with traditional print sources and other electronic sources. Good luck to us all!

Successful Marketing of Faculty Bibliographic Instruction:
Faculty Bibliographic Instruction at Andrews University

Wolfhard Touchard

Introduction

I would like to slightly change the title "Evaluating Faculty Bibliographic Instruction" to reflect my focus on successful marketing of bibliographic instruction (BI). As I researched the literature on faculty attendance in workshops and marketing Faculty BI, I found virtually nothing. It looks, at this point, as though we have stepped on virgin territory. In this presentation, therefore, I wanted to show what is being done at Andrews University to reach an attendance rate of up to 100 percent.

An organized "Faculty/Secretary BI" started at Andrews University in 1995/96. In the past, faculty only were introduced to library resources as their classes came for library orientation.

The bibliographic instruction committee felt the need for a more structured program for the faculty *and* their secretaries. We took a good look at the format of our workshops for transfer students and the community. This format needed only some minor modifications.

Methodology

Contacting the Faculty

I recognized early that contacting the faculty would be time- and nerve-consuming! At first, I approached the chair of the Christian Ministry Department of the Theological Seminary and asked to be scheduled for

---

Touchard is reference librarian and coordinator of faculty bibliographic instruction, Andrews University, Berrien Springs, Michigan.

a few minutes at the next departmental meeting. At this meeting, it became obvious that a successful faculty BI would not be accomplished without the personal touch.

It also became apparent that the secretaries needed to be part of this instruction, because they do most of the bibliographic searching. I requested and received a list of the faculty and their secretaries.

To make the invitation for our workshop brief and personal I prepared a canvass (see appendix 1), which included greetings, my name, workshop offering, invitation, outline of the workshop, grouping, and date of workshop.

I wrote attendees' names and telephone numbers on an Attendance/Registration Form (see appendix 2) in order to know who and how many were coming.

One function of the Attendance/Registration Form was to have the phone numbers of the faculty so as to remind them of their commitment that evening!! *Attendance was much higher when the faculty was called in the morning or in the afternoon, and I was encouraged to use e-mail!!*

Planning the Instruction

Our library offers 85 databases. I selected seven of the 22 that deal with religion and theology.

I knew that I would have the opportunity to work with the faculty *only once* and for only a *two-hour session*. Instead of overpowering them with all 22 databases, I decided to limit this number to those seven that are used the most.

I also had to reckon with the fact that most of our faculty are older, some are retired, and many are not very computer-friendly. They needed a hands-on experience.

To fit seven to eight databases into two hours, and using four instructors, one person had to teach two databases within a 30-minute period. Fifteen minutes for one database provides just enough time for a very general overview.

Four instructors staffed four workstations: Two religion databases were demonstrated on one; Dissertation Abstracts and Books in Print Plus on another; the World Wide Web (30-minute presentation) on still another; and databases on OCLC FirstSearch and our catalog comprises the fourth workstation.

The patrons moved from one workstation to another, while the staff taught the same databases four times during the session. This helped us to learn the databases very well!

Experience has taught me that 12 individuals are just enough for one session. This way, more personal attention can be given. I divided the participants into four groups of three patrons each.

At this point, we have to teach faculty BI on public terminals. This arrangement worked against this workshop. Older faculty felt uncomfortable being watched by students. Understandable!

Therefore, I needed to reserve the workstations, the classroom, the CD-ROMs, and the time slot at the CD-ROM workstations.

Since the faculty can't remember all they have been taught in these two hours, I provided pathfinders for the seven databases we presented. For the other databases, we have published a book, *How to Search Electronic Databases, a Survival Guide*, which is placed at every terminal. A few serious faculty members purchased their own copies.

Pre-Session

We all meet in a classroom for about ten minutes during which I introduce the outline of the workshop, stress the difference between a subject and a word search, explain Boolean Search and the use of truncations, and have prayer.

I explain the following policies and procedures:

- order procedure of books and periodicals,
- how to place materials on reserve,
- faculty loans, and
- how to place a book on hold.

I note the following services we provide:

- interlibrary loan,
- consultation,
- information desk,
- faculty reciprocal borrowing program,
- InfoPass,
- how to register a class BI,
- advertising our general workshops, and
- teaching the use of the multimedia center.

We then proceed to the terminals.

Follow-Up

I have invited individual faculty for an additional one-on-one session. One response on the evaluation mentioned that the session moved too quickly. I will try to invite this person also. Next is a visit to their offices to show them what they can get on their terminals.

Reaction from Faculty

Comments of our "Evaluation of Library Instruction" sheet (see appendix 3) were:

- (B. What was the *most useful* part of the session?) "The helpfulness of the facilitator," "the overall insight to possibilities for research," "all instructors were helpful—good clear instruction," "explanation for steps."

- (E. What other comments and suggestions do you have?) "These sessions should be *mandatory* for all faculty and staff. Excellent!" "These sessions are extremely useful. Thank you," "thank you for inviting me," "very helpful to a novice like me."

However, the most encouraging outcome of these workshops is that *faculty requested that the same workshops be given to their students*. This is most rewarding!

Attendance

Attendance included the president of Andrews University, 87 percent of faculty and secretaries of our Theological Seminary and the faculty and secretary of the undergraduate religion department. Some of the remaining 13 percent of our professors were teaching at affiliated campuses at the time. I will approach them later.

After this experience I organized a program for our agriculture department. Attendance of full-time teachers and the secretary was 100 percent. Social work and the behavioral sciences attendance was also 100 percent. Other departments have already *asked* when their turn is. We are blessed with a general air of enthusiasm for "Faculty/Secretaries Bibliographic Instruction" here at Andrews University.

APPENDIX 1: CONTACTING THE FACULTY/STAFF BY PHONE

CONTACTING THE FACULTY / STAFF by PHONE

Good _____. I am Wolfhard Touchard. Dr. _____, the library has designed a special workshop for the Theological Seminary, introducing our electronic databases to the faculty and their secretaries.

Let me briefly tell you what this workshop covers. There are over 75 databases in our library, 23 of which deal with Religion and Theology. Out of 23 databases we selected eight. They are:

    World Wide Web (I chose this database as "bait")

    Religious and Theological Abstracts

    CD-ROM version of ATLA

    Dissertation Abstracts International

    Books in Print Plus

    WorldCat

    Library Book / Media Catalog

In order to give you personal attention to each one of you, we decided to divide you into groups of three.

May I invite you to this two hour workshop which will be held June 3 (Monday) evening from 7:00 to 9:00 pm?

APPENDIX 2: WORKSHOP ATTENDEES

WORKSHOP ATTENDEES

Workshop: _____   Date: _____   Room: ____

Day: _____

NAMES	PHONE #	REMINDED
1. _____	_____	_____
2. _____	_____	_____
3. _____	_____	_____
4. _____	_____	_____
5. _____	_____	_____
6. _____	_____	_____
7. _____	_____	_____
8. _____	_____	_____
9. _____	_____	_____
10. _____	_____	_____
11. _____	_____	_____
12. _____	_____	_____
13. _____	_____	_____
14. _____	_____	_____
15. _____	_____	_____
16. _____	_____	_____

APPENDIX 3: EVALUATION OF LIBRARY INSTRUCTION

Thank you very much for attending the library training session. Please help us evaluate and improve the program by filling out this form and returning it to the library instructor or to the reference desk as soon as possible. Thanks for your input.

Class: Class instructor:

Date class was held: Library instructor:

A. Rate the following according to this scale:

     (A) Strongly agree (B) Agree (C) Undecided (D) Disagree (E) Strongly disagree

     ___ 1. I enjoyed this library session.
     ___ 2. The lesson was conveyed effectively.
     ___ 3. The coverage was what I expected.
     ___ 4. The handouts were useful.
     ___ 5. I would recommend this training session to friends.

B. What was the <u>most useful</u> part of the session?

C. What was the <u>least useful</u> part of the session?

D. Name at least one concept that you learned.

E. What other comments and suggestions do you have?

APPENDIX 4: SEARCHING AGRICULTURAL TOPICS IN SELECTED
OCLC FIRSTSEARCH DATABASES
A User Study

I. INTRODUCTION

The intent of this study was to see how many records can be found in databases, where their titles do **n o t** suggest finding materials about AGRICULTURE. For this purpose AGRICOLA and the Biological & Agricultural Periodical Index are excluded. The result of this study was so overwhelming that I decided to share these findings with the agricultural community.

II. METHODOLOGY

A. Selecting the Topics

I have taken the bulletin of the Agricultural Department and entered the title of the course as a word search. Very interesting was the use of truncation (+)! As an example I used BasicBIOSIS. I searched:

    soil (only singular records) and found 8778 records
    soils (only plural records) and found 3184 records
    soil+ (which includes all records with soil and soils) and found 9341 records

B. Databases and their Abbreviations

Appli	Applied Science & Technology Index
Basic	BasicBIOSIS
Envir	Environment
Geoba	GEOBASE
GeoRe	GeoRef
Paper	PapersFirst => only main subject areas
Proce	ProceedingsFirst => only main subject areas

C. Search Results

1. G e n e r a l

Farm Machinery   107 Geoba   34 Envir   18 Appli   8 Basic   1 GeoRe
Management of Agricultural Enterprises   266 Geoba   7 Envir
Principles of Weed Control   698 Geoba   464 Envir   238 Basic   49 Appli   3 GeoRe

2. A n i m a l   S c i e n c e

Animal Nutation   219 Envir   207 Basic   76 Geoba   14 GeoRe   11 Appli
Animal Reproduction   327 Envir   116 Basic   101 Geoba   11 GeoRe   3 Apply
Animal Science   56 Geoba   55 Envir   46 Basic   25 GeoRe   18 Appli
Canine   45 Geoba   13 Basic   1 GeoRe
Dairy Cattle Management   22 Envir   13 Geoba   2 Basic

APPENDIX 4: SEARCHING AGRICULTURAL TOPICS IN SELECTED OCLC FIRSTSEARCH DATABASES
A User Study (CONTINUED)

Equine Anatomy   2 Basic
Horse Evaluation   12 Geoba   11 GeoRe   9 Envir   9 Basci   1 Appli
Livestock Judging   36 Envir
Physiology of Farm Animals   4 Envir
Small Animal Health   30 Envir   16 Geoba   6 Basic

3. Crops and Soils

Crops   5758 Geoba   690 Basic   451 GeoRe   74 Proce
Crop+   10,211 Basic   6000 Envir   1148 GeoRe   384 Appli
Soils   73,579 GeoRe   22,500 Geoba   2791 Basic   34 Proce
Soil+   4630 Appli
Agricultural Marketing   245 Geoba   28 Envir   6 Appli   2 Basic
Cereal   111 Envir
Cereal and Crop   571 Geoba   6 GeoRe
Field Crop   1200 Basic   645 Envir   8 Appli
Forage   69 Envir
Forage and Crop   269 Geoba   77 Basic   6 GeoRe
Solanaceous   10 Basic   3 Envir   1 GeoRe
Vine Crops   28 Geoba   16 Envir   12 GeoRe
Viticulture   133 Geoba   5 Envir   2 Basic

4. Horticulture

1200 Basic   735 Paper   189 Geoba   86 Envir   23 Proce   9 GeoRe
Advanced Landscape Design   119 Envir   14 GeoRe   10 Basic
Bedding Plants   163 GeoRe   24 Geoba   10 Basic   9 Envir   1 Appli
Computer Landscape Design   16 Geoba   8 Envir   1 Basic
Diseases of Horticultural Plants   3 Envir   1 Basic
Fundamentals of Irrigation   4912 Geoba   4683 GeoRe   2610 Envir   739 Appli   491 Basic
Golf Course Management   50 Envir
Greenhouse Construction   32 Envir   15 Geoba   6 GeoRe   6 Basic
Herbaceous Plant   543 Geoba   307 Envir   193 Basic   25 GeoRe   1 Appli
History of Landscape Design   31 Geoba   5 Envir   2 Basic
Horticultural Plants   30 Envir   15 Geoba   10 Basic
Interior Plant Culture   136 Geoba   85 Envir   79 GeoRe   32 Basic   8 Appli
Introduction to Landscape Drafting   10 Basic   2 Envir   1 Geoba
Landscape Construction   181 Geoba   149 Envir   25 GeoRe   2 Basic
Landscape Design and Development   368 Geoba   32 Envir   3 GeoRe   1 Basic
Landscape Equipment   19 Geoba   10 Enivr   2 Basic   1 GeoRe
Landscape Estimating   33 Geoba   22 Envir   6 GeoRe   4 Basic
Landscape Management   930 Geoba   72 GeoRe   50 Basic   2 Appli
Landscape Site Design   21 Envir   1 GeoRe   1 Basic
Pests of Horticultural Crops   2 Geoba   2 Envir   1 Basic
Plant Environment   1903 Envir   592 Basic   22 Appli
Plant Science   290 GeoRe   131 Geoba   95 Envir   48 Basic   19 Appli
Potted Plant   97 Envir   61 Basic   37 Geoba
Turfgrass Management   8 Envir   7 Geoba   2 Basic
Urban Landscape   683 Geoba   98 Envir   69 GeoRe   7 Basic   4 Appli
Woody Plant   467 Geoba   405 Enivr   173 Basic   60 GeoRe

Appendix 5: Subject Guide for the Study of Graphic Arts

This handout is prepared for our students and faculty in the Art and Graphic Arts. This SUBJECT GUIDE is very useful for those in the industry, who struggle to keep up-to-date in an area which experiences such rapid changes.

    ADVERTISING   HF 5801 - HF 6182
    ADVERTISING LAYOUT AND TYPOGRAPHY   HF 5825
        see also   PRINTING, PRACTICAL--LAYOUT
                        PRINTING, PRACTICAL--PASTE-UP
    AIRBRUSH ART   NC 915 .A35
        see also   PHOTOGRAPHY--RETOUCHING
                        TECHNICAL ILLUSTRATION
    BOOK DESIGN   Z 116 .A3
    COLOR COMPUTER GRAPHICS   T 385
    COLOR-PRINTING   Z 258
Color separation
        see   PHOTOMECHANICAL PROCESSES   NE 2890 TR 925 - TR 997
    COMMERCIAL ART   NC 997
    COMPUTER GRAPHICS   T 385
    COMPUTER-AIDED DESIGN   TA 174   NA 2728
    COMPUTERIZED TYPESETTING   Z 253.3 - Z 253.4
    DESKTOP PUBLISHING   Z 286 .D47
    ELECTRONIC PUBLISHING   Z 286 .E43
    GRAPHIC ARTS
        (this subject covers a large spectrum of areas, therefore go to your OPAC and look under GRAPHIC ARTS)
    GRAPHIC ARTS see also PRINTING, PRACTICAL
    GRAPHIC ARTS--HISTORY
    GRAPHIC ARTS--MANAGEMENT   N 8520
    GRAPHIC ARTS--MARKETING   NC 1001.6
    GRAPHIC ARTS--PSYCHOLOGICAL ASPECTS   NC 1001.6

    GRAPHIC ARTS--SAFETY MEASURES   Z 244.5
    GRAPHIC METHODS   QA 90
Industrial design coordination   see TRADE-MARKS   T 323 - T 325
Linotype see TYPESETTING   Z 253
    LOGOTYPE   HD 59.2
        see also   TRADE-MARKS
                        SIGNS AND SYMBOLS
    OFFSET PRINTING   Z 252.5
    PACKAGING--DESIGN AND CONSTRUCTION   TS 195.2 - TS 195.4
    PAPER--PRINTING PROPERTIES   Z 237
Photo-engraving
        see   PHOTOMECHANICAL PROCESSES   NE 2890 TR 925 - TR 997
    PHOTOGRAPHY--RETOUCHING   T310

APPENDIX 5: SUBJECT GUIDE FOR THE STUDY OF GRAPHIC ARTS (CONTINUED)

PHOTOMECHANICAL PROCESSES   NE 2890   TR 925-997
PHOTO-TYPESETTING   TR 1010
PRINTING INDUSTRY--VOCATIONAL GUIDANCE   Z 243 .A2
    (these books are in the Career Information Center)
PRINTING-INK   Z 247
PRINTING MACHINERY AND SUPPLIES--MAINTENANCE AND REPAIR   Z 249
PRINTING, PRACTICAL   Z 244 - Z 245
PRINTING, PRACTICAL--ESTIMATING   Z 245
PRINTING, PRACTICAL--LAYOUT   Z 246
PRINTING, PRACTICAL--PASTE-UP   Z 246
PRINTING-PRESS   Z 249
Printing specimens
    see   TYPE AND TYPE-FOUNDING   Z 250
SCREEN PROCESS PRINTING   TT 273
SIGNS AND SYMBOLS (general)   AZ 108
TECHNICAL ILLUSTRATION   T 11.8
TRADE-MARKS   T 323 - T 325
TYPE AND TYPE-FOUNDING   Z 250
TYPE-SETTING   Z 253

    MAGAZINES
AIRBRUSH ACTION
COMMUNICATION ARTS
GRAPHIS (Switzerland)
HOW
PRINT
PUBLISH
STEP-BY-STEP

APPENDIX 6: HANDOUTS OF TWO DATABASES

> **Books in Print Plus**
> with **Book Reviews**
> CD-ROM • updated monthly

Covering all subjects. Provides access to 1.8 million books with 200,000 full-text **book reviews** (30,000 reviews are added each year) from:

Books in Print	Children's Books in Print
Forthcoming Books in Print	Paperbound Books in Print
Subject Guide to Books in Print	Supplement to Books in Print
Subject Guide to Children's Books in Print	

BASIC COMMANDS

print
mark items on the brief citation screen by pressing <Enter>
<F5>
select <brief> or <full citation>
<Enter> <Enter> <Enter>

download
<Enter> mark items on the brief citation screen
<F4>
select <brief> or <full citation>
<Enter> <Enter> <Enter>

exit <Esc> menu screen
use right arrow to Action <Enter>
scroll down to Quit Books In Print <Enter>
<$> truncation symbol

Note: **R** in front of a citation indicates that there is a **Review** available

SEARCH TECHNIQUES

AUTHOR SEARCH
for single search if item is known, use <Browse> <Enter>
select <author> <Enter>
type herriot, james <Enter>
<Enter> to highlight herriot, james
<F10> to **view** brief citations
select <Every living thing>
<Enter> to highlight title
<F10> to **view** full citation

SUBJECT SEARCH
select <subject> <Enter>
type humor <Enter>
<Enter> to highlight HUMOR

APPENDIX 6: HANDOUTS OF TWO DATABASES (CONTINUED)

\<F10\> to **view** short citations
select \<superstoe\>
\<Enter\> to highlight title
\<F10\> to **view** full citation
\<F2\> for **publisher's** information

TITLE SEARCH

select \<t i t l e\> \<Enter\>
type every living thing \<Enter\>
\<Enter\> to highlight title
\<F10\> to **view** brief citation

SERIES SEARCH

scroll down to \<se r i e s t i t l e\> \<Enter\>
type Old Testament Library \<Enter\>
\<Enter\> to highlight series title
\<F10\> to **view** short citations
\<Enter\> and select a title
\<F10\> to **view** full citation
\<F2\> for information about the **publisher**

Boolean Searching

- **or** = to give synonyms
  kw=bushes or trees
- **and** = to combine search
  kw=computers and py=1996
- **and/not** = to exclude search terms
  kw=president and/not kw=Nixon
- **cs** = combined sets
  allows Boolean Searches being combined cs=1 and cs=2
- **truncate** use $ sign expands your search
  e.g. econom$ = economics, economically, etc.

EXERCISES

type kw=reformation \<Enter\>
type kw=music \<Enter\>
type cs=1 and 2 \<Enter\>
\<F10\> to **view** brief citations
select title \<Enter\>
\<F10\> to **view** full citation
type kw=home and school \<Enter\>
type py=1995 \<Enter\>
type cs=6 and 7 \<Enter\>
\<F10\> to **view** brief citations
select title \<Enter\>
\<F10\> to **view** full citation

use of truncation

type soiL \<Enter\> ● count citations
type soils \<Enter\> ● compare the # of citations above
type soil$ \<Enter\> ● compare again the # of citations above

APPENDIX 7: DISSERTATION ABSTRACTS

DISSERTATION ABSTRACTS
CD-ROM • 1861- updated quarterly

Includes abstracts of master's theses and doctoral dissertations of over 1,000 accredited universities worldwide.

BASIC COMMANDS

access
    \<8\> \<Enter\>
    select \<Dissertation Abstracts Ondisc\> \<Enter\>

print
    mark record with the \<Spacebar\> (brown line on the left!)
    \<F2\>
    select \<print/save\>
    \<Enter\> \<Enter\>

download
    mark records with the \<Spacebar\>
    \<F2\>
    select \<print/save\> \<Enter\>
    select \<to disc file\> use arrow key
    \<Spacebar\>
    \<Enter\> \<Enter\> \<Enter\> \<Enter\> \<Enter\>
    \<Enter\> \<marked files\> (look at the green light)
    \<Enter\>
    if you need to <u>change the File name</u>
    mark records with the \<Spacebar\>
    \<F2\>
    select \<print/save\> \<Enter\>
    select \<to disk file\> use arrow key
    \<Spacebar\>
    select \<A:\UMI.OUT\>
    \<Spacebar\>
    type in your file name
    \<Enter\> \<Enter\> \<Enter\> \<Enter\> \<Enter\>
    look at the green light
    when light turns off \<Enter\>

exit
    \<Esc\>
    \<F2\>
    select \<exit\> \<Enter\>

SEARCH TECHNIQUES
KEYWORD SEARCH

type interracial marriage \<Enter\> = 14 or more citations
\<F3\> to clear line
  <u>to truncate</u> (to enlarge your search)

APPENDIX 7: DISSERTATION ABSTRACTS (CONTINUED)

type interracial marriage? \<Enter\> = 15 or more citations
\<F3\> to clear line

AUTHOR SEARCH
type au(batchelder) \<Enter\>
\<F7\> to view record and abstract
\<F3\> to start a new search

SEARCH by SCHOOL
type sc(andrews) \<Enter\>
\<F7\> to view record and abstract
\<F3\> to start a new search

SUBJECT SEARCH
type su(education) \<Enter\>
\<F7\> to view record and abstract
\<F3\> to start a new search

TITLE SEARCH
type ti(memory consistency models for shared-memory multi-processors-debugging) \<enter\>
\<F7\> to view record and abstract

SEARCH by YEAR
type su(education) \<Enter\>
\<F3\> to clear the screen
type 1996 \<Enter\>
\<F3\> to clear the screen
type #1 and #2 or your last two entries
    (you should have all the dissertations in education published in 1996)

COMBINE SETS
type #4 and #5 \<Enter\>
\<F7\>to view record and abstract

USING the INDEX
\<F6\>
select \<key words/basic index\> \<Enter\>
type depression <u>note</u> all the words starting with depress
use arrow key to make selection
\<Enter\> \<Enter\>

Discussion Groups

A Team Approach to BI: or, Growth Is Good for You (so stop complaining!)

Deborah Davis, Carolyn McPherson, Beth Stevens, and Roxann Bustos

This discussion group used a computer-generated slide show to demonstrate a version of the "team" approach to equalizing workloads in library instruction. The specifics of the Valdosta State University (VSU) method were presented to act as a catalyst for the discussion. The slide show also included the results of an "unscientific" survey done on the BI-L listserv, which attempted to collect the who, how, when, and where of library instruction as it currently is being practiced in libraries of all sizes across the country. This slide show is currently available at the following address: <http:/www.valdosta.edu/~dsdavis/loex.htm>.

Areas of discussion included moving from a traditional style of BI (i.e., one main instruction librarian designing curricula and teaching the majority of classes with minimal assistance from other librarians); to the subject specialist approach with librarians teaching in "their" areas of expertise; to variations of the *team* approach. Some teams include the subject specialist as an assignment factor, or they consider seniority: "I've paid my dues and I don't have to teach freshman orientations anymore!" Then there is the VSU extreme of total equality (information services librarians only) where everyone has the opportunity and is expected to teach any class at any level, from English composition to educational law, from undergraduate to doctoral level.

Means of implementation of new methods for BI were actively debated. VSU used what they call the "yank" method—as in removing a Band-Aid. The process is going to be painful and one is confronted with two choices: either do it slowly and prolong the agony or say, "1,2,3" and yank it off. This also can be called the "sink or swim" method. The groups seemed to agree that the implementation method really didn't make that much difference; some people were going to take to the idea of teams, and some were going to fight it. Irrefutable justification for making the change, educating staff about the process, providing ample opportunities for input, and giving librarians the means to "vent" frustrations were all presented as essentials for a successful change in method of operation or reorganization of responsibilities.

Issues of scheduling were discussed with innumerable variations being shared. Smaller libraries with the disadvantage of smaller staffs have the advantage of less scheduling to monitor. Conversely, larger libraries with more librarians to share the load have more opportunities for scheduling problems due to the sheer numbers with which they are faced.

Fighting for space and equipment seems to be a universal concern of both the large and small libraries. Many have electronic classrooms, or have them in process, or have them on their wish lists. Everyone is concerned about the pace with which electronic resources are changing and/or multiplying, and is

---

Davis is instructional services librarian, Valdosta State University, Valdosta, Georgia; *McPherson* is coordinator of collection development, Valdosta State University, Valdosta, Georgia; *Stevens* is librarian, Armstrong Atlantic University, Gary, Indiana; and *Bustos* is head of reference, Augusta State University, Augusta, Georgia.

asking the universal question, "Who on campus is responsible for computer literacy?"

We all worry about the currency of BI handouts, use of Web pages, keeping track of links that actually go someplace, whether paper sources could and should be replaced by electronic versions, how to justify having both or neither and using interlibrary loan/document delivery to supplement collection deficits (which is not really a library instruction issue, but is a concern if teaching in an area where the library's collection is not strong).

Last, and perhaps most important, issues of burnout and morale were addressed. If the job is no longer fun, but merely a way to pay the bills, something needs to change. Hence the switch to teams for VSU and other institutions. Effective teaching only can come from individuals who want to be there, sharing incredible information with authority and enthusiasm. Library instructors have a huge responsibility and frequently they need to be reminded of it. Creating a population of literate (computer or otherwise) library users is a goal worth striving for, no matter what method is chosen to achieve it.

Welcome to the 1997 LOEX Discussion on Instruction and Workload

Below are the slides from our presentation on Workload Issues in BI. Some transferred better than others, but all are legible. The subjects covered include TEAMS and results from a workload survey sent out on BI-L. The general themes of the discussion (after the slide presentation) are being written up as part of the conference proceedings. Thank you all for attending our session because we learned a lot from you. Please use the e-mail address below to make comments or ask questions.

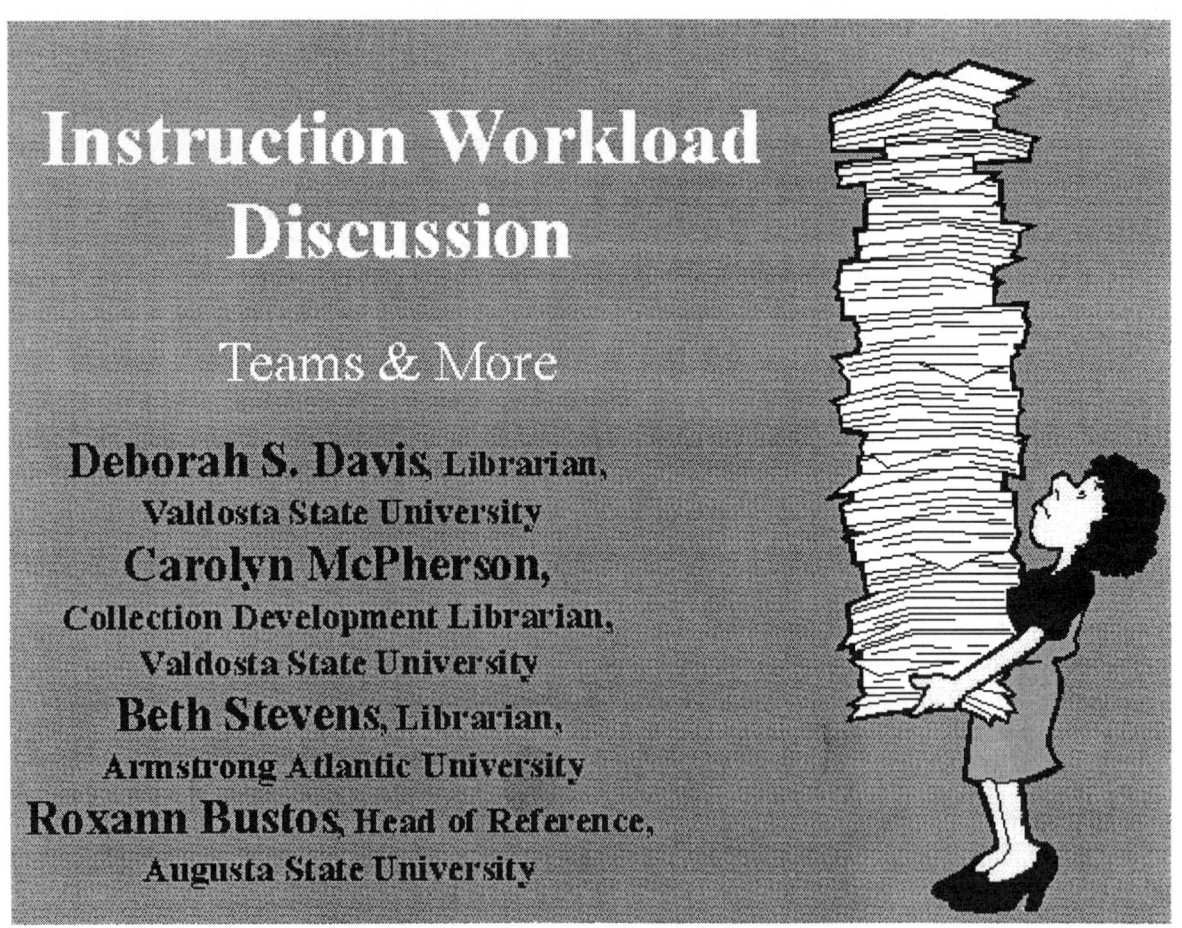

The Past

Good Old/Bad Old Days

- BI Coordinator taught 50-70% of all classes taught
  - Much night work--totally flexible schedule
  - Worked little on the desk
  - High visibility for BI Coordinator with Teaching Faculty
  - Low visibility (and credibility) for others in department with Teaching Faculty
  - Danger of burnout
  - Similarity of handouts and classes

dsdavis/bigteams

Brave New World

Or If we're really good (or bad) maybe they'll go away

- All Information Service Areas were designated teams:
  - Archives Team
  - Bibliographic Instruction Team
  - Collection Development Team
  - Computer Services Team
  - Government Documents Team
  - Information Desk Team
  - Inter Library Loan Team

dsdavis/bigteams

Team Mechanics

If it ain't broke, we'll break it!

All members of IS are on 3-5 different teams

All membership is voluntary (unless one has special expertise in an area.

No declared team leaders, thus dispensing with previous titles and privileges -- in some cases responsibilities remain the same.

Teams write goals and plans--in effect defining their reason for existence.

Teams are responsible for work in particular team's area of expertise.

Initial confusion: are the teams in an executive position to the function or are the teams there to provide the manpower to do the job. After some arguing and discussion (and burning resentments) we all agreed to the latter.

Teams meet weekly or bi-weekly (and in some cases not at all) to keep team members appraised of progress on various projects.

dsdavis/bigteams

BI Team

Down and Dirty

* Points of contention and concern:
    - Disparity in levels of experience in Teaching, Pedagogic Theory, and Desktop Publishing
    - Lack of leadership or resentment of attempts to assume leadership
    - In-fighting and misunderstandings
    - Miscommunication
    - Overwhelming nature of task
    - Unsure of team's authority to change BI for Department
    - Lack of knowledge of team members about previous BI program

* Results: BI, once the most vibrant and cutting edge of our IS programs, begins to languish.

Departmental Initiatives to Support Teams

Tolerance and Listening Are Good!

Retraining Efforts were Ongoing and Included:
- Readings on teams circulated through department.
- Meetings with Department Head and Assistant Director describing teams and expected areas of change and stability
- Individual meetings weekly with Department Head to allow team members to VENT.
- Departmental participation in Teleseminar on Teams and follow-up discussion.
- Administration of Meyers Briggs Personality Test to entire department and made results of test and interpretive material publicly available.
- Membership on specific teams was voluntary. And unless the team was one's area of specialty, no penalty attached to getting off a team that was found too frustrating.

BI Team
Baby Steps

- Some changes to the team created a framework which allowed later successes.
    - Team composition changed:
        - Head of IS joined the team and took over scheduling
            - Learned from the past that authority in that position ensures cooperation and lessens resentment.
    - We came to a formal definition of the Team's Role
        - The BI team supports and schedules Instruction
            - Handouts
            - New Lesson Plans
            - Outreach and Publicity
            - Scheduling
            - Teaching and helping non-team members in their teaching.
        - Scheduler assigns classes evenly across entire IS department.
            - All teach approximately the same number of classes.
            - All teach the same level of courses: from basic orientations to Graduate Classes.

BI Team
Strengths through sharing

* After role definition, the BI program strengthened.
  - Not concentrating all the work on one person allowed each to work on special projects and overwhelmed no one.
  - Galileo Materials blossomed–
    - Handouts went state-wide for publicity
    - Screenshows and Tutorials were given the time required.
    - Web pages became a possibility because those with the interest had time to devote to new technology
  - All members of the BI team began learning desktop publishing (not just one "in-house" expert).
  - Reference Librarians became more knowledgeable in all areas as they had to teach all types of classes (not just English 102 and library orientations.
  - Adding more people to the BI function meant more energy to pursue goals. One person didn't have to be involved in everything.
  - Other members could compensate for each other's weak spots. Example: creativity versus organization no longer has to be a choice for the program.

BI Team/IS Department
Growth is GOOD for You (so stop complaining)

* The IS department has noticed the following positive changes through the ch in the definition of BI:
  - More credibility with faculty: In the past only those librarians heavily invested in BI were considered "real faculty" by the majority of the teac faculty.
  - Everybody's Reference Desk abilities have improved by having to learn sources more intensively for teaching.
  - All are developing the skills needed for successful presentations, which could affect tenure and promotion.
  - Those who do publish and present are working with team members to d joint or team presentations.
  - No one person is completely responsible for most classes, thus we have resentment or burnout (from teaching). (Those of us who want to even h lives.)
  - Classes less standardized and boring. New faces keep it fresh.
  - Continuity in work flow. If someone is out, work can continue without interruption.

Program Description
Percent of Student Body Served by BI Annually

	1000-3,999	4,000-6,999	7,000-9,999	10,000-12,999	13,000-15,999	16,000-18,999	19,000-40,000
91-100%	97%	100%		98%			
81-90%		86%					
71-80%	75%	73%, 75%	71%		75%		
61-70%		67%,67%,62%,62%,61%	62%				
51-60%	60%	60%					
41-50%	46%, 46%	44%,45%	43%	50%,46%,46%,43%		42%	
31-40%	40%	40%,40%,33%,35%	40%,39%		35%,32%	38%	
21-30%			26%	30%	30%		21%,30%,21%
11-20%	20%			17%	18%	15%	
0-10%	6%						4%

Size of Institution (Full-Time Enrollment)

Program Description
Number of BI Sessions Per Term Taught by those with Primary BI Responsibility

	1000-4,999	5,000-9,999	10,000-14,999	15,000-19,999	20,000-40,000
75-99	75		75		
50-74	60, 50	58, 54	55	50, 50	50, 70, 65
30-49	45, 40, 40	45, 40, 40, 40, 30, 35, 39	33, 30	35, 31	
15-29	15, 17, 20, 20, 24	20, 25, 25, 26,	25, 17		
0-14	10, 10, 12, 14	8, 11, 12	10		

Size of Institution (Full-Time Enrollment)

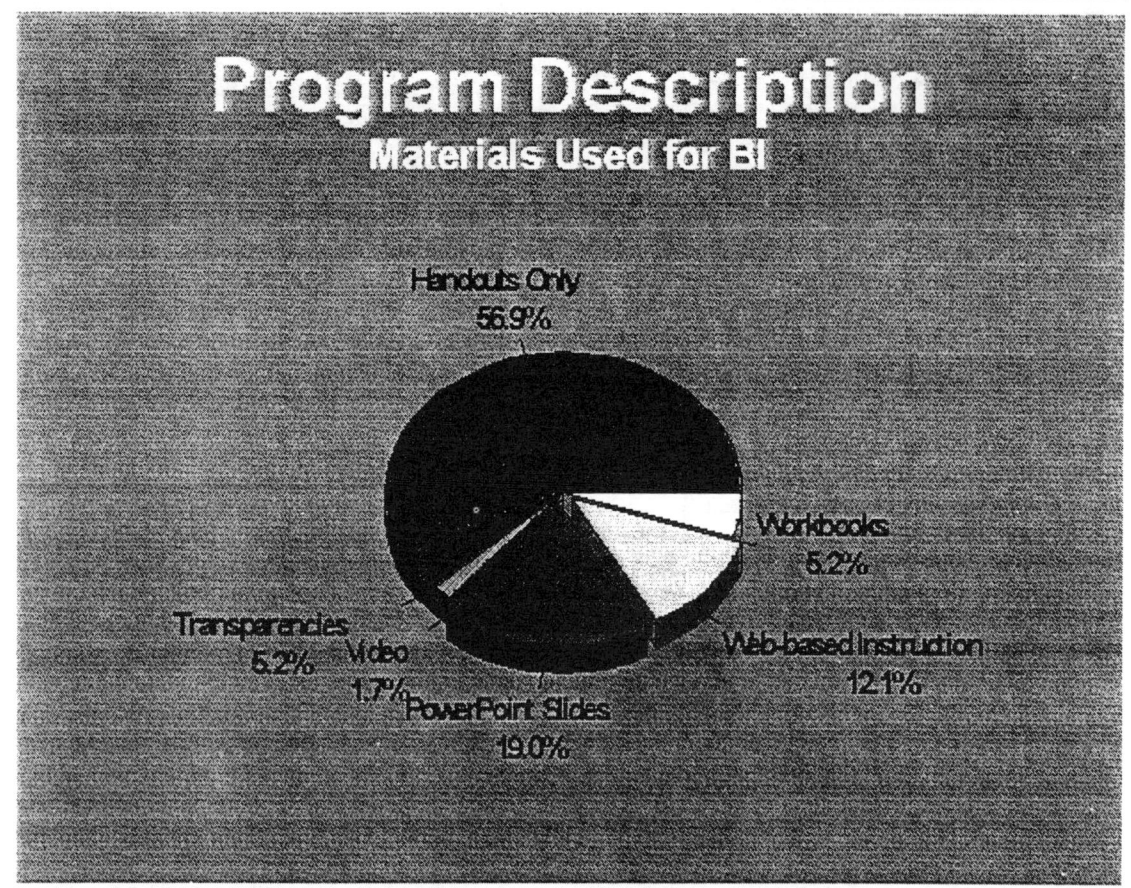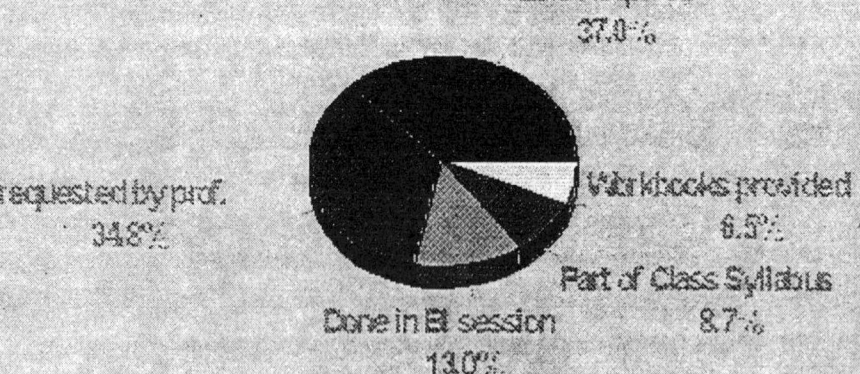

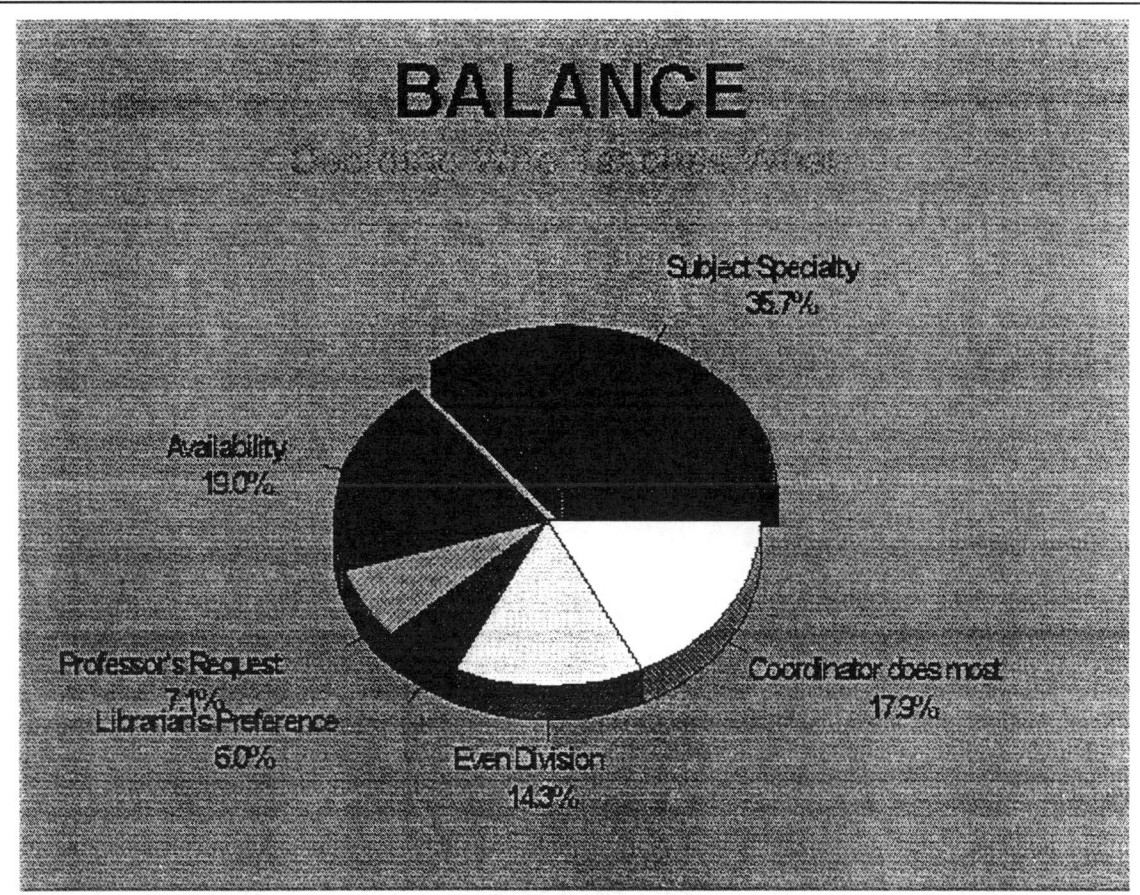

Balance
Do librarians other than BI & Ref teach?

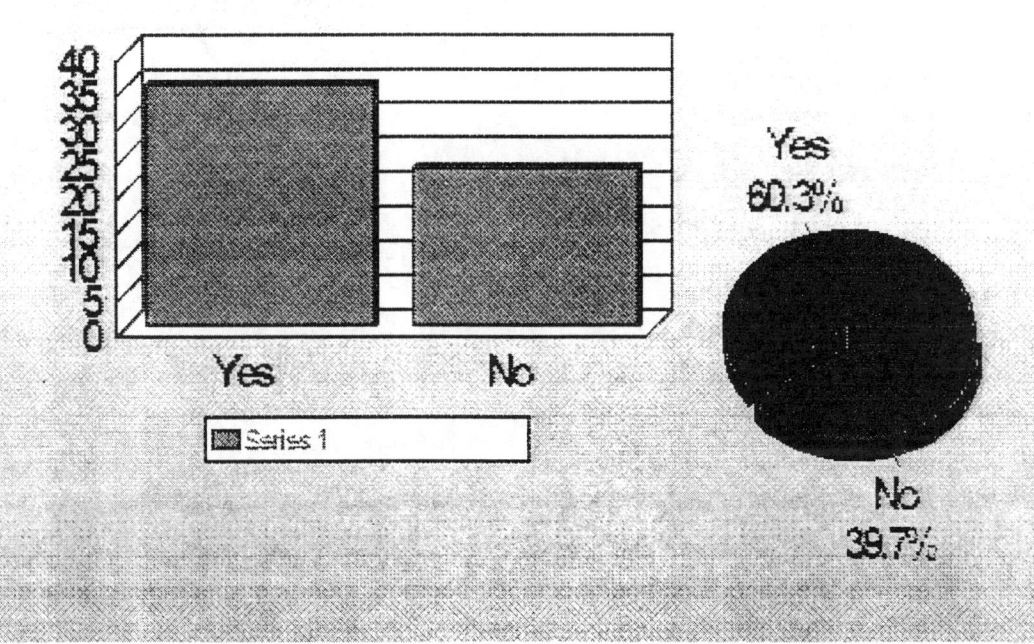

Balance: Reconciling Other Duties

- BI
- Reference
- Collection Development
- Government Docs
- ILL
- Automation
- Cataloging
- Administration
- Web Page Design

"It comes out of your nervous system"

Scheduling

How much notice do you require before teaching a BI session?
ONE OR TWO WEEKS

Who does your scheduling?
MAJORITY: single authority figure
LARGEST MINORITY: individual librarians

Does your scheduler schedule both the librarians and the facilities?
YES

Do you teach in-house or go outside the library?
MAJORITY IN-HOUSE, BUT WILL GO ELSEWHERE

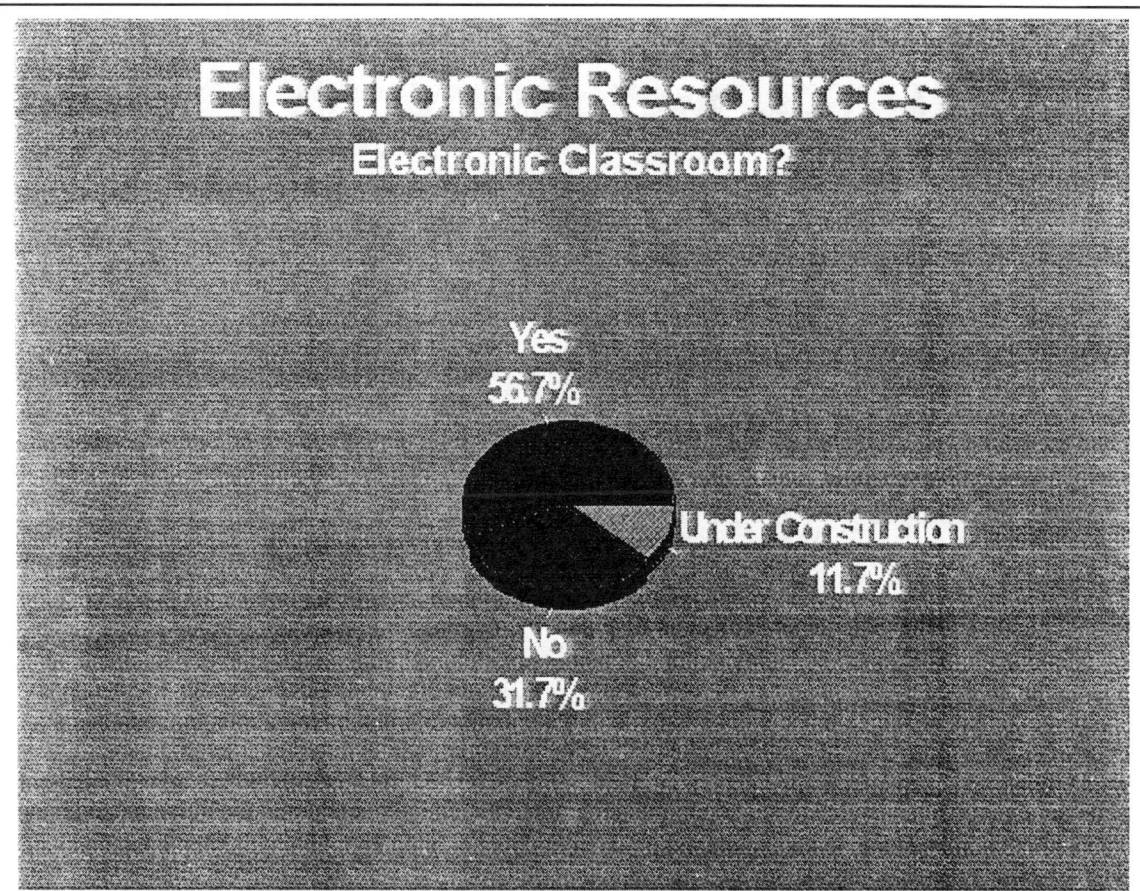
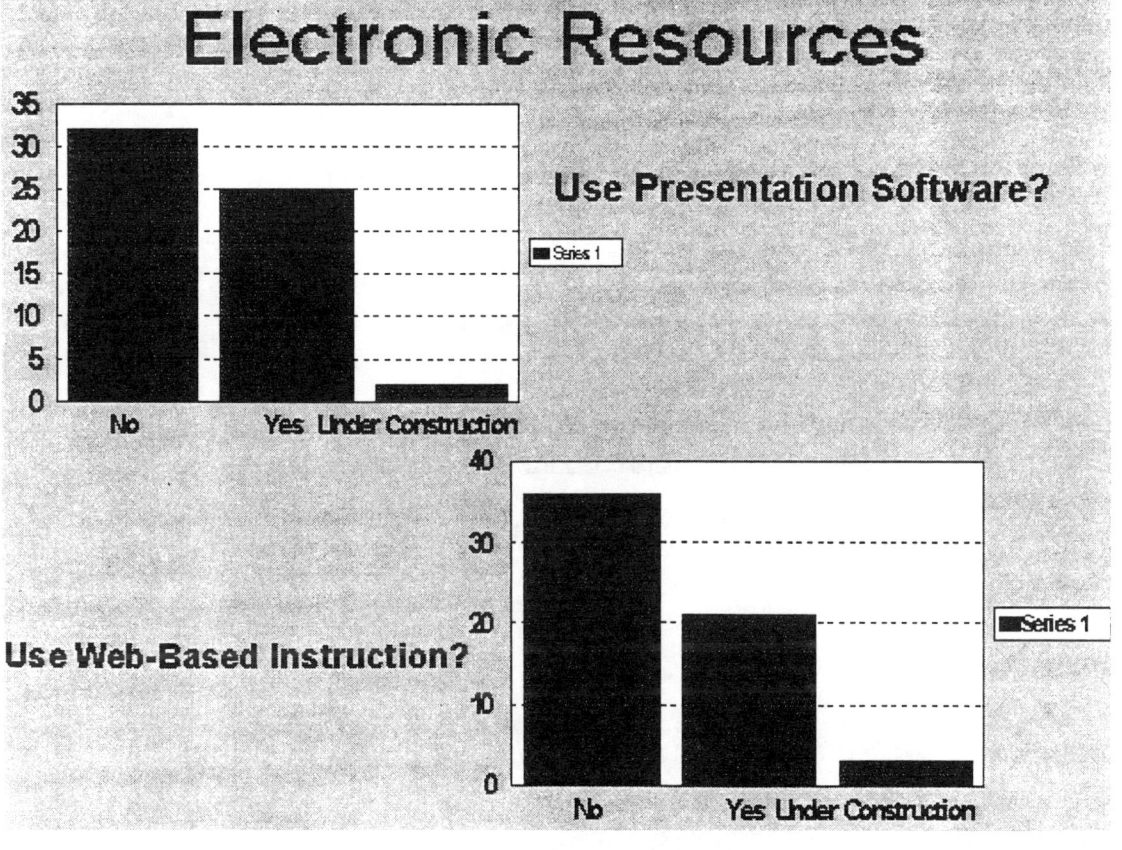

Electronic Resources
Workload Impact

Increases Workload
- More advance preparation necessary
- More "stuff" to cover
- More demand for BI
- People not satisfied with computer and want personal attention
- Require updating

Benefits Workload
- Keeps students' focus better
- Impressive to Faculty
- Can easily customize/change presentations
- Several librarians can use presentation
- Keeps instructor on track and consistent
- Not dependent on outside services
- More fun!

Please send any comments to Deborah S. Davis

Library Homepage Galileo VSU Homepage

Last updated May 15, 1997

Multiple Literacies and Competing Agendas: How Does Information Literacy Fit In?

Tasha Cooper and Loanne Snavely

Librarians recognize the importance of implementing information literacy programs at their institutions of higher learning, but they may face numerous obstacles as they attempt to do so. Competing literacies (computer literacy and environmental literacy, for example) and other curricular issues (inclusion of multiculturalism, diversity) make it difficult for faculty and administrators to find a place for information literacy. Faculty also are being asked to learn to use and incorporate new technologies into their classrooms. As a result, information literacy competes with numerous other demands on limited class time, as well as classroom autonomy. How should librarians move toward putting their ideas about information literacy programs into practice?

Discussion at this session focused on three areas: arguments used to support information literacy programs; understanding the competition and preparing arguments that recognize competing agendas; understanding individual points of view of faculty whose support is necessary for a successful program.

Participants contributed many arguments in support of an information literacy program. But how many of these are not unique to information literacy and can also be claimed by other curricular movements? What are the other competing curricular agendas? Participants were asked what other programs are competing for support on their campuses and were presented with arguments for five worthy ones: writing-across-the-curriculum; a multicultural program; a computer literacy program; an arts appreciation program; and an environmental literacy program. Participants contributed others, such as athletics, numeracy, diversity, critical thinking, and distance learning.

Participants then were asked to put themselves in the shoes of the appropriate chief administrative officers and select the one proposal or combination of proposals that would best prepare undergraduates for the future, support the educational mission, and ensure the longevity of the institution.

Individual faculty reactions to the idea of an information literacy program were then discussed. Comments such as: "I am coming up for tenure next year and I just don't have time to add anything new to my courses. I think un-tenured faculty should be exempted" and "We can now get web sites and journal articles and indexes in our offices. Why do we need a library or an information literacy program? I cover the web in my class and all my research needs are available in my office" were discussed. Participants added lack of time as a recurring competing element.

What arguments can librarians use to garner support for a comprehensive information literacy program? What can we learn from the success of other curricular programs? Writing-across-the-curriculum programs have a fairly firm foothold on many campuses. How was this achieved? What program design is best suited to information literacy? (Across-the-curriculum? Piecemeal? 100-level requirement of all students? Capstone?)

Cooper is instructional services librarian, Lycoming College, Williamsport, Pennsylvania, and *Snavely* is head, Arts Library, Pennsylvania State University, University Park, Pennsylvania.

Discussion participants were from institutions with varying degrees of success in implementing programs. Accreditation requirements were recognized as a strong motivating factor at those schools that have implemented programs. Gaining the support of one or more members of the faculty who will be outspoken advocates and moving outside the library to talk with faculty and understand their concerns were also recommended.

Varying types of programs were described, with acknowledgment that programs need to be individualized to fit a particular institution's style. Program designs included an integrated information literacy-across-the-curriculum program, which would designate certain subject-specific courses as "information" courses and require students to complete one or more of these during the course of their academic careers; an introductory/capstone combination; and an information literacy required course to be taken by all students.

Several participants noted that recognition of the ways in which information is used varies greatly by discipline and were strong advocates for discipline-integrated programs.

Lively discussion followed and ideas and humorous tales were exchanged. The importance of sharing ideas among librarians was recognized, but, probably more significantly, the importance of sharing with faculty was recognized. Participants also noted that many people (librarians as well as faculty and administrators) have widely varying understandings of the phrase information literacy, and clarity is essential for those seeking support.

Establishing an information literacy program represents many challenges, only one of which is moving from the neatly written proposal (theory) to acceptance and implementation (practice).

Library Instruction Lessons Learned the First Year

Laurel Carter

This discussion group provided a forum for first- and second-year librarians to discuss issues and solutions in four areas of our jobs: approaches to teaching, working with faculty, working with library colleagues, and apologizing gracefully. Of these four areas, approaches to teaching and working with faculty are the two that provided the most learning opportunities and issues to solve.

Defining the content of library instruction and negotiating its delivery with faculty required special attention. Some issues included balancing active learning with lectures, shifting from teaching which buttons to push to teaching concepts, and reworking assignments so they started with realistic assumptions of student knowledge and targeted defined outcomes for competency. We found that flexibility is necessary to reach a variety of faculty requests. Negotiating a later date for library instruction sessions, developing self-guided tours and other instructional materials, and teaching the faculty to teach library instruction were ways we found to provide faculty with what they need in a way that matches library goals and time limitations.

Working with faculty can be difficult because of differences in rank and different opinions about what the library should be doing and how it should be done. Whether librarians should have tenure is an issue in a number of colleges and universities, and fulfilling tenure requirements while maintaining excellence in library duties is difficult. Librarians who have liaison relationships with faculty and departments have better access to the faculty communication networks.

The mentoring program in one of the discussion participants' libraries has helped her resolve a number of these issues. The mentor guided her in interacting with faculty, improving her teaching, and working toward tenure. The discussion participants were very interested in this idea and wished more libraries used mentors.

Working with library colleagues did not seem to be much of an issue outside of revising outdated views of library instruction. Being proactive was a key to success when working with others in the library. Sometimes working with colleagues involved apologizing gracefully. Communicating was important to avoid misunderstandings and helped resolve problems. Defining responsibilities and clarifying the division of labor were also important. While apologizing is a necessary part of working with others, in certain situations an apology was unwarranted.

The discussion showed that we learned a great deal in our first two years. What we learned on the job complemented what we learned while working on the M.L.S. Finding mentors and advisers made the first years much easier and helped build confidence. Because we went to library school when the new technological tools were in place, we are a resource to our more experienced colleagues and look forward to working as a team in our individual libraries.

Carter is reference librarian, Duggan Library, Hanover College, Hanover, Indiana.

POSTER SESSIONS

Mystery to Mastery: The California State University (CSU) Information Competence Project

presented by

Sariya Talip Clay
Sallie Harlan
Judy Swanson
(California Polytechnic State University, San Luis Obispo)

Our poster session demonstrates Information Competence modules to be used in library credit courses and college-based courses throughout the general curriculum. These modules are part of a CSU (California State Universities) multi-campus project which arose out of a system-wide Information Competence Workshop held in December 1995. The project includes the library development of classroom multimedia presentations, collaborative in-class exercises, and self-paced interactive WWW instructional modules with an electronic workbook component. The purpose of the project is to teach CSU students information competence skills in an integrated process.

The instructional modules are based on 10 core competencies suggested by the CSU Work Group on Information Competence. These include:

- defining a topic
- determining information requirements
- locating and retrieving relevant information
- using technological tools
- evaluating information
- organizing and synthesizing information
- communicating information
- understanding ethical, legal and socio-political information issues
- media literacy
- judging the product and the process

The demonstration focuses on the interactive WWW-based electronic workbook which is designed to utilize split screen technologies. The design also places heavy emphasis on graphics, images, sample pages, excerpts from full-text sources, citations, and other relevant materials to provide a realistic learning environment. Using the electronic workbook, students are able to view instructional tips, examples, and exercises and simultaneously record answers on an electronic assignment sheet.

The poster session also provides information on a newly created, 3-unit Information Competence course at San Luis Obispo. This course integrates library, computer, media, and technological literacies and includes instruction on ethics, critical thinking, and communication skills. Collaborative and active learning techniques are emphasized.

Short Macromedia Director presentations developed to support class instruction are also demonstrated. These multimedia presentations utilize 3-D objects, animations, Quicktime movies, and sound to enhance the teaching of information competence concepts, skills and strategies.

Poster session 1 (Clay/Harlan/Swanson): Part 1 - Mystery to Mastery

CALIFORNIA STATE UNIVERSITY INFORMATION COMPETENCE PROJECT

http://www.lib.calpoly.edu/infocomp

As information proliferates and technology becomes more sophisticated, it is imperative that a person be "information competent" i.e. be able to find, evaluate, use, and communicate information efficiently and effectively. Therefore, incorporating information competence into the core curriculum and library instruction has become increasingly important.

Our poster session demonstrates Information Competence modules to be used in library credit courses and college-based courses throughout the general curriculum. These modules are part of a CSU (California State Universities) multi-campus project which arose out of a system-wide Information Competence Workshop held in December 1995. The project includes the library development of classroom multimedia presentations, collaborative in-class exercises, and self-paced interactive WWW instructional modules with an electronic workbook component. The purpose of the project is to teach CSU students information competence skills in an integrated process.

The instructional modules are based on 10 core competencies suggested by the CSU Work Group on Information Competence. These include: defining a topic; determining information requirements; locating and retrieving relevant information; using technological tools; evaluating information; organizing and synthesizing information; communicating information; understanding ethical, legal and socio-political information issues; media literacy; and evaluating the product and the process.

WEB-BASED TUTORIALS

Instructional Section

Workbook Section

‡Certain materials are included under the Fair Use exemption of the U.S. Copyright law and have been prepared according to the Multimedia Fair Use Guidelines and are restricted from further use.

Poster session 1 (Clay/Harlan/Swanson): Part 2 - California State University Information Competence Project

3-Unit Information Competence Course at Cal Poly San Luis Obispo

LIB 304X: Information Competence. Instruction on finding, evaluating, using, and communicating information in all its various formats. Integrates library literacy, computer literacy, media literacy, technological literacy, ethics, critical thinking, and communication skills. 3 lectures. No prerequisites.

Course Outline

1. Introduction to the course, covering goals, expectations, assessment; explanation of groups/ collaborative learning format, and information competence concepts. Instruction on developing a viable research topic using critical thinking skills.

2. Instruction on determining the information requirements for a research question, problem, or issue.

3. Instruction on locating and retrieving relevant information. Emphasis on access points and search concepts/strategies using Polycat.

4. Instruction on using technological tools to access information. Emphasis on database selection, access points, search concepts/strategies. Instruction on communicating information using a variety of formats and technologies. Introduction to electronic page layout design with emphasis on user interface.

5. Instruction on evaluating information for relevance, currency, reliability, coverage/completeness, and accuracy. Introduction to Microsoft PowerPoint and its uses as a computer-based slidemaking presentation tool.

6. Instruction on organizing and synthesizing information. Introduction to Adobe PDF (Portable Document Format).

7. Instruction promoting awareness of the ethical, legal and socio-political issues surrounding information and information technology. Introduction to HTML (HyperText Markup Language).

8. Instruction on using, evaluating and treating critically information received from the mass media. Introduction to Adobe Pagemill (a WYSIWYG HTML editor).

9. Instruction on judging the product and the process. Comparison of the various electronic formats and their appropriate uses.

10. Presentation of student projects.

The course attempts to teach students information competence. Beginning sessions focus on the need for information competence and its application in university course work and lifelong learning. Each week provides in-depth instruction on a specific competence. Weeks 4 - 9 include instruction on various presentation formats and tools. The course concludes with student presentations of projects.

For more information, see the Expanded Course Outline at: **http://www.lib.calpoly.edu/infocomp/project/index.html**

Poster session 1 (Clay/Harlan/Swanson): Part 3 - Unit Information Competence Course

Classroom for the New Millennium: Design, Use and Management of a Library Instruction Multimedia Room

Donna Lehman and Charlene Loope, Reference Librarians
Thomas Cooper Library
University of South Carolina, Columbia

In keeping with this year's conference theme of "Theory and Practice," this poster session presented our library's rationale for creating an electronic classroom and the instructional methods we have found to be effective in this environment. In describing instruction in the electronic classroom, we organized the session into four sections: Technology, Design, Management and Instruction.

Technology – The multimedia classroom contains thirty IBM compatible workstations as well as an instructor's station at the front of room. This station allows the instructor to connect and operate all projection, audio, and video equipment from one central point.

Design – In designing the classroom, much thought was given to the room's location within the library, the arrangement of equipment and furniture, and the placement of the instructor's controls. Lighting, comfort and overall atmosphere were also taken into consideration in the design phase. In addition, steps were taken to insure that the room complied with the Americans with Disabilities Act.

Management – The classroom is managed by a librarian who acts as the classroom supervisor. This person is the main referral for scheduling the room, for basic maintenance, troubleshooting and appearance.

Instruction – Since opening in the fall of 1996, 103 instruction sessions were led by librarians in the classroom and approximately twenty hours of instruction took place in the room each week. We anticipate that these numbers will increase as awareness of this resource becomes more widespread on campus. Instruction sessions in the room have reached students, faculty, staff and our library colleagues. This classroom has benefited our instruction program in a variety of ways including allowing for greater flexibility in instruction and active, hands-on learning for students.

The following pages describe in detail the four sections of this poster session and include additional resources for design and instruction in an electronic classroom.

Poster session 2 (Lehman/Loope): Part 1 - Classroom for the New Millennium

Technology Purchases

- Sony VPH-1272Q Superdata Ex Multiscan Graphics/Data Video Projector (with an Analog RGB interface module, support bracket and suspension support, and cabling): *$17, 493.00*

- Elmo Visual Presenter, with twin light option kit: *$3,000.000*

- Elmo Slide/Video Unit: *$2809.00*

- Sony VHS Video Cassette Recorder: *$375.00*

- Sony Audio Cassette Deck: *$185.00*

- Performer Stereo Switcher: *$1, 092.00*

- DA-lite Boardroom Electrol Projection Screen (60" x 80") with video format spectre surface and 3-position control switch: *$1,299.60*

- Ethernet Adapter 5PK: *$479.00 each*

- Ethernet Adapter 20 PK: *$1706.00*

- PCs: Dell 590/XL Base with 256K Cache and IM Video RAM, Keyboards, 32MB RAM, and Multisync Color monitors: approximately *$3,250.00 each*

- 32 Mouse pads: *$1.00 each*

- 32 Surge protectors, with 6 outlet extensions: *$2.50 each*

- 40 Chairs without arms: *$92.50 each*

- HP LaserJet series IV laser printer: *$1,950.90*

- Storage cabinet: *$177.00* (for audio equipment)

- Counter-high instructor's table: *$260.00*

- Instructor's adjustable stool: *$251.00*

- 28 Computer workstations (30" x 36" x 26" h) : *$71.50 each*

- 2 Computer workstations (30" x 36" x 30" h) (wheelchair accessible) : *$73.50 each*

Total expenditures: $28,502.50

Poster session 2 (Lehman/Loope): Part 2 - Technology Purchases

Classroom Design

Location of classroom within the library
The Multimedia Classroom is located on a quiet floor of the library apart from the main flow of pedestrian traffic. The room contains no windows and is removed from areas that could produce noise distractions.

Arrangement of equipment and furniture
All 28 workstations face the front of the classroom at a slight angle to improve visibility of the projection screen from all locations in the room. The instructor station is located at the front of the room near the projection screen facing the student workstations. This location allows the instructor easy access to the screen and the white board, and improved visibility and audibility to the class.

Placement of controls
All of the controls for the classroom are within arm's reach of the instructor's station. This feature improves the flow of instruction and minimizes down time in the classroom. The central control panel is located on the instructor's desk. This panel, called the "Elmo," operates all of the computer and audio/visual equipment in the room. The video equipment cabinet and the light switches are also adjacent to the instructor's desk.

Lighting, comfort, overall atmosphere
The Multimedia Classroom has a theater-like atmosphere that is conducive to teaching and learning. The walls and carpeting are a neutral color. The room does not have windows, so glare and other visual distractions are not problematic. The lighting is designed to be versatile and to accommodate the many functions of the room. Four rows of lights operate independently of each other and all are equipped with dimmer switches.

ADA compliance
The classroom is located in an easily accessible location in the library. Two student workstations are adapted for wheelchair access, and screen enlargement software is available for use on any of the workstations. The instructor's desk was also designed to meet ADA height and width requirements.

Poster session 2 (Lehman/Loope): Part 3 - Classroom Design

Management of the Multimedia Classroom

Classroom Supervisor
We have a permanent classroom supervisor/librarian who is in charge of day-to-day operations of the classroom. The supervisor's schedule is not fixed, but flexible so that she can be available at the times the classroom will be in use. She is the main referral for scheduling the room, for basic maintenance, troubleshooting and appearance. She works closely with the Bibliographic Instruction coordinator to ensure that the room is being utilized and operating efficiently. She reports to the head of the reference department and in addition to her other duties, works several hours each week at the reference desk.

Scheduler
The room is scheduled via GroupWise - a software program used throughout the library. This scheduler is accessible to only a few librarians (including the classroom supervisor and the Bibliographic Instruction coordinator). Only these people have authorization to schedule the classroom. The fact that the schedule is accessible from each desk PC allows for ease of scheduling and easy checking of what is happening in the classroom at any given time.

Equipment and Policies
Each person who teaches in the room receives training in classroom equipment use and policies. The classroom supervisor schedules time with each new librarian in order to introduce them to the equipment and how to best use the facility for teaching. Everyone who uses the classroom is aware of the policies:

- No food or drink allowed

- Only University classes or seminars with trained instructors may use the room

- It is not used as a "computer lab" for individual student use

- Library-related classes/instruction have priority over other uses

- The classroom utilizes a security system which identifies each user affiliated with the University when logging on

Poster session 2 (Lehman/Loope): Part 4 - Management of the Multimedia Classroom

Instruction in the Multimedia Classroom

Quick Facts
- Approximately 20 hours of instruction takes place in the room each week
- Since opening in the fall of 1996, 103 instruction sessions have been led by librarians in the electronic classroom
- Most sessions in the classroom are conducted by librarians, but any member of the university community may use the room for instruction

Who and What Are We Teaching?

Students
- Course-related instruction in all subject areas led by librarians
- Heavy use by the Freshman Year Seminar course to teach use of email
- Use by other faculty members for various teaching activities
(i.e., viewing videos, conducting writing workshops, exploring Internet resources)

Faculty and Staff Members
- Workshops on how to use networked resources (CD-ROMs, Internet databases)
- Internet searching workshops
    → How to Search; Evaluating Internet Resources; Grant Funding Sources on the Web
- OPAC instruction

Librarians
- Professional development seminars
- Product demonstrations by vendors
- Training opportunities for librarians from USC and from around the state

Benefits to the Instruction Program
- Greater flexibility is possible during instruction sessions
- Librarians excited about using the classroom
- Active, hands-on learning for students
- Opportunity for students to begin actual research during instruction
- Library instruction becoming integrated into more courses

Poster session 2 (Lehman/Loope): Part 5 - Instruction in the Multimedia Classroom

Software Used in the Classroom

The classroom is connected both to the University mainframe and the library's Local Area Network, which runs using Novell Netware Version 4.1. This allows for great variety and flexibility in teaching. Not only can librarians give hands-on instruction in the use of the library's online catalog and indexes on CD-ROM, we can also instruct professors in the use of the Internet and teach students how to use their e-mail accounts. English composition instructors have even used the word processing software in the classroom to conduct a "writing laboratory" for their students. to begin writing an assignment in a word processing program while helping each edit and clarify their writing.

Available on each machine is:
- Wordperfect 6.1
- Word for Windows 95
- Microsoft Office
- Lan Work Place
- Quattro Pro for Windows
- Paradox for Windows
- Netscape and Explorer for searching the World Wide Web
- mainframe access to the Internet (including e-mail and Lynx)
- mainframe access to the library's OPAC
- Access to the library LAN and to the 40 CD-ROMs available on it (covering all subject areas)

Examples of classes taught in the classroom are:

An educational psychology graduate class learns to search ERIC on CD-ROM, and find the Buros Mental Measurements page on the World Wide Web

How to search the online catalog and the Humanities Index for an English 101 class assignment

Faculty learn how to find grant and funding sources in their research areas on the Web

Library staff members learn how to search the Library of Congress catalogs to verify citations

Dialog instructors teach local librarians how to effectively search Dialog databases

Poster session 2 (Lehman/Loope): Part 6 - Software Used in the Classroom

Tips for Teaching in the Electronic Classroom

This handout provides a practical set of precautions and suggestions for dealing with a few of the special circumstances presented in the electronic classroom. How do you make sure that everyone is able to keep up with your instruction? What steps can you take to make a session in the electronic classroom particularly effective and worthwhile? And how do you deal with unexpected technical problems?

Keep It Together . . .

- Wait for everyone to become settled and attentive before beginning a session. Students with little computer experience may be left behind if they miss the first step.

- Pause before you hit the enter key or click on a hyperlink! Give students an opportunity to see the operation or search you have just performed before you execute it.

- When switching from one application to another, be certain to give a step-by-step account of how to perform the switch. Try to anticipate the possible problems students may experience and ask if anyone "has a different screen" than the one you are projecting.

- Build time into your session to walk around the classroom in order to monitor students' needs for assistance. Some students may be hesitant to ask for help if they have to interrupt you while you are speaking from the instructor's station. Taking the time to roam around the room periodically will make you more accessible and encourage students to seek help.

Time Well Spent . . .

- Allow time for students to conduct searches on topics pertinent to their own interests or research. Offer the opportunity to print or download search results in the classroom.

- Make certain that the instruction setting matches the actual environment in which students will be working. Access to the system and databases in the

Poster session 2 (Lehman/Loope): Part 7 - Tips for Teaching in the Electronic Classroom electronic classroom should match as closely as possible access at the public workstations.

•Particularly in large classes, consider having a second person available in the classroom to assist students with any difficulties they may encounter. This will save the instruction session from being interrupted if a student needs individual attention to correct technical problems.

•When teaching a specific course-related session, collaborate with the course instructor to provide relevant examples in your instruction session. Also invite the course instructor to comment on the search results. *For example: Which periodical titles are most like what he or she expects students to cite?*

•Bring print resources into the electronic classroom. The overhead projector is a great way to demonstrate a print resource. Feel free to mix the media – demonstrate that electronic information is not superior to print information.

•Don't try to include too many electronic databases in one session. Choose only as many resources to demonstrate as will comfortably fit in the time period allotted.

•As you perform demonstrations, include fairly detailed verbal descriptions of what you are doing. Some students may learn best through listening and will be better able to follow the class.

Don't Hit the Panic Button . . .

•If you experience technical problems and cannot gain access to the electronic resources you need, have a back-up plan. It may be useful to have a general Power Point presentation or set of overheads available in the electronic classroom as back-up materials.

•Use a technical problem as an opportunity to (briefly!) explain the library's network, why such a problem may occur, or where else we might look for information.

•Use down time due to technical problems to consult with students individually about paper topics or research strategies.

Poster session 2 (Lehman/Loope): Part 7 - Tips for Teaching in the Electronic Classroom (continued)

Classroom for the New Millennium:
Additional Resources

Introduction: This bibliography lists resources about electronic classrooms. Both journal articles and web sites are included. This is not an exhaustive list of sources, but rather a general introduction to the literature and some items we have found to be particularly useful.

I. Articles

Aiken, Milam and Delvin Dawley. "Designing an Electronic Classroom for Large College Courses." T.H.E. Journal, vol. 23, n2, Sept. 1995, pp. 76-77.

This article describes a new electronic classroom in use at the University of Mississippi School of Business which was particularly designed for large, regularly scheduled classes.

Barker, Bruce and Bruce Harris. "Establishing and Using an Electronic Classroom: The Western Illinois University Experience." 1993. ED 360958. (Paper presented at the regional "Teaching with Technology" Conference, Moline, IL, April 23-24, 1993.)

Describes a new electronic classroom at the Western Illinois University which uses advanced technologies for large image video projection as well as the ability to project microscopic views. The design, hardware, development and costs are described.

Glogoff, Stuart. "Library Instruction in the Electronic Library: The University of Arizona's Electronic Library Education Centers." Reference Services Review, Summer 1995, pp. 7-12.

This article profiles the two Electronic Library Education Centers at the University of Arizona libraries which allow students to actively participate in their library instruction sessions.

Poster session 2 (Lehman/Loope): Part 8 - Classroom for the New Millennium: Additional Resources

Watkins, Beverly. "The Electronic Classroom." <u>Chronicle of Higher Education</u>, vol. 38, n.2, Sept. 4, 1991, pp. 26-28.

Describes the Vanderbilt University experience with an electronic classroom. It is being used increasingly by faculty in all disciplines and is encouraging the development of new teaching ideas and techniques.

II. World Wide Web Sites:

Zauha, Jan "Electronic Classroom Planning, Renne Library, Montana State University, Bozeman". URL: http://www.lib.montana.edu/~alijz/eleclass.html

This site contains links to other Internet sites which discuss or display current options for electronic classrooms. Included is a discussion of equipment and design issues with regard to Montana State's electronic classroom.

"Classroom Products and Technology Infrastructure: A Buyer's Guide". URL: http://www.syllabus.com/classproducts.html

This site is a "guide to the products that support technology integration on campus." It includes descriptions of authoring tools, projectors, multimedia presentation systems and peripherals. The site is copywritten by Syllabus Press, Inc. and is part of the larger "Syllabus Mart" site which describes more software and hardware and is available at http://www.syllabus.com/syllmart.html.

"The University of Iowa Libraries Information Arcade - The Electronic Classroom". URL: http://www.arcade.uiowa.edu/arcade/classroom.index.html

This is a good descriptions of the electronic classroom at the University of Iowa's Information Arcade. It includes sections describing their policies, software availability, handbook for instructors, etc.

Poster session 2 (Lehman/Loope): Part 8 - Classroom for the New Millennium: Additional Resources (continued)

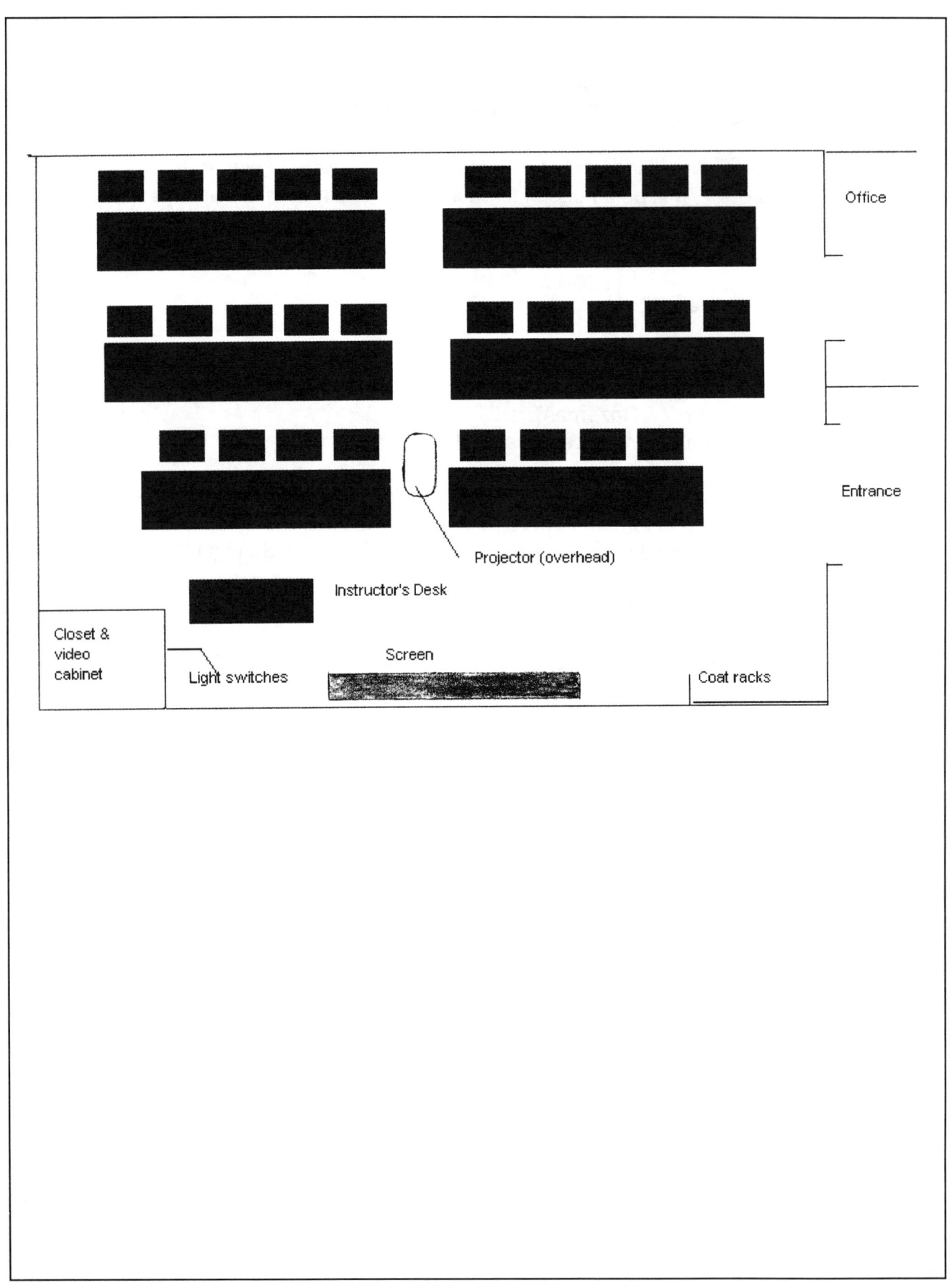

Poster session 2 (Lehman/Loope): Part 8 - Classroom for the New Millennium: Additional Resources (continued)

Library Instruction Web Pages: The Carleton Library Experience

25th National LOEX Library Instruction Conference Poster Session

May 8-10, 1997, Charleston, South Carolina

Many libraries are exploring ways to provide some types of library instruction via the World Wide Web. This poster session demonstrates how this has been done at Carleton College, a 4-year liberal arts college.

- **Background**
- **Advantages of Web-Based Library Instruction**
- **Disadvantages of Web-Based Library Instruction**

- **Tips for Instruction Page Development**
- **Sample Topics for Web-Based Library Instruction**
- **Where to Learn More about Web-Based Library Instruction**

Carleton Library Instruction Page

Maintained by Terry Metz, temetz@carleton.edu
Last updated: May 5, 1997
URL: http://www.library.carleton.edu/instruction/loex/index.html

Poster session 3 (Metz): Part 1 - Library Instruction Web Pages

Background

Contents: <u>About Carleton College</u> | <u>About the College Library</u> | <u>About Library Instruction at Carleton</u> | <u>Carleton Library Instruction Pages</u> | <u>Tools Used in These Efforts</u>

About Carleton College

<u>Carleton College</u> is a highly selective liberal arts college offering 1,900 men and women degrees in 33 fields of study and 7 interdisciplinary programs. It is consistently ranked among the top liberal arts institutions nationally for the quality of its educational enterprise.

The campus, athletic fields, and arboretum are situated on 900 acres in historic <u>Northfield, MN,</u>, which is located 45 miles south of <u>Minneapolis/St. Paul</u>.

Return to Contents

About the College Library

<u>Carleton College's Laurence McKinley Gould Library</u> houses one the finest undergraduate library collections in the U.S. The building, which was extensivley remodeled and expanded in 1985, houses over 500,000 volumes, 1,500 active journal subscriptions, and is automated with an <u>Innovative Interfaces</u> library automation system.

The library participates in <u>MINITEX</u> (a statewide cooperative library network), <u>OCLC</u>, <u>CNI</u>, and is a member of the <u>Oberlin Group Libraries</u>.

The library employs 9 librarians and 16 support staff. Librarians are classified as administrative staff and do not serve on faculty curricular committees.

Return to Contents

About Library Instruction at Carleton

Library instruction has not been a leading component of library service at Carleton College during the past few decades. From the early 1980s until the middle 1990s one librarian was responsible for devoting half of her time to library instruction duties. Most instruction was arranged for an interested, but small, cadre of faculty who generated library instruction demand. Traditionally, there has been no formal library instruction for incoming students and faculty.

Beginning this past academic year, the half-time of a second librarian has also been devoted to library instruction. In addition, the two librarians involved have begun using Web pages to support their instruction efforts.

Return to Contents

Carleton Library Instruction Pages

The Web <u>pages devoted to library instruction</u> were created in the early spring of 1996. This site has now grown to a family of over 50 pages.

Return to Contents

Tools Used in These Efforts

- **Hardware**
    - operating a Web server (on a Macintosh computer) since late summer 1994
    - current device is a Power Macintosh 7100/66 using 32MB RAM
- **Software**
    - Web server - WebStar 2.0
    - HTML authoring - BBEdit Lite 4.0, Adobe PageMill 2.0, & Claris Home Page 2.0

Return to Contents

<u>LOEX Poster Session Main Menu</u>

Maintained by <u>Terry Metz, temetz@carleton.edu</u>
Last updated: May 6, 1997
URL: http://www.library.carleton.edu/instruction/loex/background.html

Poster session 3 (Metz): Part 2 - Background

Advantages of Web-Based Library Instruction

Just-in-Time Delivery

Users can access your materials seven days a week, twenty-four hours a day. Materials can be printed on demand.

Easy to Update

Corrections and revisions to your instruction materials are instantaneous. You don't need to prepare and duplicate many copies of paper handouts every time your revise the content of your materials. In addition, your site can grow and become more rich over time.

Multi-Platform

Any networked computer can access your materials.

Attracts Young Adults

Many "Generation X" age students enjoy using the Web.

Multimedia

Your materials can include images, sounds, or video, in addition to text.

Enhances Library's Image

Highlights the library's willingness to adapt new technology.

Disadvantages of Web-Based Library Instruction | LOEX Poster Session Main Menu

Maintained by Terry Metz, temetz@carleton.edu
Last updated: May 6, 1997
URL: http://www.library.carleton.edu/instruction/loex/advan.html

Poster session 3 (Metz): Part 3 - Advantages of Web-Based Library Instruction

Disdvantages of Web-Based Library Instruction

May Reduce Face-to-Face Contact

Instruction received remotely via the Web may reduce the personal contact between librarians and users.

Access Not Universal

Not all library users (especially students) have convenient access to networked computers required to access the Web.

Learning Curve for Producers

Composers and producers of Web publications and instructional materials must develop expertise in Web authoring techniques and tools. This does not take a trivial amount of time and effort. However, this drawback can be ameliorated by teaching student employees to author Web pages and maintain Web server.

Advantages of Web-Based Library Instruction | LOEX Poster Session Main Menu

Maintained by Terry Metz, temetz@carleton.edu
Last updated: May 5, 1997
URL: http://www.library.carleton.edu/instruction/loex/disadvan.html

Poster session 3 (Metz): Part 4 - Disadvantages of Web-Based Library Instruction

Tips for Instruction Page Development

You've decided you want some library instruction Web pages. Now what? Here is a step-by-step outline for developing them.

1. Define your purpose
2. Assemble a team
3. Prepare a Plan
    - Identify your objectives
    - Decide how to use the technology
    - Establish the "look and feel" of the site
    - Create content
    - Identify future support requirements

4. Collect and convert site content
5. Maintain and update your site

- Where You Might Go From Here
    - Learn how to produce HTML pages.

LOEX Poster Session Main Menu

Maintained by Terry Metz, temetz@carleton.edu
Last updated: May 5, 1997
URL: http://www.library.carleton.edu/instruction/loex/tipsoutline.html

Poster session 3 (Metz): Part 5 - Tips for Instruction Page Development

Learn More about Web-Based Library Instruction

Contents: Examples of Web-Based Library Instruction Sites | Web-Based Information Literacy Initiatives | Other Lists of Web-Based Library Instruction Sources | Other Organizations with Web-Based Instruction Interests

---

Examples of Web-Based Library Instruction Sites

Beardsley, Sylvia. (University of Wisconsin - Parkside)
    Information Literacy Skills Workbook
    <http://www.uwp.edu/library/toc.html>

    A component of UWP's Information Literacy Program.

Davis, Deborah. (Valdosta State University)
    Welcome to the Searching Page
    <http://www.valdosta.edu/~dsdavis/main.htm>

    Search strategy basics. The author also maintains a collection of course-specific guides.

Engle, Michael. (Cornell University)
    Library Research at Cornell: A Hypertext Guide
    <http://www.library.cornell.edu/okuref/research/tutorial.html>

    "...a simple and effective strategy for finding information for a research paper, writing the paper, and documenting the sources you find."

Georgia State University Libraries.
    OLLI Tutorial
    <http://wwwlib.gsu.edu/databases/olli/ollitutor/>

    A basic orientation to using OLLI, the library's online catalog.

Gustavus Adolphus College Library.
    Library Research Tutorial
    <http://www.gac.edu/Academics/Resources/Library/tutorial.html>

    A tutorial "...intended to clarify the research process and describe strategies can be used for various parts of the process."

Holcomb, Athena. (University of Central Florida)
    LUISQuest
    <http://pegasus.cc.ucf.edu/~library/luisquest/00luisq.htm>

    Gives a basic orientation to using the LUIS, the library's online catalog.

James Madison University Libraries.
    Go for the Gold
    <http://www.jmu.edu/libliaison/masonal/new_gold/modules.htm>

    Designed to help library users "...formulate and conduct an effective information search that includes a variety of reference sources, such as encyclopedias, library catalogs, indexes, bibliographies, statistics sources, government publications, and resources available on the Internet.."

Laverty, Cory. (Queen's University)

Poster session 3 (Metz): Part 6 - Learn More about Web-Based Library Instruction

Tutorials
<http://stauffer.queensu.ca/inforef/instruct/tutor.htm>

Eight online aids to various tools and research guides.

Mateer, Karen. (Augsburg College)
Augsburg College Internet Basics
<http://www.augsburg.edu/library/aib/>

"If you know nothing about the Internet and want to be introduced to it gently, this is the source for you...[you will] become literate about the 'information superhighway.'"

Metz, Terry. (Carleton College)
Web Search Tools Research Page
<http://www.library.carleton.edu/websearch/welcome.html>

Examines Web search tools--what are they? how do they function? how do you use them effectivley?

New Mexico State University Libraries.
Library Shortcuts
<http://lib.nmsu.edu/projects/tutorial/index.html>

An online respository of instructional materials for users of New Mexico State University's libraries.

Parker-Gibson, Necia. (University of Arkansas)
Jumpstart!
<http://www.uark.edu/libinfo/refdept/instruction/index.html>

Basic library orientation with a quiz.

Salt Lake Community College Library.
Library Tutorial: The Quick and Painless Guide on How to Start Getting Around the Library
<http://www.slcc.edu/lr/library/libwork/tutorial.htm>

Basic library orientation.

Scholz, Ann. (Purdue University)
PLUTO: Purdue Libraries Undergraduate Tutorial Online
<http://thorplus.lib.purdue.edu/library_info/instruction/tutorials/pluto/index.html>

"PLUTO teaches new users of the Purdue Libraries' system how to search for information in electronic databases. It focuses on keyword search concepts and methods."

University of British Columbia Libraries.
Stars Tutorial: Startup Research Skills
<http://unixg.ubc.ca:7001/0/tutorial/stars/start.html>

Gives a basic orientation to using the UBCLIB, the library's online information system.

University of California, San Diego, Science and Engineering Library.
Guide to Compendex on Inn-View
<http://scilib.ucsd.edu/electclass/Compendex.html>

A tutorial for an online index..

University of Cincinnati Libraries.
Library Instruction 101: How to Use the Library
<http://www.libraries.uc.edu/libinfo/freshman.html>

A tutorial is designed to teach basic library skills and research strategies.

Poster session 3 (Metz): Part 6 - Learn More about Web-Based Library Instruction (continued)

University of Delaware Libraries.
>   Virtual Library Tutor
>   <http://www.lib.udel.edu/tutor/>
>
>   Designed primarily for an introductory level English course assignment.

University of Northern Colorado, Library/Learning Center.
>   UNC Libraries Library Tutor
>   <http://www.univnorthco.edu/library/libtutor/libtutor.htm>
>
>   A Web-based tutorial used for college research paper classes at UNC.

University of Utah.
>   Internet Navigator
>   <http://medstat.med.utah.edu/navigator/>
>
>   A multi-institutional Internet course, sponsored by the Spencer S. Eccles Health Sciences Library and the Utah Academic Library Consortium (UALC), complete with quizzes.

University of Waterloo Libraries.
>   UW Electronic Library Resources by Discipline
>   <http://www.lib.uwaterloo.ca/discipline/discip.html>
>
>   Several dozen examples of topical electronic pathfinders.

University of Wisconsin - Green Bay Libraries.
>   Library Research at UWGB: A Hypertext Guide
>   <http://www.uwgb.edu/~library/tutorial.htm>
>
>   Modeled on Michael Engle's Library Research at Cornell.

Valdez, Esteban. (University of California-San Diego)
>   Contemporary Issues 50: Information & Academic Libraries
>   <http://orpheus.ucsd.edu/ugl/ci50/>
>
>   "...an introductory course for teaching research methods primarily, but not exclusively, delivered through libraries. It provides a basic approach to information arrangement and access, with an emphasis on technology and the UCSD library system."

Return to Contents

Web-Based Information Literacy Initiatives

Bartelstein, Andrea, and Zald, Anne.
>   Teaching Students to Think Critically about Internet Resources
>   <http://weber.u.washington.edu/~libr560/NETEVAL/>
>
>   A University of Washington workshop exposing faculty to the issues of evaluating Internet resources.

California State University System.
>   CSU Information Compentence Project
>   <http://multiweb.lib.calpoly.edu/infocomp/index.html>
>
>   "This site has been constructed to provide a focal point for the Information Competence initiatives within the California State University system. The site is currently maintained by the Kennedy Library at Cal Poly, San Luis Obispo."

Colorado Department of Education.

Poster session 3 (Metz): Part 6 - Learn More about Web-Based Library Instruction (continued)

Colorodo Model Information Literacy Guidelines
<http://www.cde.state.co.us/infolitg.htm>

A list of curricular objectives.

Evans, Linda, et al. (Maricopa County Community College)
Report on Information Literacy
<http://hakatai.mcli.dist.maricopa.edu/ocotillo/report94/rep7.html>

Identifies models offering a "...springboard for other experiments in preparing students for life and work in the Information Age.

Griffith University, Australia.
Information Literacy Blueprint
<http://www.gu.edu.au/gwis/ins/infolit/blueprnt.htm>

A strategic plan for introducing information literacy at the university level.

Holman, Jill. (University of Oregon)
Get Ready: The Basics of Information Technology for Incoming Students
<http://libweb.uoregon.edu/getready/>

A pilot project "...designed to introduce all incoming students to the basics of information technology use."

Shapiro, Jeremy, and Hughes, Shelley.
Literacy as a Liberal Art
<http://www.educom.edu/web/pubs/review/reviewArticles/31231.html>

Offers an argument for introducing information literacy into the liberal arts curriculum.

This article appeared in print in **Educom Review**, 31(2), March/April 1996, pp. 31.

University of Washington.
UWired
<http://www.washington.edu/uwired/>

"...a model project for integrating electronic communication and information navigation skills into instruction and learning on campus.

University of Wisconsin-Parkside, Library/Learning Center.
Information Literacy Program
<http://www.uwp.edu/library/>

An 8-unit program that is almost entirely on the Web.

Return to Contents

Other Lists of Web-Based Library Instruction Sources

Ashton, Sarah. (University of Sheffield)
Information Skills Training
<http://netways.shef.ac.uk/rbase/infskll.htm>

Over 25 links to Web-based library instruction examples.

California State University System.
IC [Information Competency] Sites on the Web
<http://www.lib.calpoly.edu/infocomp/related.html>

Poster session 3 (Metz): Part 6 - Learn More about Web-Based Library Instruction (continued)

"The following Web sites are examples of how other institutions are approaching the topic of Information Competence. Gathered here are some background reports and projects as well as some online tutorials and courses that have been developed on the Web." Maintained by CSU Information Compentence Project

Curnoles, Bud. (University of Maryland)
Bibliographic Instruction
<http://umbc7.umbc.edu/~curnoles/bibinstr.html>

A Webliography of over a dozen sources.

Laverty, Cory. (Queen's University)
Library Instruction on the Web
<http://stauffer.queensu.ca/inforef/tutorials/cla/clahome.htm>

Includes over 20 links plus advice on how to create Web-based library instruction tutorials.

University of California Berkeley Library Web.
Bibliographic Instruction Resources on the Internet
<http://www.lib.berkeley.edu/TeachingLib/BIResources.html>

"This site is a collection of materials related to bibliographic instruction, and hopefully, a source of ideas and inspiration for other librarians and instructors."

University of Washington UWired Project.
Other Sites about Evaluating Information on the Internet
<http://weber.u.washington.edu/~libr560/NETEVAL/resources.html/>

Links to a dozen resources.

University of Washington UWired Project.
Teaching & Technology Links
<http://www.washington.edu/uwired/links.html>

Links to twenty resources.

University of Waterloo Libraries.
Instruction Uses of the Web
<http://www.uwaterloo.ca/web-docs/Guidelines/instruction.html>

Over a dozen links.

Return to Contents

Organizations with Library Instruction Interests

ACRL
Instruction Section
<http://www2.colgate.edu/instruction/1>

"The mission of the Instruction Section (IS) of the Association of College and Research Libraries (ACRL) is to foster the profession of academic and research librarianship and to enhance the ability of academic and research librarians involved in bibliographic instruction to serve effectively the library and information needs of current and potential library users."

ACRL/CNI
ACRL/CNIInternet Education Project
<http://www.cwru.edu/orgs/cni/base/acrlcni.html>

Poster session 3 (Metz): Part 6 - Learn More about Web-Based Library Instruction (continued)

This project, a collaboration of the Association of College and Research Libraries (ACRL) and the Coalition for Networked Information (CNI), "intends to provide an effective method for librarians to display and share instructional materials that they have designed for teaching about seeking and evaluating information in a networked environment. It is the hope of the Committee that sharing these resources will assist librarians in responding to the challenge posed by digital technologies."

ALA/LIRT
> Library Instruction Round Table (LIRT)
> <http://diogenes.baylor.edu/Library/LIRT/>
>
> LIRT is a round table of the American Library Association which advocates library instruction as a means for developing competent library and information use as a part of lifelong learning. LIRT membership represents all types of libraries (academic, public, school, and special) committed to this goal.
>
> The LIRT Web site includes access to LIRT's mission statement, committee information, electronic discussion forums (LIRT-L and LIRT-S), publications (including the LIRT Newsletter), summer and midwinter conference programs and activities, and links to other major professional instruction sites.

Instruction Section
> Emerging Technologies in Instruction Committee
> <http://www.lib.ncsu.edu/staff/kamorgan/etech.html>
>
> The Committee on Emerging Technologies in Instruction (ETech) is one of a number of committees of the Instruction Section (IS), a part of the Association of College and Research Libraries (ACRL).
>
> ETechs's charge is "to promote and facilitate the use of emerging technologies in bibliographic instruction; to act as a resource and information-sharing vehicle for those who use electronic technologies in bibliographic instruction. Principle areas of interest include new or innovative applications of these technologies in bibliographic instruction."

LOEX
> LOEX Clearinghouse for Library Instruction
> <http://www.emich.edu/public/library/index.html>
>
> LOEX (Library Orientation and Exchange) is a self-supporting, non-profit educational clearinghouse for all sorts of materials used in library instruction.

Return to Contents

Other Organizations with Web-Based Instruction Interests

Brandt, D. Scott.
> Internet-related Tutorials on the World Wide Web
> <http://www.psd.k12.co.us/intro/tutorials.html>
>
> Created for a presentation at the 1997 Computers in Libraries Conference, this resource contains links to Internet tutorials covering topics for the Internet beginner and specialized tutorials for searching the Internet.

Carvin, Andy.
> EDWeb
> <http://k12.cnidr.org:90/>
>
> Contains resources on educational technology and trends in computer based education.

Kilby, Tim.
> The Web-Based Training Information Center
> <http://www.clark.net/pub/nractive/wbt.html>

Poster session 3 (Metz): Part 6 - Learn More about Web-Based Library Instruction (continued)

A non-profit resource for individuals and organizations interested in developing and delivering training using Web technology. The site contains recommendations for creating web-based training modules as well as a wealth links to outside resources.

Scholz-Crane, Ann.
>   Web-Based Instruction Resource Center
>   `<http://crab.rutgers.edu/~scholzcr/cil/>`

Created for a postconference presentation at the 1997 Computers in Libraries Conference, this resource provides links to library tutorials, other tutorial examples, HTML resources, software, clip art, and additional information.

University of New Brunswick - Continuing Education Centre.
>   World Wide Web Courseware Developers Listserv Home Page
>   `<http://www.unb.ca/web/wwwdev/>`

This site contains information of interest to persons developing courseware that is to be delivered in part or totally over the World Wide Web.

Return to Contents

LOEX Poster Session Main Menu

Maintained by Terry Metz, temetz@carleton.edu
Last updated: May 2, 1997
URL: http://www.library.carleton.edu/instruction/loex/more.html

Poster session 3 (Metz): Part 6 - Learn More about Web-Based Library Instruction (continued)

THE ONE MINUTE PAPER: A SIXTY SECOND ASSESSMENT TECHNIQUE

by
Sharon Lee Stewart, M.A.
The University of Alabama

INTRODUCTION

A paradigm shift has occurred in the field of education, leading classroom teacher/researchers to assess learning as opposed to researcher studying instruction. Some of the ensuing classroom assessment techniques can be adapted to library instruction, even for the one-time, fifty minute presentations. The one minute paper is such a device.

Poster session 4 (Stewart) Part 2 - Introduction

ADVANTAGES OF CLASSROOM ASSESSMENT

- Learner-centered
- Teacher-directed
- Mutually beneficial
- Ungraded
- Usually anonymous
- Quick and easy to use
- Integral to teaching

Poster session 4 (Stewart) Part 3 - Advantages of Classroom Assessment

ANGELO'S* SEVEN AXIOMS OF CLASSROOM ASSESSEMENT

- Don't ask if you don't want to know.
- Don't ask for feedback unless you can respond to it.
- Don't collect more data than you can easily turn into information.
- Ask first which method is appropriate to answer your questions; not which questions are appropriate to fit your method.
- Don't simply <u>adopt</u> methods and

techniques from others, <u>adapt</u> them.
- If an assessment is worth doing, it's worth teaching students to do well.
- Always ask: how will knowing the answer to this help improve student learning? (If you can't think of an answer, ask yourself if it's worth doing.)

* Thomas A. Angelo, along with K. Patricia Cross, are well known in the field of classroom assessment. ERIC has assigned the identifier "Cross Angelo Classroom Assessment Model" to the concept they have developed.

ONE MINUTE PAPER

1. What was the most important thing you learned during this class?

_____
_____
_____
_____

2. What important question remains unanswered?

_____
_____
_____
_____

Adaptations can include asking about the "clearest" and "muddiest" points.

Poster session 4 (Stewart) Part 5 - One Minute Paper

APPROPRIATE USES OF THE MINUTE PAPER

- Most useful in lecture or lecture/discussion courses.
- Works well at the end or beginning of class sessions.
- Important when a great deal of new information is presented.
- Quick to administer (one minute) and easy to analyze.
- Well suited to large classes.

USE IN LIBRARY INSTRUCTION

- Technique can be used to fine tune instruction and eliminate extraneous information.
- Unanswered questions can be researched and answered through the classroom instructor.

Poster session 4 (Stewart) Part 7 - Use in Library Instruction

Bibliography

Library Instruction and Information Literacy—1996

Hannelore B. Rader

The following is an annotated list of materials dealing with information literacy including instruction in the use of information resources, research, and computer skills related to retrieving, using, and evaluating information. This review, the twenty-third to be published in *Reference Services Review*, includes items in English published in 1996. A few items are not annotated because the compiler could not obtain copies of them for this review.

The list includes publications on user instruction in all types of libraries and for all levels of users, from beginning levels to the most advanced. The items are arranged by type of library and are in alphabetical order by author (or by title if there is no author) within those categories.

Overall, as shown in figure 1, the number of publications related to user education and information literacy decreased by **30 percent** from 1995 to 1996. These figures are approximate and are based on the published information that was available to the reviewer. However, since the availability of this information does not vary greatly from year to year, these figures should be reliable.

Publications dealing with user instruction in academic libraries continue to be the largest number, although they decreased by **46 percent.** The number of publications about user instruction in public libraries decreased and they remain the smallest number in the group; school library publications increased by **18 percent**; special library publications increased by **5 percent;** publications for all levels increased by **15 percent**.

User education publications in libraries continue to deal with teaching users how to access, retrieve, and organize information, including electronic information resources through online searching, online system use, and bibliographic computer applications. An increasing percentage deals with evaluative research of user education.

It is noteworthy that in 1996 articles dealing with instruction in the use of electronic information and the World Wide Web increased substantially as did articles dealing with information literacy, resource-based and active learning, and integrating information literacy into the curriculum both in the schools and in higher education. In fact, for the first time there are publications treating the topic of information literacy and higher education accreditation.

It is also significant that librarians and faculty are increasingly forming partnerships to integrate electronic information and information literacy instruction into the curriculum. The climate for these activities is ideal as teachers and faculty are rethinking curricula and teaching styles in the technological information environment and in terms of distance education and virtual universities and virtual libraries.

The continuing growth of electronic information has made librarians more aware of the need for assistance and instruction to all types of information seekers. For the first time in the 23 years this review of the literature has been compiled, **Web site addresses** have been included where available. Librarians are becoming more concerned that library users will need

---

Rader is university librarian, University of Louisville, Kentucky.

Type of Library	# of 1995 Publications	# of 1996 Publications	% Change
Academic	197	107	-46%
Public	05	04	-20%
School	38	45	+18%
Special	18	19	+05%
All Types	13	15	+15%
TOTAL	271	190	-30%

Figure 1: Number of Publications Related to User Education and Information Literacy, 1995 and 1996

more training and skills development in using the World Wide Web so they can become more critical and evaluative information consumers. As a result, librarians are increasingly placing information skills instruction on the World Wide Web while addressing instructional needs of remote users and building virtual libraries.

Academic Libraries

Affleck, Mary Ann. "Burnout among Bibliographic Instruction Librarians." *Library and Information Science Research* 18 (Spring 1996): 165-183.

Describes the use of the Maslach Burnout Inventory and a Role Questionnaire with bibliographic instruction librarians' colleges in New England via mail to assess the relationship between levels of burnout and role stress, formal educational preparation, and faculty rank/status.

Alberlico, Ralph, and Elizabeth A. Dupuis. "The World Wide Web as an Instructional Medium." In *New Ways of "Learning the Library" and Beyond*. Ed. by Linda Shirato, 27-36. Ann Arbor, MI: Pierian Press, 1996.

Discusses the impact of new media on library instruction such as using the World Wide Web as an instructional medium. Gives several examples.

Archer, Sarah B. "Using Performance Techniques to Activate Your Library Instruction." In *New Ways of "Learning the Library" and Beyond*. Ed. by Linda Shirato, 37-40. Ann Arbor, MI: Pierian Press, 1996.

Describes dynamic and effective delivery styles teachers can use to enhance library instruction.

Arp, Lori. "New Paradigms: Using the Management Techniques of Instruction to Buy (into) a New Curriculum." *RQ* 36 (Fall 1996): 59-65.

Discusses the need for librarians to use appropriate management techniques to bring programmatic changes into the curriculum to enable students to gain necessary information skills. Cites several case studies.

Avery, Chris, and Kevin Ketcher. "Do Instruction Skills Impress Employers?" *College and Research Libraries* 57 (May 1996): 249-258.

The ACRL Instruction Section conducted a pilot project to investigate the perceived importance of library instruction skills to employers and whether instruction experience or coursework is important in getting a job for which library instruction is a stated responsibility. Findings show that employers consider skills or experience in library instruction in the hiring process.

Banks, Julie, et al. "Library Luncheon and Update: Teaching Faculty about New Technology." *Journal of Academic Librarianship* 22 (March 1996): 128-130.

Describes a method to interest faculty in learning about new technology and finding ways to integrate information literacy into the curriculum.

Bast, Carol M. "Shepardizing: An Indispensable Legal Research Tool." *Research Strategies* 14 (Spring 1996): 112-119.

Provides basic information to enable librarians to help legal researchers use *Shepard's* citators.

Baumann, Melinda J. "Creating and Maintaining Electronic Classrooms: The Virginia Academic Library Experience." *Virginia Libraries* 42 (January-March 1996): 8-10.

Gives an overview of librarians' experiences with electronic classrooms in Virginia academic institutions.

Blake, Michael, et al. *Teaching the New Library: A How-to-Do-It Manual for Planning and Designing Instructional Programs*. New York: Neal-Schuman, 1996.

Gives an overview of the changing teaching environment in the emerging library. Includes many helpful hints for instruction librarians.

Bradford, Jane I., et al. "Designing and Implementing a Faculty Internet Workshop: A Collaborative Effort of Academic Computing Services and the University Library." *Research Strategies* 14 (Fall 1996): 234-245.

Describes the planning and holding of a three-day Internet workshop for faculty at Stetson University in Florida. Includes information on instructional materials, contents of the sessions, exercises, and evaluation.

Branch, Katherine, and Debra Gilchrist. "Library Instruction and Information Literacy in Community and Technical Colleges." *RQ* 35 (Summer 1996): 476-483.

Gives detailed analysis of the history of instruction in community colleges and surveys current developments in regards to information literacy and faculty-librarian partnerships.

Brandt, D. Scott. "Evaluating Information on the Internet." *Computers in Libraries* 16 (May 1996): 44-46.

Purdue University librarians discuss the Internet and offer their views on evaluating information on the Internet in terms of teaching it in the library instruction program.

Brown, Lyn S. *Development, Implementation, and Evaluation of an Information Literacy Program for the Undergraduate School of Philadelphia College of Bible.* Ann Arbor, MI: University Microfilms International, 1996.

Describes the information literacy programs for undergraduates at the Philadelphia College of Bible including information retrieval skills and instructional methods and materials.

Buchanan, Lori E., et al. *Integrating Electronic Information Sources into the Curriculum.* Washington, DC: ERIC Document, 1996. ED 400811.

Describes the integration of technology-based library resources into the curriculum to help students obtain important information seeking skills using an active learning environment at Austin Peay State University in Tennessee.

Burke, John J. "Using E-Mail to Teach: Expanding the Reach of BI." *Research Strategies* 14 (Winter 1996): 36-43.

Discusses an effort at Fairmont State College in West Virginia, where librarians used e-mail and a listserv to provide instruction to registrants at a 16-part Internet seminar. Gives benefits and disadvantages as well as instructional method used.

Burks, Steven S., et al. "The Evolution of Innovation in Teaching LS101." In *New Ways of "Learning the Library" and Beyond.* Ed. by Linda Shirato, 93-105. Ann Arbor, MI: Pierian Press, 1996.

Gives history, politics, and descriptive details including handouts for library studies, a two-credit course at Saint Michael's College in Vermont.

Carder, Linda, et al. *Using Situational Leadership to Reach the Whole Population.* Washington, DC: ERIC Document, 1996. ED 406998.

Using Paul Hersey's Situational Leadership Model, librarians can accurately assess students' levels of experience and ability to offer the appropriate information instruction. This model is especially applied to adult learners.

Cordell, Roseanne M. "Enhancing Library Instruction with Multimedia Presentations." In *New Ways of "Learning the Library" and Beyond.* Ed. by Linda Shirato, 41-53. Ann Arbor, MI: Pierian Press, 1996.

Describes a dynamic multimedia presentation for library instruction at Indiana University, South Bend. Provides software evaluation techniques and technical considerations.

Cox, Andrew. "Hypermedia Library Guides for Academic Libraries on the World Wide Web." *Program* 30 (January 1996): 39-50.

Describes a new way to do user instruction by placing library guides on the World Wide Web.

Daragan, Patricia, and Gwendolyn Stevens. "Developing Lifelong Learners: An Integrative and Developmental Approach to Information Literacy." *Research Strategies* 14 (Spring 1996): 68-81.

Describes first part of a four-year, course-integrated library instruction program based on William Perry's developmental model. Introduces Perry's levels and gives results of evaluations of the program.

Davis, Marta A. "Current Relevance of Zetetics to Library Research and Library Instruction." *Illinois Libraries* 78 (Fall 1996): 230-233.

Explains zetetics, theories of research, and epistemology and discusses relevance to library science. Includes use of an information matrix to help library users understand what information they have and what they need to find.

Davis, Marta A. "Tackle Box Strategy: Using a Matrix to Facilitate Library Research Strategy." *Research Strategies* 14 (Fall 1996): 205-213.

Presents aids to help students grasp the concept of controlled vocabulary in search strategy. Provides a matrix to allow students to graphically record the progress of the search.

Davis, Rose P. "Library Instruction in an Electronic Environment: A Teacher's Perspective." *Mississippi Libraries* 60 (Summer 1996): 33-34.

Discusses bibliographic instruction for college and university students in the evolving electronic information environment in Mississippi academic institutions.

Day, Pam A., and Kimberly L. Armstrong. "Librarians, Faculty, and the Internet." *Computers in Libraries* 16 (May 1996): 56-58.

Discusses how librarians at Illinois State University work in teams with faculty to teach them the Internet.

Dempsey, Paula R. "Focusing on the Experts: Mapping Resources in an Interdisciplinary Focus Area." *Research Strategies* 14 (Summer 1996): 175-183.

Describes search strategy instruction for students in interdisciplinary master's programs at DePaul University in Chicago.

DeHart, Brian. "Job Search Strategies: Library Instruction Collaborates with University Career Services." *The Reference Librarian* 55 (1996): 73-81.

Provides information on a library instruction program for students at DePaul University where librarians and career counselors collaborate to create this program.

Dewald, Nancy H. "Computer-Mediated Communication in Library Credit Courses." *Research Strategies* 14 (Summer 1996): 169-176.

Discusses the advantages of computer-mediated communication in two library credit courses and provides several elements for success.

Dickens, Janis L. "Education for the 21st Century." *College and Research Libraries News* 57 (July/August 1996): 439-440+.

Reports on a meeting of the Consortium of College and University Media Centers held in April 1996. The meeting focused on the use of different types of multimedia in education, the need for appropriate classrooms, and faculty development.

Dilmore, Donald H. "Librarian/Faculty Interaction at Nine New England Colleges." *College and Research Libraries* 57 (May 1996): 274-284.

Presents the results of a study of librarian/faculty interaction at nine small (1,000 to 4,000 students) college libraries. Examines several activities used by librarians to build cooperation with faculty and presents faculty perceptions of library efforts to provide service.

Dougherty, Christopher B., and Patti Fantaske. "Defining Expectations or Problem-Solving Skills." *New Directions for Higher Education* 96 (Winter 1996): 55-66.

Research in the past 20 years has shaped an understanding of effective problem-solving skills and their place in the undergraduate curriculum. Provides background and framework for innovative teaching techniques to teach problem-solving skills to undergraduates in various disciplines.

Duesterhoeft, Kiane M., and Nancy A. Cunningham. "The Role of Assessment in the Development and Evaluation of Library Instruction." In *New Ways of "Learning the Library" and Beyond*. Ed. by Linda Shirato, 65-83. Ann Arbor, MI: Pierian Press, 1996.

Provides a detailed description of planning the assessment of library orientation and course-integrated instruction programs at St. Mary's University in Texas. Gives samples of evaluation instruments.

Duggua, Hilary F., and Lisa J. Haddow. "Meeting the Information Needs of Aquaculture Students—Delivering User Education and Training to the Consumer." In *Information Across the Waves*. Southampton, England: International Association of Aquatic and Marine Science Libraries and Information Centers, 1996.

Describes bibliographic instruction for graduate students in marine science at the University of Stirling.

Exploring Internet 7: Information Literacy. Restructuring Learning in an Electronic Environment. Teleconference transmitted 7 November 1996. Host Bill Erbes, presenter Hannelore Rader. Chicago: D&F Associates, 1996. Videotape.

Traces the evolution of information literacy, explains the requirements for training teachers of information literacy, and explores national and international trends in the field.

Fjallbrant, Nancy. "EDUCATE–a Networked User Education Project in Europe." *IFLA Journal* 22 (1996): 31-34.

Describes the EDUCATE Project to produce self-paced user education for formal and informal learning situations for students. The programs can be distributed through networks such as the World Wide Web. Programs have been developed for physics, electrical engineering, and electronic engineering.

Flak, Jean. "Working Reference at Indiana State University." *Library Mosaics* 7 (November/December 1996): 17.

Gives an overview of a patron assistance program that teaches searching and information skills.

Ford, Barbara. "All Together Now." *School Library Journal* 42 (April 1996): 48.

Advocates that academic and school libraries work together to actively coordinate library instruction.

George, Rigmor, and Rosemary Luke. "The Critical Place of Information Literacy in the Trend Towards Flexible Delivery in Higher Education Contexts." *Australian Academic and Research Libraries* 27 (September 1996): 204-212.

Discusses relationships among the faculty, the curriculum, and academic librarians and the role of bibliographic instruction in Australian academic libraries.

Gremmels, Gillian S. "Active and Cooperative Learning in the One-Shot BI Session." In *New Ways of "Learning the Library" and Beyond.* Ed. by Linda Shirato, 85-91. Ann Arbor, MI: Pierian Press, 1996.

Describes cooperative techniques used to provide cooperative learning in a one-hour library instruction session at Wartburg College in Iowa.

Greenfield, Louise, et al. "A Model for Teaching the Internet: Preparation and Practice." *Computers in Libraries* 16 (March 1996): 22-25.

Gives tips on planning and teaching a session on listservs.

He, Peter W., and Trudi E. Jacobson. "What Are They Doing with the Internet? A Study of User Information Seeking Behaviors." *Internet Reference Services Quarterly* 1 (1996): 31-51.

Summarizes a survey of library users regarding their Internet use. It was found that users want new access points and individual training.

Henshaw, Robert G. *The Internet and Instruction: Outreach and Support Strategies for Mainstream Faculty in Higher Education.* Chapel Hill, NC: University of North Carolina-Chapel Hill, 1996.

This master's thesis in information science elaborates on outreach and support efforts to faculty to bring the Internet into instructional activities.

Herring, Doris B., and Mary Alice Hunt. "How Well Prepared Are Florida Community College Librarians to Promote and Teach Information Literacy Skills?" *Florida Libraries* 39 (September/October 1996): 97-98.

Summarizes a survey of junior and community college librarians in Florida to assess their skills in teaching information skills to students.

Holland, Maurita P., and Christina K. Powell. "Two Goals, One Course: Using Library School Students as Research Mentors." *Research Strategies* 14 (Fall 1996): 196-204.

Reports on a collaborative effort involving the School of Information and Library Studies, the College of Engineering, and Engineering Library and the University of Michigan. Library science students served as mentors to beginning students in engineering and engineering librarians served as lecturers. Evaluations indicate that the collaboration was successful.

Jacobson, Trudi E., and Janice G. Newkirk. "The Effect of CD-ROM Instruction on Search Operator Use." *College and Research Libraries* 57 (January 1996): 68-76.

Reports survey results of 675 CD-ROM users. User status and department affiliation/major were significantly correlated to search skill. Although more testing is needed, instruction in searching does produce more sophisticated CD-ROM searchers.

Jafari, May, and Anthony Stamatoplos. "Promoting Active Learning in the Electronic Classroom: Making the Transition from Presentation to Workshop." In *New Ways of "Learning the Library" and Beyond.* Ed. by Linda Shirato, 107-112. Ann Arbor, MI: Pierian Press, 1996.

Highlights a new approach to teaching the library portion of English composition and discusses style changes in instruction. Points out issues related to active learning and the electronic classroom.

Jeffries, Shellie. "Apples and Apples: A Comparison of Bibliographic Instruction Programs in Libraries." *Illinois Libraries* 78 (Fall 1996): 242-246.

Summarizes a survey in Illinois to assess bibliographic instruction programs for college and university students.

Judd, Vaughan C., and Betty J. Tims. "Integrating Bibliographic Instruction into a Marketing Curriculum: A Hands-On Workshop Approach Using Interactive Team-Teaching." *Reference Services Review* 24:1 (Spring 1996): 21-30.

The article describes rationale for secondary data workshops to introduce students to government data in marketing courses. Outlines workshops and provides sample scenarios.

Kaczor, Sue A., and Trudi E. Jacobson. "Bibliographic Instruction for the Internet: Implications of an End-User Survey." *Research Strategies* 14 (Fall 1996): 214-223.

Focuses on survey data collected at the University of SUNY-Albany in 1995 on how patrons learned to use the Internet and the library Internet instruction program.

Kautzman, Amy M. "Teaching Critical Thinking: The Alliance of Composition Studies and Research Instruction." *Reference Services Review* 24:3 (Fall 1996): 61-66.

Examines the pace of composition studies in academia and how library instruction fits within this course. Proposes a model for integrating critical thinking and library skills into a single, one-hour session.

Khamadi, S.I.D. "Moi University Library's Bibliographic Instruction Programme: A Proposal for Change." *Library Review* 45 (1996): 44-49.

Talks about the library instruction program at Moi University and how it should change.

Koltay, Zsuzsa, et al. "Technologies for Learning: Instructional Support at Cornell's Albert R. Mann Library." *Library Hi Tech* 14 (1996): 83-98.

Describes Cornell University's instructional technology support program that integrates print and digital libraries and offers information literacy skills instruction.

Koltay, Zsuzsa. *Supporting Digital Instructional Technology: The Role of the Academic Library.* Washington, DC: ERIC Document, 1996. ED 403914.

Lists librarians' expertise in information work and technology and discusses how to use these skills to position libraries more into the teaching and learning process and building partnerships with faculty.

Konrad, Lee, and James Stemper. "Same Game, Different Name: Demystifying Internet Instruction." *Research Strategies* 14 (Winter 1996): 4-21.

Describes the development of a series of Internet training workshops for students and library staff at the University of Wisconsin-Madison. It is viewed as a natural extension of existing BI programs. Offers advice for developing Internet training programs.

Koss, Andrea I. *Information Needs of Kent State University Masters of Business Administration Students.* Washington, DC: ERIC Document, 1996. ED 401911.

Addresses information needs of the master's of business administration students. Based on data from surveying the students, the need for bibliographic instruction emerged.

Kunkel, Lilith E., et al. "What Do They Know? An Assessment of Undergraduate Library Skills." *Journal of Academic Librarianship* 22 (November 1966): 430-434.

Examines variables affecting scores on a test of library skills and finds that the best predictor of the score is the frequency with which students receive library research assignments. Gives implications for bibliographic instruction.

Laverty, Corinne. "The Cooperative Jigsaw: A New Approach to Library Learning." In *New Ways of "Learning the Library" and Beyond.* Ed. by Linda Shirato, 113-123. Ann Arbor, MI: Pierian Press, 1996.

Defines cooperative learning and group working in terms of improving library instruction. Provides examples from Queen's University in Canada.

Learning for Life: Information Literacy and the Autonomous Learner: Proceedings of the Second National Information Literacy Conference, November 30-December 1, 1995. Adelaide, Australia: University of South Australia Library, 1996.

This conference featured speakers on a variety of topics concerned with continuing education and information literacy.

Leckie, Glories J. "Desperately Seeking Citations: Uncovering Faculty Assumptions about the Undergraduate Research Process." *Journal of Academic Librarianship* 22 (May 1966): 201-208.

Discusses information seeking problems associated with the typical research paper. Suggests that faculty assume more responsibility for teaching information retrieval skills and provides a stratified methodology.

Lee, Catherine A. "Teaching Generation X." *Research Strategies* 14 (Winter 1996): 56-59.

Discusses four characteristics of Generation X, today's students, and the impact of these traits on bibliographic instruction. Includes six guidelines for developing appropriate instruction programs based on this information.

Lippincott, Joan K. "New Initiatives in Teaching Learning Strategies." *College and Research Libraries News* 57 (April 1996): 216-217.

Describes initiatives within the Association of College and Research Libraries and the American Association of Higher Education to help librarians and faculty cooperate within the framework of the electronic environment and student demands to improve teaching and learning.

Loomis, Abigail, and Deborah Fink. "Meta-Learning: A Transformational Process for Learning and Teaching." In *New Ways of "Learning the Library" and Beyond.* Ed. by Linda Shirato, 19-25. Ann Arbor, MI: Pierian Press, 1996.

Discusses learning styles, the meta-learning process that includes observation, reflection, characterization, expansion, and transformation.

MacInnis, Jamie A. *A Survey of the Library Use and Instruction Experiences of Learning Disabled College Students*. Chapel Hill, NC: University of North Carolina-Chapel Hill, 1996.

This master's thesis in library science didn't summarize the survey in a learning-disabled college students in terms of their library use and instruction experiences.

Mader, Sharon. "Instruction Librarians: Leadership in the New Organization." *RQ* 36 (Winter 1996): 192-197.

Examines critical issues in transforming libraries for the future–leaders and qualities of leadership. Presents the view that instruction librarians are ready to become leaders for the libraries of the future.

Mardikian, Jackie. "Targeted BI: Teaching Electronic Resources in the Biomedical Sciences." *Research Strategies* 14 (Winter 1995): 44-49.

Discusses teaching sessions designed by librarians to teach biomedical researchers how to access Internet and other electronic resources. Includes hands-on experience.

Martorana, Janet, and Carol Doyle. "Computers On, Critical Thinking Off: Challenges of Teaching in the Electronic Environment." *Research Strategies* 14 (Summer 1996): 184-191.

Describes the University of California at Santa Barbara Library's instruction program and networked computer classroom. Shows how the program focuses on teaching critical thinking.

McAlpine, Iain. *A Combined Video and CAI Package on Advanced Level Library Skills for Open Learning Students*. Washington, DC: ERIC Document, 1996. ED 396732.

Describes video and computer-assisted learning materials developed at the University of Southern Queensland in Australia to teach library users advanced keyword and subject searching of library catalogs and CD-ROMs.

Miller, Lisa K. "Cooperative Learning Users Groups: Modeling Cooperation." In *New Ways of "Learning the Library" and Beyond*. Ed. by Linda Shirato, 125-131. Ann Arbor, MI: Pierian Press, 1996.

Describes library exercises incorporating the principles of cooperative learning and provides examples from Paradise Valley Community College in Arizona.

Nissen, Karen R., and Barbara A. Ross. "A Mentor/Research Model to Teach Library Skill: An Introduction to Database Searching." *T.H.E. Journal* 24 (September 1996): 96-98.

Describes a humanized approach to teaching students efficient database searching. The skills students learned are easily transferable to online searching of the Internet.

Oberman, Cerise. "Library Instruction: Concepts and Pedagogy in the Electronic Environment." *RQ* 35 (Spring 1996): 315-323.

Discusses library instruction in terms of preparing users cognitively to properly interpret and use information and teach users the power of information to contribute to the quality of social and political life.

Orr, Debbie, et al. "Teaching Information Literacy Skills to Remote Students Through an Interactive Workshop." *Research Strategies* 14 (Fall 1996): 224-233.

Provides information about an Australian information literacy program at Central Queensland University for off-campus students. Evaluations indicate that this new learning environment offers distinct benefits.

Parks, Joan, and Dana Hendrix. "Integrating Library Instruction into the Curriculum through Freshman Symposium." *Reference Services Review* 24:1 (Spring 1996): 65-72.

Introduces Southwestern University (Texas) Library's major library instruction effort to integrate a module within the required first-year foundation course for students.

Perry, Stephen, and Lutishoor Salisburg. "The Ten Most Effective Ways to Search WorldCat on First-Search: A Practical Guide for Scholars and Practitioners." *RQ* 35 (Summer 1996): 505-518.

Recommends encouraging critical thinking skills in training and instruction sessions to enable scholars and others to acquire more sophisticated searching skills for electronic information resources.

Peterson, Lorna. "A Survey of U.S. Libraries on the Use of Audio Tape Orientation Tours." *Research Strategies* 14 (Winter 1996): 22-35.

Explores the use of both English and multilingual audiotape orientation tours in U.S. libraries. Gives results of a survey indicating that such tours are rarely used.

Piette, Mary I., et al. "Meeting the Masses: Making It Happen." In *New Ways of "Learning the Library" and Beyond*. Ed. by Linda Shirato, 55-65. Ann Arbor, MI: Pierian Press, 1996.

Describes a successful library instruction program at Utah State University. In partnership with academic support services, faculty input and technology librarians revamped library instruction and continue to improve based on student evaluations.

Pixey, Anne M., and Daniel Xiao. "Touring the Campus Library for the World Wide Web." *Reference Services Review* 24:4 (Winter 1996): 7-14+.

Describes a World Wide Web-accessible, interactive Virtual Library Tour at Texas A&M University's Evan Library. It combines technical computer issues and library instruction expertise.

Ramey, Mary Ann. "Student Choice: A Modular Approach to Library Instruction." *Research Strategies* 14 (Fall 1996): 246-251.

Discusses the modular library instruction approach for one-hour sessions at Georgia State University. The modules are available to the university community. Advantages of this teaching method are pointed out.

Rabinowitz, Celia. "Research in Teaching: A Course to Bridge the Theory-Practice Gap." *Research Strategies* 14 (Spring 1996): 82-92.

Gives a brief review of the literature and describes a course for education students to help conduct theoretical and practical research. The goal is to educate teachers who can read the literature critically and understand how it fits into their professional development.

Rettig, James. "Sired by a Hurricane. Dam'd by an Earthquake." *Reference Librarian* 54 (1996): 75-94.

Discusses trends in library reference services with a focus on the needs of individual users. Highlights various reference issues including library instruction.

Riggs, Donald. "Working with Faculty." *College and Research Libraries* 57 (November 1996): 498-499.

Discusses the importance of good librarian-faculty partnerships now and in the future in terms of faculty teaching and motivating students for library use and helping the faculty rethink how they teach with electronic resources.

Robles, Kimberly, and Neal Wyatt. *Reference Training in Academic Libraries*. Washington, DC: ERIC Document, 1996. ED 398929.

Surveys training programs in small and medium-sized academic libraries. Training documents include library instruction.

Scholz, Ann Margaret, et al. "PLUTO: Interactive Instruction on the Web." *College and Research Libraries News* 57 (June 1996): 346-349.

Describes PLUTO (Purdue Libraries Undergraduate Tutorial Online) and online orientation program, including two quizzes.

Searing, Susan E. "Meeting the Information Needs of Interdisciplinary Scholars: Issues for Administrators of Large University Libraries." *Library Trends* 45 (Fall 1996): 315-342.

Gives an overview of administrative issues in supporting interdisciplinary library use at large universities including library use education.

Shapiro, Jeremy J., and Shelley K. Hughes. "Information Technology as a Liberal Art." *Educom Review* 31 (March/April 1996): 31-35.

Discusses information literacy as a new liberal art and provides a prototype information literacy curriculum.

Slade, Alexander L., and Marie A. Kascus. *Library Services for Off-Campus and Distance Education. The Second Annotated Bibliography*. Washington, DC: ERIC Document, 1996. ED 393459.

This bibliography on distance education library services contains references to 518 items published after 1990 and includes a section on bibliographic instruction.

Smith, Susan. "Z. Smith Reynolds Library: Its Role in Wake Forest University's Access 2000 Project." *North Carolina Libraries* 54 (Winter 1996): 153-157.

Describes the library's role in training faculty, staff, and students to use the new technology on campus.

Snyder, Carolyn A., et al. *Role of Libraries in Distance Education*. SPEC Lot 216. Washington, DC: ERIC Document, 1996. ED 398930.

Summarizes a survey of 119 Association of Research Libraries members regarding their current distance education initiatives. Library instructional support is high on the list of initiatives.

Sonntag, Gabriela, and Donna M. Ohr. "The Development of a Lower-Division, General Education, Course-Integrated Information Literacy Program." *College and Research Libraries* 57 (July 1996): 331-338.

Discusses the reforms in higher education as related to information literacy. Describes the model at California State University-San Marcus, where librarians successfully integrated information literacy into the lower division's general education curriculum.

Staines, Gail M. "Moving Beyond Institutional Boundaries: Perceptions Toward BI for Transfer Students." *Research Strategies* 14 (Spring 1996): 93-107.

Explores different perceptions of librarians at community colleges and four-year institutions toward library instruction for transfer students based on a survey. Findings indicate that bibliographic instruction programs differ in these institutions in part due to different faculty expectations. Suggests that collaborative efforts between the institutions could help transfer students.

Stelling, Prue. "Student to Student: Training Peer Advisors to Provide BI." *Research Strategies* 14 (Winter 1996): 50-55.

Discusses the use of a peer advisor to teach students effective library use for library research assignments. Gives details on training such peer advisors.

Still, Julie. "Multifaceted Evaluation of User Education." In *New Ways of "Learning the Library" and Beyond*. Ed. by Linda Shirato, 133-143. Ann Arbor, MI: Pierian Press, 1996.

Summarizes the use of traditional and non-standard evaluations of library instruction at Trenton State College in New Jersey.

Stover, Mark, and Steven D. Zink. "World Wide Web Home Page Design: Patterns and Anomalies of Higher Education Library Home Pages." *Reference Services Review* 24:3 (Fall 1996): 7-20.

Discusses the relative quality of university library home pages. Lists the top 20 home pages based on the authors' ranking.

Tate, Marsha, and Jan Alexander. "Teaching Critical Evaluation Skills for World Wide Web Resources." *Computers in Libraries* 16 (November-December 1996): 49-54.

Provides a two-part lesson plan and a checklist for teaching critical evaluation skills for resources on the Web.

Thompson, Gary B. "Library Instruction for Changing Times." *College and Research Libraries News* 57 (July/August 1996): 437-438.

The 25th Canadian Workshop on Instruction in Library Use, held in May 1996, focused on the challenges for academic librarians in supporting teaching and learning in an electronic environment.

Touchard, Wolfhard. "Introducing New Library Technology to Faculty and Their Secretaries at Andrews University." *Christian Librarian* 39 (September 1996): 104.

Describes a program of library instruction and technology for faculty and their secretaries.

Vander Meer, Patricia F., and Galen E. Rike. "Multimedia: Meeting the Demand for User Education with a Self-Instructional Tutorial." *Research Strategies* 14 (Summer 1996): 145-158.

Describes the use of a multimedia self-instructional tutorial to introduce library services and teach basic skills in a cost-effective manner. Evaluations indicate no significant differences between traditional workbook instruction and the tutorial.

Varner, Caroll H., et al. "Library Instruction and Technology in a General Education 'Gateway' Course: The Student's View." *Academic Library Journal* 22 (September 1996): 355-359.

Summarizes the finding gained through group discussions with freshmen. It was found that library instruction and hands-on technology training must be better integrated into the general education gateway course to be effective.

Wagner, Robin, and Kim Breighner. *Faculty as Partners: A Four Tiered Training Approach to the Web*. Washington, DC: ERIC Document, 1996. ED 405836.

Describes the library training team at Gettysburg College in Pennsylvania, composed of software specialists and bibliographic instruction librarians who work with faculty as partners to bring technology into the teaching.

Ward, Dane M. "More to Research Than ERIC: A Quick Attack on Database Dependency." *Research Strategies* 14 (Spring 1996): 108-111.

Advocates teaching students a three-step process for formulating a search strategy before they begin their research projects at the ERIC terminals.

Watkins, Nan. "A Case in Point: Individual Library Instruction of International Students." *North Carolina Libraries* 54 (Summer 1996): 76-79.

Describes techniques for providing individualized library instruction for international students at Western Carolina University in North Carolina.

Weimer, Maryellen. "Challenges of College Teaching." In *New Ways of "Learning the Library" and Beyond*.

Ed. by Linda Shirato, 1-7. Ann Arbor, MI: Pierian Press, 1996.

Discusses challenges of college teaching in terms of lack of preparation for such teaching and in terms of the changing characteristics of current college students.

Weinstein, Claire E. "Strategic Learning: The Merging of Skill, Will, and Self-Regulation." In *New Ways of "Learning the Library" and Beyond.* Ed. by Linda Shirato, 9-17. Ann Arbor, MI: Pierian Press, 1996.

Explains that people have a need to want to learn, a need to want to use what they are learning, and a need to want to manage their learning in order to be successful at it. Provides details and examples of skill, will, and self-regulation in the learning process.

Wiggins, Marvin E. "Planning Electronic Classrooms: Beginning, Expanded and Enriched." In *New Ways of "Learning the Library" and Beyond.* Ed. by Linda Shirato, 145-151. Ann Arbor, MI: Pierian Press, 1996.

Covers the planning of electronic classrooms from the beginning to the most sophisticated based on 28 years of experience at Brigham Young University.

Willingham, Patricia, and Carl Pracht. *Using Library Handbooks for Reduction in Reference Staff.* Washington, DC: ERIC Document, 1996. ED 401891.

At Southeast Missouri State University, librarians developed library handbooks for students and faculty to instruct them in library use. The handbooks are successful because they target specific audiences.

Woodard, Patricia. "Librarian and Faculty Collaboration in Honors 301.88: An Interdisciplinary Computer Applications Course." *Research Strategies* 14 (Summer 1996): 132-144.

Describes the collaboration between librarians and faculty to plan and teach an honors course. Includes the use of electronic research tools, desktop publishing, and graphics software.

Zahner, Jane, and Jack Hasling, Jr. "Building on Brainstorms: Sociological Perspectives to Library Research." In *New Ways of "Learning the Library" and Beyond.* Ed. by Linda Shirato, 153-161. Ann Arbor, MI: Pierian Press, 1996.

Describes a team teaching effort in sociology at Valdosta State University in Georgia where a library and faculty member collaborate to teach students information and research skills.

Zarnosky, Maggie. "The 'Net' Advantage: Library Instruction Using the World Wide Web." *Library Instruction Roundtable News* (December 1996): 5.

Describes the use of the World Wide Web as an instructional tool and home pages to reinforce classroom presentations at the Virginia Tech University Libraries.

Zastrow, Jan. "The Inner Workings of a Document Delivery Project." *Computers in Libraries* 16 (October 1996): 20-24.

Describes a special project at Kapiolani Community College in Hawaii to enhance library services through document delivery including bibliographic instruction, customized searches, a Web site, and evaluation results.

Public Libraries

Balas, Jane. "Building Virtual Libraries." *Computers in Libraries* 16 (February 1996): 48-50.

Discusses the Internet Public Library at the University of Michigan's School of Information. The Web address is <http://ipl.sils.umich.edu>.

Batt, Chris. "The Libraries of the Future: Public Libraries and the Internet." *IFLA Journal* 22 (1996): 27-30.

Discusses how public libraries worldwide can become more relevant to people's lives due to the Internet and the public's need for information.

Matsco, Sandra, and Sharon Campbell. "Writing a Library Home Page." *Public Libraries* 35 (September-October 1996): 284-286.

Provides tips and ideas for developing a library home page.

Robinson, John. "Links to Literacy Multimedia Software and Internet Applications." *Feliciter* 42 (April 1996): 28-29+.

Describes a computer-assisted information literacy program at North York Public Library in Canada.

School Libraries

Burdick, Tracy A. "Success and Diversity in Information Seeking: Gender and the Information Search Styles Model." *School Library Media Quarterly* 25 (Fall 1996): 19-26.

Reviews a study about gender difference in the information search process. It was found that differences were less related to gender than to styles of information seeking.

Callison, Daniel. "Science Instructional Resource Plans." *Indiana Media Journal* 18 (Winter 1996): 61-114.

Describes instruction guides for science prepared by students in the 1995 school media specialist course at Indiana University.

Caywood, Carolyn. "Guide and Seek." *School Library Journal* 42 (July 1996): 35.

Librarians should develop programs to help children, teens, and parents evaluate material found on the World Wide Web. The piece includes a Web address to assist parents.

Chatam, Barbara. "Elementary School Study Skills Questions Box." *Catholic Library World* 67 (September 1996): 30-32.

Describes the Question Box Program used in second through sixth grades to teach students skills to use reference books in the media center.

Chatman, Arleen. "Resource-Based Teaching and Learning: Reading, Writing, and Researching in History-Social Science." *Social Studies Review* 36 (Fall 1996): 35-36.

The library/media resource center can become the center for active social studies learning in the middle grades to teach students information skills.

Cushman, Kathleen. "Information, Literacy, and the Essential School Library." *Ohio Media Spectrum* 48 (Spring 1996): 23-26.

Discusses how teachers and librarians cooperated within the curriculum to ensure that elementary and high school students gain learning information skills.

Darrow, Rob. "Strategies for Starting the Big Six—Just Do It!" *Journal of the California Library Association* 20 (Fall 1996): 33-35.

Explains the problem-solving approach to library and information skills teaching at Clovis Unified School District.

Ehlert, Adrienne G. *An Integrated Process Model for Teaching Information, Technology and Subject-Area Skills*. Chapel Hill, NC: University of North Carolina, 1996.

This master's thesis in library science discusses how to teach information skills integrated into the curriculum in elementary and high school.

Eisenberg, Michael B. *Computer Skills for Information Problem-Solving Learning and Teaching Technology in Context*. Syracuse, NY: Clearinghouse on Information and Technology, 1996.

Discusses computer literacy and how to teach computer skills for solving information problems.

Gold, Etta. "Do Spiders Live on the Web?" *School Library Journal* 42 (July 1996): 34.

Describes a program at the Miami-Dade Public Library to introduce the Web to a group of toddlers, middle-school students, and parents.

Gordon, Mark. "The Essential Library: Partner in School Design." *Indiana Media Journal* 18 (Summer 1996): 9-22.

Describes experiences in the Central Park East Secondary School in New York where teachers and media specialists cooperate to teach information skills within the curriculum.

Griggs, Shirley, and Rita Dunn. "Learning Styles of Asian-American Adolescents." *Emergency Librarian* 24 (September-October 1996): 8-13.

Reviews research, defines cultural values, and discusses implications for teaching.

Hunt, Rebecca N. "Learning in the Library: An Assessment of Library Services to Home Schoolers." *Feliciter* 42 (July-August 1996): 62-69.

Explains how public libraries can fulfill the needs of home-schooled children and provide them with necessary information skills.

"Information Literacy Guidelines, Assessment for Information Literacy and Assessment of School Library Media Programs." *Indiana Media Journal* 18 (Summer 1996): 39-71.

This is a draft of guidelines for school library media programs to assess information literacy and school library media programs in Colorado. It provides aims and objectives.

"Into the Curriculum." *School Library Media Activities Monthly* 13 (October 1996): 12-31.

Gives seven library media activities designed to use with specific curriculum units in art, health, reading and language arts, science, and social studies. Specifies library media skills, objectives, grade levels, instructional roles, and evaluations. (This journal provides an "Into the Curriculum" section each month.)

Johnson, Douglas A., and Michael B. Eisenberg. "Computer Literacy and Information Literacy: A Natural Combination." *Emergency Librarian* 23 (May-June 1996): 12-16.

Discusses the teaching of information and computer skills within the school curriculum through partnerships between teachers and media specialists.

Kaser, Linda R. "How to Prepare for and Teach Library Media Skills 'a la Cart'." *School Library Media Activities Monthly* 12 (April 1996): 30-31+.

Talks about methods of teaching information skills to elementary and high school students.

Kirsch, Robert, and James Bradley. "Introducing a Problem-Solving Method and Library Resources in a Science Class Research Assignment." *Book Report* 14 (March/April 1996): 14-15.

This is an excerpt from the book *Skills for Life: Library Information Literacy for Grades 9-12* published in 1993 by Linworth Publisher. It discusses the teaching of information and problem-solving skills in a science class.

Knierim, Janella. "Media Specialists and Classroom Teachers as Co-Planners, Co-Facilitators, Co-Operators, Co-Ordinators, and Co-Designers of Instruction." *Indiana Media Journal* 18 (Winter 1996): 19-25.

Discusses teacher-librarian cooperation to ensure that students learn important information skills.

Lincoln Public Schools. *Guide to Integrated Information Literacy Skills*. Lincoln, NB: The Schools, 1996.

Covers information science, information technology, and computer skills in an integrated information literacy environment.

Levitov, Deborah. "Lincoln Public Schools' Guide to Integrated Information Literacy Skills (GIILS)." *Nebraska Library Association Quarterly* 27-28 (Winter 1996-Spring 1997): 19-20.

Describes the integrated information skills program in Nebraska's Lincoln Public School System.

Lewis, Mary K., and Champelli, Lisa. "Information Literacy Video Programs for the Professional Collection." *Indiana Media Journal* 18 (Summer 1996): 192-195.

Reviews video programs of information literacy programs for professional collections in schools.

McConnell, Terry. "Library Technology Adds Immediacy to Research Assignments." *Book Report* 14 (March/April 1996): 11+.

Discusses the use of technology in teaching information skills and research techniques within the school curriculum.

Miller, Donna P., and J'Lynn Anderson. *Developing an Integrated Library Program. Professional Growth Series*. Washington, DC: ERIC Document, 1996. ED 406989.

Gives detailed instruction for integrating library resources and skills into the classroom curriculum using team teaching.

Nahl, Diane, and Violet H. Harada. "Composing Boolean Search Statements: Self-Confidence, Concept Analysis, Search Logic, and Errors." *School Library Media Quarterly* 24 (Summer 1996): 199-207.

Reports results of a test of secondary students' abilities to interpret and construct search statements. Reviews related research and influences of other factors influencing search behavior of students.

Neuman, Delia, et al. "The Science Library Catalog: A Springboard for Information Literacy (and) Notes from ERIC." *School Library Media Quarterly* 42 (Winter 1996): 105-112.

Provides relevant information for school media specialists developing children's information skills.

Pungente, John J. "Getting Started on Media Literacy." *Emergency Librarian* 24 (November/December 1996): 9-11.

Provides a list of resources for teachers and librarians in Canada to help them teach information skills.

Rankin, Virginia. "Get Smart: The Crucial Link Between Media Specialists and A+ Student Projects." *School Library Journal* 42 (August 1996): 22-26.

Describes a special project at Odle Middle School in Belevue, Washington, where teachers and library media specialists cooperated to teach students research and information skills.

Robinson, David E. "Cooperative Discipline Model of Library Media Skills Instruction." *School Library Media Activities Monthly* 13 (October 1996): 34-35.

Describes models to teach information skills integrated within a discipline to students in elementary and high schools.

Rubric for the Assessment of Information Literacy: Based on the Information Literacy Guidelines for Colorado Students, Teachers, and School Library Media Specialists. Denver, CO: State Library and Adult Education Office, 1996.

Addresses searching behavior, retrieval, problem solving, and information seeking behavior with appropriate evaluation techniques.

Secondary Utah Library Media/Information Literacy Core Curriculum Standards: Levels 7-12. Salt Lake City, UT: Utah Office of Education, 1996.

Provides core curriculum standards for library media/information curriculum for grades 7-12.

Stripling, Barbara K. "Quality in School Library Media Programs: Focus on Learning." *Library Trends* 44 (Winter 1996): 631-656.

Gives historical overview of instruction in school library media programs from 1950 to the present and discusses the developing roles of the school library media specialist.

Symonds, Ann K. "Intelligent Life on the Web and How to Find It: Part I of http://the.thinking.librarian's web.guide." *School Library Journal* 42 (March 1996): 106-109.

Describes how the Web is used in the high school library to support student projects; also discusses evaluation.

Teaching Information Literacy Using Electronic Resources for Grades 6-12. Worthington, OH: Linworth, 1996.

Gives guidelines for high school and middle school students in regards to teaching library and electronic information skills.

Terry, Christine, et al. "Into the Curriculum." *School Library Media Activities Monthly* 13 (September 1996): 11-28.

Gives five fully developed library media activities designed for use with units in reading, language arts, science, and social studies. Includes library skills instruction.

Thome, Richard. "The Fourth R Is Research." *Electronic Learning* 16 (October 1996): 58.

Discusses the need for research skills for students from K-12 and lists essential research skills.

Vandegrift, Kay E. "Build a Web Site with a Brain: Part 2 of http://the.thinking.librarian's web.guide." *School Library Journal* 42 (April 1996): 26-29.

Provides the beginner with tips on planning for a Web site and includes defining the purpose, maintenance, and copyright.

Walster, Diane, and Lynda Welborn. "Colorado's Information Literacy Guidelines." *School Library Media Activities Monthly* 12 (March 1996): 21-27.

Examines the five guidelines for information literacy in Colorado. The guidelines are designed to enable students to construct meaning from information, create a quality product, learn independently, work in groups, and use information and information technologies responsibly.

Walter, Virginia A., and Christine Borgman. "The Science Library Catalog: A Springboard for Information Literacy." *School Library Media Quarterly* 24 (Winter 1996): 105-110.

Describes the University of California at Los Angeles' prototype information retrieval system for literacy.

Wells, Melissa. "Portfolio Assessment with a Library Media Component." *Journal (California School Library Association)* 19 (Spring 1996): 23-25.

Describes information skills instruction at Clark Intermediate School in the Clovis Unified School District in California.

Whitmore, Marilyn P. *Empowering Students: Hands-On Library Instruction Activities*. Pittsburgh: Library Instruction Publications, 1996.

This source book for the busy instruction librarian includes many lesson plans.

Williams, Dorothy, and Shonagh Morrison. "Curriculum Change and Libraries in Independent Schools in Scotland." *Scottish Education Review* 28 (November 1996): 120-138.

Summarizes surveys of 75 independent schools in Scotland regarding level of library services including information skills programs.

Williams, Tracy J. "Creating Partnerships between the Library Media Specialist and Classroom Teachers." *Indiana Media Journal* 18 (Winter 1996): 1-18.

Discusses how teachers and librarians work together to bring information skills instruction into the curriculum.

Wolcott, Linda. "Planning with Teachers: Practical Approaches to Collaboration." *Emergency Librarian* 23 (January-February 1996): 9-14.

Addresses curriculum-planning processes in schools in which teachers and librarians collaborate to ensure that students learn appropriate skills. Provides several scenarios to help librarians in their collaboration with teachers.

Wolfgram, Linda M. "Information Literacy Books for the Professional Collection." *Indiana Media Journal* 18 (Summer 1996): 189-191.

Lists resource books on information literacy for teachers and library media specialists to place into their professional collection.

Special Libraries

Barsh, Adel, and Meliza Jackson. "Information Needs of Special Populations: Serving People with Mental Illnesses Using Computer Aided Instruction in a Multimedia Library for Outpatients." *Reference Librarian* 53 (1996): 47-61.

Report the experiences of Western Psychiatric Institute and Clinic in regard to teaching the mentally handicapped person information skills in the computer environment.

Berry, Catherine E. "Library Induction Programmes: How Do We Do That?" *The Law Librarian* 27 (March 1996): 41-43.

Discusses library instruction programs for law students in the United Kingdom where these programs are called library induction programmes. Gives information on planning, needs assessment, methodology, and evaluation.

Biffen, Kate. "Student Tours USA Fashion." *Library Association Record* 98 (January 1996): 30-31.

Describes a bibliographic instruction program for college students at the Mountbatten Library of the Southampton Institute in England.

Chiu, Cathy. "One-Stop Research: Using WWW for BI." *Journal of the East Asian Libraries* 109 (June 1996): 1-20.

Describes bibliographic instruction using the World Wide Web for East Asian studies at the University of California, Santa Barbara.

Curtis, Karen L. "Teaching Roles of Librarians in Nursing Education." *Bulletin of the Medical Library Association* 84 (July 1996): 416-422.

This paper, presented at the 1994 Illinois Library Association Conference, discusses the emergence of teaching roles for nurses as information skills are integrated into the curriculum.

Daragon, Patricia, and Gwendolyn Stevens. *Developing Life-Long Learners: An Integrative and Developmental Approach to Information Literacy*. New London, CT: Center of Advanced Studies, U.S. Coast Guard Academy, 1996.

Based on data for entering first-year college students in the U.S. Coast Guard Academy regarding their information literacy levels, this investigation assessed an across-the-curriculum information literacy skills program based on Perry's theory of cognitive development and improved students' information skill and online research techniques.

DeBrower, Amy M., and Robert F. Skinder. "Designing an Internet Class for a Scientific and Technical Audience." *Special Libraries* 87 (Summer 1996): 139-146.

Describes the development of "Introduction to the Internet," a formal training class for staff members of a scientific and technical research and development laboratory. The one-day course covers theoretical Internet concepts, hands-on instruction in browser software functionality, important Internet resources, and information discovery and retrieval techniques.

Earl, Martha, et al. "Faculty Involvement in Problem-Based Library Orientation for First-Year Medical Students." *Bulletin of the Medical Library Association* 84 (July 1996): 411-415.

Describes a survey of library instruction programs in medical libraries in the southeast conducted by East Tennessee State University College of Medicine.

Earl, Martha. "Library Instruction in the Medical School Curriculum: A Survey of Medical College Libraries." *Bulletin of the Medical Library Association* 84 (April 1996): 191-195.

This survey of medical libraries assessed their instructional programs within the curriculum. It was conducted by East Tennessee State University College of Medicine.

Freeman, Mark. "An Information Systems Approach to Teaching IT Skills to Students of Library and Information Studies." *Education for Information* 14 (1996): 233-237.

Proposes to teach library and information studies students information technology skills by starting with databases and related software, spreadsheets as data analysis tools, and graphics and word processing as data presentation tools. This will develop an appreciation of the way in which information systems are used in business. This is particularly appropriate for library and information science studies where students should be trained as information managers.

Hannigan, Gale G., et al. "Computers and Medical Information: An Elective for Fourth-Year Medical Students." *Medical Reference Services Quarterly* 15 (Winter 1996): 81-88.

Talks about teaching end-user searching skills for MEDLINE to medical students at Texas A&M University Health Science Center's College of Medicine.

Hannigan, Gale G., and Katherine Edwards. "Medical Information in the Medical School Curriculum." *Medical Reference Services Quarterly* 15 (Spring 1996): 71-76.

Discusses the relationship between librarians and faculty toward integrating medical information and research skills into the medical curriculum.

Hightower, Barbara. *The Effect of Faculty Library Attitudes and Experiences on Undergraduate Use of the Geology Library at the University of North Carolina at Chapel Hill*. Chapel Hill, NC: University of North Carolina at Chapel Hill, 1996.

This master's thesis in information science summarizes a study of the effect that librarians' attitudes have on undergraduates' utilization of the Geology Library.

Maple, Amanda, et al. "Information Literacy for Undergraduate Music Students: A Conceptual Framework." *Notes* 52 (March 1996): 744-753.

Focuses on music students and examines the four elements of an information gathering process as specified in the Association for College and Research Libraries' "Model Statement of Objectives for Academic Bibliographic Instruction."

Minchow, Rochelle L. "Changes in Information-Seeking Patterns of Medical Students: Second-Year Students' Perceptions of Information Management Instruction as a Component of a Problem-Based Learning Curriculum." *Medical Reference Services Quarterly* 15 (Spring 1996): 15-40.

Discusses the changes taking place in the medical curriculum at the University of California, Irvine. Librarians and faculty are integrating information skills into the curriculum.

Murphy, Sharon C. "Nursing Sites on the World Wide Web." *Journal of the New York State Nurses Association* 27 (March 1996): 19-21.

Gives an overview and Web addresses of Web sites for nursing.

Oberg, Lisa A. "The Moving Target: Internet Instruction at the University of Washington Health Sciences Libraries and Information Center." *Medical Reference Services Quarterly* 15 (Fall 1996): 73-79.

Describes bibliographic instruction and Internet teaching for students in the health sciences at the University of Washington.

Oliver, Ron. "The Influence of Instruction and Activity on the Development of Skills in the Usage of Interactive Information Systems." *Education for Information* 14 (1996): 7-17.

Describes an Australian study in which students were given instruction in using a CD-ROM encyclopedia. Assessment revealed that the instruction and practice provided low-order syntactic knowledge and skills but failed to provide semantic knowledge and understanding required for successful use of the more powerful features of the interactive information system.

Romans, Larry. "GODORT Education Committee Handout Diskettes." *Documents to the People* 24 (September 1996): 188-193.

Describes detailed finding aids for using government information.

All Levels

Bolles, Charles. *Idaho's Network of Libraries: A Statewide Plan for Multi-Type Library Cooperation and Resource Sharing 1996-1999*. Washington, DC: ERIC Document, 1996. ED 398937.

Describes status of multi-library cooperation and resource sharing in Idaho and outlines possible new infrastructure for the future. The eight stated goals include user preparation to enable citizens to get and use information.

Courtois, Martin P. "Cool Tools for Web Searching." *Online* 20 (May/June 1996): 29-36.

Lists and discusses a variety of search engines for the World Wide Web.

Farah, Barbara D. "Information Literacy: Retooling Evaluation Skills in the Electronic Information Environment." *Journal of Educational Technology Systems* 24 (1996): 127.

Garlock, Kristen L., and Sherry Piontek. *Building the Service-Based Library Web Site: A Step-by-Step Guide to Design and Options*. Washington, DC: ERIC Document, 1996. ED 391528.

Includes six chapters giving directions and instructions to librarians on all aspects of building home pages for different types of libraries.

Glossbrenner, Alfred. "Save Veronica!" *Online User* 2 (July-August 1996): 48.

Argues that Veronica is a better tool than most World Wide Web search engines for finding information. Gives comparisons.

Notess, Greg R. "Internet Ready Reference Resources." *Database* 19 (April/May 1996): 88-91.

Explains some of the Internet information resources in terms of online factual databases from business.

Rader, Hannelore B. "Library Instruction and Information Literacy–1995." *Reference Services Review* 24 (Winter 1996): 77-96.

Presents the 22nd review of the literature in library orientation, instruction, and information literacy for all types of libraries.

Rader, Hannelore B. "User Education and Information Literacy for the Next Decade: An International Perspective." *Reference Services Review* 24:2 (Summer 1996): 71-75.

Reviews the need for information skills for all types of persons and all ages so they can be successful in the Information Society. Discusses how librarians are uniquely qualified to provide information skills training worldwide.

Shonrock, Diana D. *Evaluating Library Instruction.* Chicago: American Library Association, 1996.

Produced by the Research Committee of the Library Instruction Roundtable, this monograph discusses types of evaluations and assessments for library instruction. It provides a variety of model tests, questionnaires, checklists, and evaluation instruments for library instruction in different types of libraries. This is a useful guide for librarians involved in user instruction.

Silberman, Mel. *Active Learning. 101 Strategies to Teach Any Subject.* Boston: Allyn and Bacon, 1996.

Explains active learning and provides many specific and practical strategies to teach any subject matter. Can be used to provide active learning in any type of situation and for any level from young children to older adults.

Sloan, Steve. "The Virtual Pathfinder: A World Wide Web Guide to Library Research." *Computers in Libraries* 16 (April 1996): 53-54.

Talks about automated pathfinders on the Web in terms of effectiveness and limitations based on the experiences at the University of New Brunswick.

U.S. Department of Education. *Getting America's Students Ready for the 21st Century. Meeting the Technology Literacy Challenge.* Washington, DC: U.S. Department of Education, 1996. <www.ed.gov>.

This report to the nation on technology and education challenges everyone to work toward making all students technology- and information-literate to prepare them for productive lives in the 21st century.

Strasser, Dennis. "Tips for Good Electronic Presentations." *Online* 20 (January/February 1996): 78-81.

Gives practical advice and tips for anyone interested in using presentation software for instruction.

Wilhelm, Tony. *Latinos and Information Technology Preparing for the 21st Century.* Claremont, CA: The Tomas Rivera Center, 1996.

The report explores how Latinos will be impacted by the transformations underway in the economy and in technology. The need for education, information technology, and computer literacy constitutes an important training mandate, especially for Latinos.

Zorn, Peggy, et al. "Advanced Searching: Tricks of the Trade." *Online* 20 (May/June 1996): 15-28.

Discusses skilled Web searching and recommends Altavista as the best search engine although professional library help still will be needed.

Web Sites

Alexander, Jan, and Marsha Tate. "Teaching Critical Evaluation Skills for World Wide Web Resources." <http://www.science.widener.edu/~withers/webeval.htm>.

Grassian, Esther. "Thinking Critically about World Wide Web Resources." <http://www.ucla.edu/campus/computing/bruinonline/rainers/critical.html>.

Kirk, Elizabeth. "Evaluating Information Found on the Internet." <http://milton.mse.jhu.edu:8001/research/education/net.html>.

Ormondroyd, Joan, et al. "How to Critically Analyze Information Sources." <http://urisref.library.cornell.edu/skill26.htm>.

Smith, Alastair. "Criteria for Evaluating of Internet Information Resources." <http://www.vuw/ac/nz/~agsmith/evaln/index.htm>.

Tillman, Hope. "Evaluating Quality on the Net." <http://www/tiac.net/users/hhope/findqual.html>.

Examples of Good Web Sites

BI-L is the premier listserv for instruction librarians. Subscribe: listserv@bingvmbcc.binghamton.edu

ACRL/Instruction Section Web site: <http://www2/colgate/edu/instruction/>

LIRT (Library Instruction Roundtable) Web site: <http://diogenes.baylor.edu/library/LIRT>

Participants

Roster 1997

Mary Ellen Armentrout
Otterbein College
Westerville OH 43081
marmentrout@otterbein.edu

Judith Arnold
Western Michigan University
Kalamazoo MI 49008
judith.arnold@wmich.edu

Priscilla Atkins
Hope College
Holland MI 49424
atkinsp@hope.edu

Nicole Auer
Virginia Polytechnic Institute
Blacksburg VA 24062-9001
auern@vt.edu

Pam Bach
Xavier University
Cincinnati OH 45207-5211
Bach@xavier.xu.edu

Laura Baker
University of Tennessee-
 Chattanooga
Chattanooga TN 87403
laura_baker@utc.edu

Aggie Balash
Manatee Community College
Venice FL 34293

Margaret (Peggy) Bates
Coastal Carolina University
Conway SC 29528
peggyb@coastal.edu

Paul Beavers
Wayne State University
Detroit MI 48202
pbeaver@cms.cc.wayne.edu

Jeff Beck
Wabash College
Crawfordsville IN 47933
beckj@wabash.edu

Susan Beck
New Mexico State University
Las Cruces NM 88003
susabeck@lib.nmsu.edu

Colleen Bell
University of Oregon
Eugene OR 97403-1299
cbell@darkwing.uoregon.edu

Lenora Berendt
Loyola University-Chicago
Chicago IL 60626-5311
lberend@orion.it.luc.edu

Patricia Berge
Marquette University
Milwaukee WI 53201-3141
bergep@vms.csd.mu.edu

Goodie Bhullar
University of Missouri
Columbia MO 65201
ellisgb@showme.missouri.edu

Mary Jo Blackport
Olivet College
Olivet MI 49076
mjblackport@olivetnet.edu

Sarah Blakeslee
California State University-
 Chico
Chico CA 95929
sarah_blakeslee@macgate.
 csuchico.edu

Lisa Blankenship
University of Northern
 Colorado
Greeley CO 80639
llblank@bentley.univnorthco.
 edu

Jane Bradford
Stetson University
DeLand FL 32720
jane.bradford@stetson.edu

D. Scott Brandt
Purdue University
West Lafayette IN 47907-1530
techman@purdue.edu

Virginia Brohard
Houston Community College
Houston TX 77004
brohard_v@hccs.cc.tx.us

Roxann Bustos
Augusta State University
Augusta GA 30904-2200
rbustos@aug.edu

Judy Butler
David Lipscomb University
Nashville TN 37204
butlerjm@dlu.edu

Marie Byers
David Lipscomb University
Nashville TN 37204-3951
byersmp@dlu.edu

Judy Cantwell
Houston Community College
Stafford TX 77477

Joan Carey
Clark College
Vancouver WA 98663
careje@library.clark.edu

Patricia Carroll-Mathes
Ulster County Community
 College
Stone Ridge NY 12482
caroll@sunyulster.edu

Betsey Carter
The Citadel
Charleston SC 29409

Laurel Carter
Hanover College
Hanover IN 47423
carterl@hanover.edu

Sariya Talip Clay
Cal Poly State University
San Luis Obispo CA 93407
stclay@sci-fi.lib.calpoly.edu

Jean Coates
Davidson College
Davidson NC 28036
jecoates@davidson.edu

Tasha Cooper
Lycoming College
Williamsport PA 17701
cooper@lycoming.edu

Leslie Czechowski
Grinnell College
Grinnell IA 50112-0811
czechowl@ac.grin.edu

Ann Daily
Texas A&M University
College Station TX 77843-5001
a-daily@tamu.edu

Eileen Daniel
Glendon College, York University
Toronto, Ontario, Canada
edaniel@yorku.ca

Deborah Davis
Valdosta State University
Valdosta GA 31698
dsdavis@valdosta.edu

Melinda Dermody
Lake Forest College
Lake Forest IL 60045
dermody@lfc.edu

Katherine Dickson
U.S. Naval Academy
Annapolis MD 21402
dickson@nadn.navy.mil

Kathleen Donovan
Harvard University
Cambridge MA 02138
donovaka@hugsel.harvard.edu

Linnea Dudley
Marygrove College
Detroit MI 48221-2599
marygrov@mlc.lib.mi.us

Diane Dustin
Monroe County Community College
Monroe MI 48161
ddustin@monroe.cc.mc.us

Tami Echavarria
University of California, San Diego
La Jolla CA 92093
techavarria@ucsd.edu

Carla Ellard
University of Texas-Pan American
Edinburg TX 78539
carla@panam.edu

Tracy Elliott
Columbus State University
Columbus GA 31907

Margaret Fain
Coastal Carolina University
Conway SC 29528
margaret@coastal.edu

Tonya Fawcett
Cedarville College
Cedarville OH 45314
fawcettt@cedarville.edu

Honey Fein
Ulster Community College
Stone Ridge NY 12484
honey@mhv.net

Kyzyl Fenno-Smith
Pierce College
Lakewood WA 98498-1999
kfenno@ctc.ctc.edu

Elaine Filsinger
Lock Haven University of PA
Clearfield PA 16830
efilsing@eagle.lhup.edu

Deborah Fink
University of Colorado-Boulder
Boulder CO 80309-0184
deborah.fink@colorado.edu

Marcella Flaherty
Harvard University
Cambridge MA 02138
flaherma@hugsel.harvard.edu

Rosmarie Fouad
Idaho State University
Pocatello ID 83209
fouarosm@isu.edu

Olga Francois
Pierce College
Lakewood WA 98498-1999
ofrancoi@ctc.ctc.edu

Joanne Galanis
St. Louis Community College
St. Louis MO 63135
jgalania@fv.stlcc.cc.mo.us

Marie Garrett
University of Tennessee
Knoxville TN 37996-1000
magarrett@utk.edu

Cheryl Ghosh
University of Cincinnati
Cincinnati OH 45221
cheryl.ghosh@uc.edu

Chandra Gigliotti
Hampden-Sydney College
Hampden-Sydney VA 23943
chandrag@tiger.hsc.edu

Jan Glover
Yale School of Medicine
New Haven CT 06520-8014
janis.glover@yale.edu

Melanie Golder
Southern Methodist University
Dallas TX 75275
mgolder@mail.smu.edu

Andrea Gower
Idaho State University
Pocatello ID 83209
goweandr@isu.edu

Gail Gradowski
Santa Clara University
Santa Clara CA 95053
ggradowski@scuacc.scu.edu

Esther Grassian
UCLA
Los Angeles CA 90095-1450
estherg@library.ucla.edu

Denise Green
University of Illinois-
 Springfield
Springfield IL 62794-9243
green@uis.edu

Marcia Grimes
Wheaton College
Norton MA 02766
mgrimes@wheatonma.edu

L. Emily Grimm
University of Cincinnati
Cincinnati OH 45221
emily.grimm@uc.edu

Mimi Gronlund
Northern Virginia Community
 College
Alexandria VA 22311
nvgronm@nv.cc.va.us

Donna Gunter
University of North Carolina-
 Wilmington
Wilmington NC 28403

Marianne Hageman
University of St. Thomas
St. Paul MN 51105
mdhageman@stthomas.edu

Trudi Hahn
University of Maryland
College Park MD 20742
th90@umail.umd.edu

Susan Hahn
University of Oklahoma
Norman OK 73019-0528
shahn@aardvark.ou.edu

Julie Hansen
Southern Illinois University at
 Edwardsville
Edwardsville IL 62026
jhansen@siue.edu

Sallie Harlan
Cal Poly State University
San Luis Obispo CA 93407
sharlan@sci-fi.lib.calpoly.edu

Laura Harmon
Linda Hall Library
Kansas City MO 64110
harmonl@lhl.lib.mo.us

Meg Hawkins
Manatee Community College
Bradenton FL 34206
hawkinm@mail.firn.edu

Patricia Herrling
University of Wisconsin
Madison WI 53706
pherrling@doit.wisc.edu

Patricia Herron
University of Maryland
College Park MD 20742
ph20@umail.umd.edu

Beth Hillemann
Macalester College
St. Paul MN 55105
hillemann@macalester.edu

Carole Hinshaw
University of Central Florida
Orlando FL 32816-2666
chinshaw@pegasus.cc.ucf.edu

Jill Hobgood
St. Mary's College
Notre Dame IN 46556
jhologood@saintmarys.edu

Ruth Hodges
South Carolina State University
Orangeburg SC 29117
LB_Hodges@scsu.edu

Gretchen McCord Hoffmann
University of Houston
Houston TX 77204-2091
gmhoffmann@uh.edu

Jill Holman
University of Oregon
Eugene OR 97403-1299
holman@darkwing.uoregon.
 edu

Martha Hooker
University of Maryland
College Park MD 20742
mh47@umail.umd.edu

Caroline Hopkinson
Armstrong Atlantic State
 University
Savannah GA 31419
Caroline@pirates.armstrong.
 edu

Janice Houck
University of Maryland-
 University College
College Park MD 20742
jhouck@polaris.umuc.edu

Karen Hovde
Northern Illinois University
DeKalb IL 60115
c60kjhl@cso.wpo.niu.edu

Pam Howard
Columbus State University
Columbus GA 31907

Jon Hufford
Texas Tech University
Lubbock TX 79409-0002
lijrh@ttacs.tm.edu

Mary Huntsman
Campbellsville University
Campbellsville KY 42718
mhunt@cambellsvil.edu

Sandra Hussey
Georgetown University
Washington DC 20057-1174
shussey@guvaz.georgetown.
 edu

Lydia Jackson
Southern Illinois University
Edwardsville IL 62026
ljackso@siue.edu

Rebecca Jackson
George Washington University
Washington DC 20052
rjackson@gwis2.circ.gwu.edu

Heather Jagman
North Central College
Naperville IL 60540
hejagm@noctrl.edu

Elaine Jayne
Western Michigan University
Kalamazoo MI 49008
elaine.jayne@wmich.edu

Carolyn Johnson
Arizona State University-West
Phoenix AZ 85069-7100
iccrj@asuvminre.asu.edu

Lisa Kammerlocher
Arizona State University-West
Phoenix AZ 85069-7100
lisa.kammerlocher.asu.edu

Joan Kaplowitz
UCLA
Los Angeles CA 90095-1798
jkaplowi@library.ucla.edu

Jodee Kawasaki
Montana State University
Bozeman MT 59717-3320
alijk@gemini.osos.montana.
  edu

Andrea Kenny
Edgewood College
Madison WI 53711
kenny@edgewood.edu

Amy Knapp
University of Pittsburgh
Pittsburgh PA 15260
aknapp+@pitt.edu

Dave Kohut
St. Xavier University
Chicago IL 60655
kohut@sxu.edu

Lee Konrad
University of Wisconsin-
  Madison
Madison WI 53711
mrlee@macc.wisc.edu

Michael Kruzich
University of Michigan-
  Dearborn
Dearborn MI 48128
mikruzich@umich.edu

Helene LaFrance
Santa Clara University
Santa Clara CA 95053
hlafrance@mailer.scu.edu

Dena Lahue
Faulkner University
Montgomery AL 36109-3398
dlahue@faulkner.edu

Pamela Lakin
Alfred University
Alfred NY 14802
flakin@bigvax.alfred.edu

Nancy Lambert
University of South Carolina-
  Spartanburg
Spartanburg SC 29303
nlambert@sc.edu

Linda Lambert
Seattle Pacific University
Seattle WA 98119
11ambert@spu.edu

Denise Landry-Hyde
Texas A&M University-Corpus
  Christi
Corpus Christi TX 78412
dlandry@tamucc.edu

Barbara Lay
University of Maryland
College Park MD 20742
bl35@umail.umd.edu

Donna Lehman
University of South Carolina
Columbia SC 29208
lehmand@tcl.sc.edu

Susan Levendosky
Ball State University
Muncie IN 47306
00selevendos@bsu.edu

Carla List
SUNY-Plattsburgh
Plausburgh NY 12901-2697
listck@splava.cc.plattsburgh.
  edu

Jana Lonberger
Georgia Institute of
  Technology
Atlanta GA 30332-0900
jana.lonberger@library.gatech.
  edu

Julie Long
St. Mary's College
Notre Dame IN 46556
jlong@saintmarys.edu

Abbie Loomis
University of Wisconsin-
  Madison
Madison WI 53706
loomis@doit.wisc.edu

Charlene Loope
University of South Carolina
Columbia SC 29208
loopec@tcl.sc.edu

Carol Lunce
Southern Methodist University
Dallas TX 75275-0135
clunce@mail.smu.edu

Beth Mark
Messiah College
Grantham PA 17027
bmark@messiah.edu

Ruth Martin
Cedarville College
Cedarville OH 45314
martinr@cedarville.edu

Karen Mateer
Augsburg College
Minneapolis MN 55454
mateer@augsburg.edu

Frank McBride
Alfred University
Alfred NY 14802
fmcbride@bigvax.alfred.edu

Pamela McKay
Worcester State College
Worcester MA 01602
pmckay@worc.mass.edu

Susan McMillan
York College of Pennsylvania
York PA 17405
smcmilla@ycp.edu

Carolyn McPherson
Valdosta State University
Valdosta GA 31698
cmcphers@valdosta.edu

Terry Metz
Carleton College
Northfield MN 55057
temetz@carleton.edu

Marsha Miller
Indiana State University
Terre Haute IN 47809
libmill@cml.indstate.edu

Rosanne Moore
Christian Brothers University
Memphis TN 38104
rmoore@bucs.cbu.edu

Pixey Anne Mosley
Texas A&M University
College Station TX 77843-5000
pmosley@tamu.edu

Alfred Mowdood
Kent State University
Kent OH 44242-0001
amowdood@kentvm.kent.edu

Priscilla Munson
Clemson University
Clemson SC 29634-3001
wprisci@clemson.edu

Cathy Neis
Aquinas College
Grand Rapids MI 49506
neiscat@aquinas.edu

Stacey Nickell
Paducah Community College
Paducah KY 72002
sanick00@pop.uky.edu

Roger Niles
Wofford College
Spartanburg SC 29303
nilesro@uofford.edu

Julia Nims
Bowling Green State
    University
Bowling Green OH 43403
jknims@bgnet.bgsu.edu

Sue Norman
Dickinson College
Carlisle PA 17013
normans@dickinson.edu

Daniel Norstedt
University of Wisconsin-
    Eau Claire
Eau Claire WI 54702
norsteda@uwec.edu

Fran Nowakowski
Dalhousie University
Halifax, Nova Scotia, Canada
fcn@is.dal.ca

Cerise Oberman
SUNY-Plattsburgh
Plattsburgh NY 12901
obermacg@splava.cc.
    plattsburgh.edu

Jan Orf
University of St. Thomas
St. Paul MN 55113
jmorf@stthomas.edu

Gina Overcash
Davidson College
Davidson NC 28036
giovercash@davidson.edu

Catherine Palmer
University of California-Irvine
Irvine CA 92623-9557
cpalmer@uci.edu

Maria Perez-Stable
Western Michigan University
Kalamazoo MI 49008
maria.perez-stable@wmich.edu

Mary Jane Petrowski
Colgate University
Hamilton NY 13346
mjpetrowki@colgate.edu

Barbara Petruzzelli
SUNY-New Paltz
New Paltz NY 12561
petruzzb@npvm.newpaltz.edu

Cindy Pierard
University of Kansas
Lawrence KS 66045
cpierard@ukans.edu

Gayle Poirier
Louisiana State University
Baton Rouge LA 70803
notgap@unix1.sncc.lsu.edu

Phillip Powell
College of Charleston
Charleston SC 29424
powellp@cofc.edu

Neville Prendergast
University at Buffalo
Buffalo NY 14214
nprender@msmail.buffalo.edu

Ward Price
University of Texas-Pan
    American
Edinburg TX 78539
wprice@panam.edu

Alice Primack
University of Florida
Gainesville FL 32611
aliprim@cantread

Celia Rabinowitz
St. Mary's College of
    Maryland
St. Mary's City MD 20686
cerabinowitz@osprey.smcm.
    edu

Patrick Ragains
University of Nevada, Reno
Reno NV 89557
ragains@admin.unr.edu

Marea Rankin
University of Tennessee at Chattanooga
Chattanooga TN 37403
marea-rankin@utc.edu

Dan Ream
Virginia Commonwealth University
Richmond VA 23284
dream@gems.vcu.edu

Gretchen Revie
Grinnell College
Grinnell IA 50112
revie@ac.grin.edu

Lori Ricigliano
University of Puget Sound
Tacoma WA 98416
ricigliano@ups.edu

Tom Riedel
University of Wyoming
Laramie WY 82071-3334
triedel@uwyo.edu

Donna Ring
Western Michigan University
Kalamazoo MI 49008
donna.ring@wmich.edu

Eleanor Rodini
University of Wisconsin-Madison
Madison WI 53706
rodini@doit.wisc.edu

Janell Rudolph
University of Memphis
Memphis TN 38152-6500
nrudolph@memphis.edu

Helen Salmon
University of Guelph
Guelph, Ontario, Canada
hsalmon@uoguelph.ca

Stephen Sanders
Southeastern Louisiana University
Hammond LA 70402
ssanders@selu.edu

Gita Satyendra
Saddleback College
Mission Viejo CA 92692
satyendra_g@sccd.cc.ca.us

Janice Sauer
University of South Alabama
Mobile AL 36688
jsauer@jaguar1.usouthal.edu

Jane Schillie
Radford University
Radford VA 24142
jschilli@mnet.edu

Elsa Schwartz
Lock Haven University of PA
Lock Haven PA 17745
eschwart@eagle.lhup.edu

Jerry Seay
College of Charleston
Charleston SC 29424
seay@spinner.cofc.edu

Tracy Seneca
DePaul University
Chicago IL 60614-3210
tseneca@wppost.depaul.edu

Linda Shirato
Eastern Michigan University
Ypsilanti MI 48197
lib_shirato@online.emich.edu

Greg Sidberry
University of North Texas
Denton TX 76203
gsidberr@library.unt.edu

Dena Siegel
Ball State University
Muncie IN 47306
dsiegel@lib.bsu.edu

Loanne Snavely
Penn State University
University Park PA 16802
11s@psullas.psu.edu

Linda Snodgrass
Worcester State College
Worcester MA 01602
lsnodgrass@worc.mass.edu

Jan Squire
University of Northern Colorado
Greeley CO 80639
jsquire@bentley.univnorthco.edu

Glenn Ellen Starr
Appalachian State University
Boone NC 28608
starrge@appstate.edu

Arena Stevens
Indiana University Northwest
Gary IN 46408
astevens@iunhawl.iun.indiana.edu

Beth Stevens
Armstrong Atlantic State University
Savannah GA 31419
stevenbe@pirates.armstrong.edu

Sharon Stewart
University of Alabama
Tuscaloosa AL 35487
sstewart@ualvm.ua.edu

Sharon Stoerger
Danville Area Community College
Danville IL 61832
stoerger@jaguar.dacc.cc.il.us

Judy Swanson
Cal Poly State University
San Luis Obispo CA 93407
jswanson@calpoly.edu

Miriam Thompson
Grand Rapids Community College
Grand Rapids MI 49503
mthompso@grcc.cc.mi.us

Joyce Thomson
St. Mary's University
Halifax, Nova Scotia
joyce.thomson@stmarys.ca

Ann Thornton
New York Public Library
New York NY 10016
athornton@nypl.org

Kathleen Tiller
University of Dayton
Dayton OH 45469
tiller@data.lib.udayton.edu

Ann Tolzman
American Graduate School of
    International Management
Glendale AZ 85306
tolzmana@t-bird.edu

Lily Torrez
University of Texas-Pan
    American
Edinburg TX 78539
lily@panam.edu

Wolfhard Touchard
Andrews University
Berrien Springs MI 49104-
    1400
touchard@andrews.edu

Jane Tuttle
Columbia College
Columbia SC 29203
jtuttle@colacoll.edu

Sarah Vasse
Orange County Community
    College
Middletown NY 10940
vassesj@sorazz.sunyorange.cc.
    ny.us

James Ward
David Lipscomb University
Nashville TN 37204
wardje@dlu.edu

Kappa Waugh
Vassar College
Poughkeepsie NY 12604-0020
kawaugh@vassar.edu

Kathleen Webb
University of Dayton
Dayton OH 45469
webb@data.lib.udayton.edu

Barbara Weeg
University of Northern Iowa
Cedar Falls IA 50613-3675
barbara.weeg@uni.edu

Jeanie Welch
University of North Carolina-
    Charlotte
Charlotte NC 28223

David White
Augusta State University
Augusta GA 30904-2200
dwhite@aug.edu

Betsy Whitley
Western Carolina University
Cullowhee NC 28723
bwhitley@wcu.edu

Alis Whitt
College of Charleston
Charleston SC 29424
whitt@spinner.cofc.edu

Shelle Witten
Paradise Valley Community
    College
Phoenix AZ 85032
witten@pvc.maricopa.edu

Vicki Young
Xavier University
Cincinnati OH 45207-5211
young@xavier.xu.edu

Diane Zwemer
UCLA
Los Angeles CA 90095
dzwemer@library.ucla.edu